Antigua And The Antiguans, Volume 2 (Of 2) A Full Account Of The Colony And Its Inhabitants From The Time Of The Caribs To The Present Day

Mrs. Lanaghan

Alpha Editions

This Edition Published in 2021

ISBN: 9789355399625

Design and Setting By
Alpha Editions
www.alphaedis.com
Email – info@alphaedis.com

#

TABLE OF CONTENTS

CHAPTER XXIX   - 1 -

CHAPTER XXX   - 9 -

CHAPTER XXXI   - 21 -

CHAPTER XXXII   - 31 -

CHAPTER XXXIII   - 41 -

CHAPTER XXXIV   - 51 -

CHAPTER XXXV   - 59 -

CHAPTER XXXVI   - 66 -

CHAPTER XXXVII   - 74 -

CHAPTER XXXVIII   - 79 -

CHAPTER XXXIX   - 86 -

CHAPTER XL   - 94 -

CHAPTER XLI   - 100 -

CHAPTER XLII   - 106 -

CHAPTER XLIII   - 110 -

CHAPTER XLIV   - 117 -

CHAPTER XLV   - 124 -

CHAPTER XLVI   - 134 -

CHAPTER XLVII   - 145 -

CHAPTER XLVIII   - 153 -

CHAPTER XLIX   - 160 -

\#

CHAPTER L   - 170 -

CHAPTER LI   - 178 -

CHAPTER LII   - 189 -

CHAPTER LIII   - 208 -

SUPPLEMENTAL CHAPTER   - 218 -

\#

CHAPTER XXIX

Caribs: Domestic state—Treatment of their women—Children—Their early tuition—Superstitious cruelties—Hatred of the Arrowawks—Female children—Occupation of the men—Canoes—Bows and arrows—Cottages —Cooking utensils—Native cloth—Food—Fishing—Decoy fish— Spirituous liquors—Personal appearance—Amusements—The Carib house —Extermination of the Caribs from Antigua—Remarks upon their history.

From a view of the religion of the Caribs, which we have endeavoured to give some account of in the last chapter, we will proceed to notice their domestic ties. Alas! we have a very sad picture here. The ineffable sympathies of the soul, the pure friendship, the chaste pleasures of the connubial state, were never known, or at least never appreciated by them. Proud of excelling in strength and courage, the chief marks of priority among this rude and savage people, the Caribs treated their women in every respect as beings of a far inferior nature—to despise and degrade them by every possible means was esteemed as a manly virtue. Although given as a reward to successful combatants, their wives were looked upon as no better than captives; every species of drudgery fell to their share; while their husbands passed the day in sleep, unless engaged in war, or in absolute want of a new weapon. When the men engaged in fishing, the women were obliged to attend to carry the tackle and bring home the fruits of their sport; but after cooking it, they were not allowed to partake of it with their husbands, or even to eat in their presence. In the island of Cuba at this day this custom is still extant, for a late traveller remarks, "In some of the first houses the men sit down to dinner while their wives wait behind their chairs." But to return to the Carib women. All their services were received without gratitude or even complacency—no cheering word or kind look (and how women appreciate those little endearments none but a woman can tell) mitigated their incessant toil or lightened their heavy burdens. They were not allowed to approach their husbands but with the most abject homage, to look up to them as exalted beings, to obey their every wish, and that without uttering a word of complaint or giving a single look of discontent—all this was expected of the Carib woman. Wearily must their days have passed, without a hope in this world, and scarcely one in the other—trouble and sorrow must indeed have been their lot!

Having considered the Carib's appreciation of the nearest and dearest tie in this world, we will proceed to take a view of his behaviour to his offspring. Perhaps there is not a stronger passion implanted by nature in the breast than that of parental love; even in the brute creation, there is a wonderful degree of instinct in the care of their young. The most stupid and sluggish, the most fearful and timid animals, become active and desperate in defence of their infant progeny, and will suffer any cruelty rather than permit their precious charge to be hurt or destroyed. If then this feeling exists so strongly in the breasts of animals devoid of reason, how much more should this be the case with man, raised as he is far above all terrestrial beings, endowed with a rational and comprehensive mind, and capable of enjoying the delights which flow from reciprocal affections! But in many instances we have to blush for our fellow creatures, and while we admire the instinct and parental feelings of brutes, deplore the inferiority of our own race.

The passions of savages, while they last, are more violent and enthusiastic than those of men who are placed in civilized society, and consequently under some degree of restraint. Thus it was with the Caribs during the infancy of their male children; no duty, however irksome, or ceremony, however severe, which was fondly hoped would tend to make them formidable warriors, was regretted or postponed. The father freely lost his own blood to sprinkle his male child as soon as it was born, in the hopes that he might be endowed with a portion of his own courage.[1] As the child grew, he was taught all the arts requisite for his savage life—to draw the bow, wield the club, make and manage his canoe, swim skilfully, catch fish, and prepare the poison to dip his arrows in; he was also instructed in lessons of patience and fortitude, inspired with courage to attack his foes by having the deeds of his fathers related to him, and familiarized to look upon death and danger with contempt.

So far the Carib performed the part of a good parent; but superstition exerted her gloomy powers, and the cruelties inflicted on the young Carib by the being from whom he derived his existence, exhibits a mournful and sanguinary picture, capable of harrowing up the deepest feelings of the soul. The dawn of manhood was the hour in which these trials were to be endured; and at this time the young warrior changed his infant name for one of greater importance and more significant in expression. With regard to their female children, but little fatherly attention was paid them; their education devolved upon their mothers, who taught them to cull the cotton and weave the cloth, and, in a word, instructed them in all the duties necessary to the comfort of their future lords and tyrants. If very handsome, they were reserved to grace the triumph of some successful warrior, while those of less beauty were allotted to men of inferior worth.

The principal occupation of the Carib, the one, as before remarked, which absorbed the greatest portion of his time and attention, was war. The study of his life was to render himself an adept in those arts which would enable him to capture a greater number of his enemies, and spread desolation wherever he went. When not thus engaged, his days were passed in listless apathy. Enveloped in his mantle, and stretched upon his *hemack* beneath the shade of some luxuriant tree, he enjoyed the breeze of his native isle without alloy; and unless the calls of hunger aroused him, or his weapon or canoe required repair, he seldom or ever stirred. But when the war-cry arose, when an expedition against the Arrowawks was intended, or when his countrymen invited him "to seize his war-club," and avenge the death of some friend, whose bones lay whitening on another shore, he started from his repose, and grasped his spear; while the fire emanating from his dark eyes, his black hair streaming in the blast, his strong form vibrating from the intensity of his ardour, conspired to render him what he wished to be—the formidable-looking warrior.

But although the Carib was generally during peace fond of indolence, yet when he chose to exert his powers, his arts and manufactures displayed a degree of ingenuity surpassing what could have been expected from his tools. His canoe was formed of the trunk of large trees, principally that of the ceibar, or silk cotton, as being more substantial, and of larger bulk. His bow and arrows were fabricated with a degree of nicety almost unequalled; some of them inlaid with pieces of tortoiseshell, or the bones of fish finely polished. His cottage was also built with some degree of taste, and neatly thatched with plaited cocoa-nut leaves; and was situated in some of the loveliest spots. They also possessed the art of fabricating vessels for cookery, and other domestic uses, from the clay of the island, which is still in use in Antigua, the negroes making pots for boiling their victuals, *yubbas*, (or frying-pans,) water-jars, and several other utensils. Of this clay it is said excellent bricks might be made; and there are several waste spots of land belonging to government, which might be turned into extensive brickfields: the bricks used in the island are all imported.

But to return to our subject: while the men were thus employed, the women were far from idle: they wove the cloth from the cotton and bark of trees, and stained it of various colours. Of this cloth, which was very substantial, they made their beds, which were suspended from posts by the two ends, and obtained the name of *hemacks*, from being made by the southern islanders of the rind of a tree of that name. Columbus was so pleased with them, that he took the pattern, and used them for the bedding of his crew. They are still used at the present day under the appellation of *hammocks*. Of the leaves of the cocoa-nut and palmetto they also made baskets; while the fibres were twisted into ropes. The negroes also follow them in this particular, making rope, and also baskets, which they call *"catacous."*

The Caribs have often been likened to the ancient Jews in some of their customs; but they did not follow that peculiar people in abstaining from blood, as they frequently drank that of the Arrowawks in their inhuman festivals. It is true, they refrained from eating many kinds of flesh, which were generally reckoned luxuries by others; but "if it was from religious motives, we are nowhere sufficiently informed," as Goldsmith justly observes. Their greatest treat, however, was human flesh, which they devoured with avidity whenever they could procure it. The Arrowawks, or inhabitants of Cuba, and the adjacent islands, as before remarked, were their principal prey. Sometimes they ate this horrible food raw; at other times they roasted or boiled it; but the fat was all preserved for the use of their children, both as food, and to anoint their bodies, in hopes of rendering them hardy and valiant; and for this reason they were also frequently immersed in a *bath of blood.*

Another of their viands, and indeed the principal part of their food, was fish. These they caught in nets, composed of the twisted fibres of the cocoa-nut; or else speared them at night as they rose to the surface of the water to breathe. A similar practice is still pursued in Scotland; and the dexterity consists in throwing a spear at the salmon as it springs from the water. A fuller account would be inconsistent with my present work; but I refer my readers to Sir W. Scott's well known novel of "Guy Mannering," where it is accurately and vividly described. To resume our subject:—Columbus mentions seeing some fishermen making use of very curious assistants in securing their finny prey, namely, decoy fish. These were a species of small fish, which abounded in these seas, called "reves." Fastening a string round their tails, they were lowered into the water, and, made cunning by the hand which fed them, these tiny ensnarers encountered their brethren of the deep; and winding about them, all were drawn up together.

In looking over the accounts of different countries, everyone must be struck with the propensity man has of indulging in spirituous liquors. While the inhabitants of fruitful and sunny districts imbibe the luscious juice of the grape, the Kamtschadale ranges his barren and inhospitable clime in search of a species of grass, from which to obtain a supply of fermented drink. The Tartar, in his wild state, roaming from pasture to pasture, placing his whole wealth in his horses and cattle, silently enjoys the intoxicating qualities of his brandy procured from the milk of his mares, and sighs not for the richest cup ever quaffed by the lip of mortals. So likewise the Carib was not without his stimulants—his festive board was not without its cup. From the bark of the palm and cocoa-nut tree, they procured a liquor clear as crystal, which they allowed to ferment, and of which they were very fond; but their principal drink was mobby, made from the sweet potatoe, (a native of this island,) which they also drank in a fermented state. But still drunkenness was not one of their crimes; it was reserved for their conquerors to teach them that vice. We are told of an old Carib addressing a planter in the following manner—"Our people are become almost as bad as yours. We are so much altered since you came among us, that we hardly know ourselves; and we think it is owing to so melancholy a change that the hurricanes are more frequent than they were formerly. It is an evil spirit who has done all this; who has taken our best lands from us, and given us up to the dominion of the Christians." Alas! poor Caribs, it was an evil spirit which had come among you—the evil spirit of lawless and unchristian *men*. Why was your country invaded and your rights trampled on? Why were your wives and children torn from you?—and you yourselves condemned to death?—yea, worse than death—to vile and endless slavery, till time, the end of all things, consigned you to your silent graves?—are questions which will arise, but whose answer can only be given in these words—"What is, is best."

To resume our description of these ancient possessors of Antigua— these warlike Caribs. Vanity is a passion which to a greater or lesser degree pervades the breast of almost every mortal, and the savage in his native wilds feels the force of it in the same manner, although, perhaps, not to the same *extent*, as the giddy fair who whirls round the vortex of dissipation within the purlieus of May Fair. When first discovered by the Spaniards, the Caribs were habited in different fashions; some appeared in complete dresses of native cloth, stained of a dark red; others had only a cotton girdle rolled round their loins; while others, again, were arrayed in "Nature's garb." But although this plain and scanty dress forbid much fancy or variety, they were far from unadorned. Their hair was arranged in a thousand fantastic shapes; some had it braided with small pieces of gold, shells or shining stones; others decorated it with the teeth and bones of their enemies; and some, again, placed large bunches of parrots' feathers upon the top of the head. Nor were all their decorations confined to their head-dresses; they stained their bodies with various colours, and in a variety of figures, and, as before alluded to, caused themselves much pain in thus ornamenting their persons, by their great propensity for altering their natural features. It does not appear if this was intended to heighten their beauty, and render them captivating in the eyes of the "nice-judging fair," or if to make them more hideous in the sight of their enemies; but most probably it was for the latter purpose, although it has been said "that women always like the monsters!"

Their amusement, which has also been before observed, was war; nothing else seemed to please or interest them, it was "their gain, their glory, their delight!" They had their dances, but they were rather a serious ceremony than indulged in as a pastime. Their principal assemblies were held before starting upon a warlike expedition, when a leader or chief was elected with the barbarities before described; or upon the return of a victorious warrior, when these ceremonies concluded with a dance.

In the foregoing review, the character of the red Caribs, the aborigines of Antigua, has been described; but in different islands were found different tribes. Guadaloupe was inhabited by a race of Amazons, who, upon the first appearance of Columbus, rushed out of a wood, armed with bows and arrows, and attacked the crew with such determined fury, that he was obliged to open a fire upon them before they would disperse; that they were also cannibals was evident from the relics of their disgusting feasts found in their huts. Some of the other islands were inhabited by a similar race; but the people of Hispaniola, Cuba, Jamaica, and Porto Rico were decidedly of a different family—mild, temperate, and indolent, they were a certain prey to the ferocious cannibals.

The Caribs of Antigua were first conquered by the Spaniards in 1521, and after trying to make them work as slaves without effect, they were finally driven from off the island. As in the other islands, fire and sword came among them, and the ancient people of the soil are no more. Their manners and customs, their hopes and fears, their enjoyments and distresses, are almost buried in oblivion, only now and then, here and there, we find a few traces of them in the wide page of history. There are, however, vestiges of their dwellings still to be met with in different parts of the island, one of which I had the curiosity to enter. It appeared to have consisted of two distinct buildings, the materials of which were composed of the stone which is common in all parts of the island, cemented with a rough kind of mortar. The one nearest the north is about fifty feet long and twenty-five broad; in the middle is a circular hollow; small square window-places are on all sides, and the door-place fronts the west. I stood before that open door, and memory carried me back to "by-gone" ages. The sun had set, but his golden beams still lingered in the west, and tinged the clouds with a thousand beautiful colours. Not a single living creature was in sight, but one poor solitary ground-dove, who sat by the ruined walls and uttered her plaintive notes. The negroes are of an opinion that this bird is the harbinger of death; be that as it may, her melancholy cry on such a spot called up many an image. Who might not have stood upon the very place where I was standing and watched that glorious sun while he set? The formidable-looking Carib, his meek, degraded, uncomplaining wife; his miserable, wretched victim, the unhappy Arrowawk! All might have once stood there and gazed upon that very scene. And those crumbling walls! what tales might not they have told! how many scenes of bloodshed might not they have witnessed! how many harsh, discordant notes of revelry, from the wild beings who once inhabited them, might not they have echoed to! how many piercing shrieks for mercy from those poor wretched creatures, immolated upon that family altar for the darkling ceremonies of superstition, or for the daily meal, might not they have heard!

The other adjoining building has the appearance of a square tower, and must, in its day, have been a place of some strength; it is considerably higher than the one before described. I felt inclined to believe it was built by the buccaneers, who, many years ago, made these islands their place of resort. In the island of St. Thomas is still standing a kind of castle, built by that renowned and formidable captain of pirates, "Blackbeard."[2] However, all Antiguans agree in calling the building mentioned the "Carib's House."

To a contemplative mind, how many emotions arise upon taking a review of history. We see whole nations swept away from the surface of the globe, and others springing up to form the connecting link in the grand chain of nature. We see the stupendous powers of the Omnipotent, at whose beck myriads start into life—at whose frown they vanish away like chaff before the wind. We are inclined to ask, Where now is mighty Rome, the empress of the world? Lost in the abyss of her own power and greatness. Greece, too, with all her brave sons—her disinterested patriots— her wise and just lawgivers—where are they? All, all are fled, their very existence almost forgotten; and as a favourite traveller remarks, "Greece remembers her sons no more." He whose reckless ambition sighed for worlds to conquer, is himself conquered by the strong hand of death. The prince and peasant, the rich and poor, the bond and free, alike fall beneath those all-powerful shafts.

"The boast of heraldry, the pomp of power,
And all that beauty, all that wealth ere gave.
Must wait alike the inevitable hour;
The paths of glory lead but to the grave."

While surveying these things, the mind is lost in the boundless depths of imagination. We are led to reflect upon the transitory state of existence we pass in this nether world; and the truth flashes upon us, that however great we may be in our own estimation—however great in our own conceit, we are but in reality as the bubble on the water, the ephemera of a summer's day. Reader! didst thou ever examine the interior of an ant-hill? didst thou ever notice how its busy little inmates are hurrying to and fro, intent upon their different occupations? Some are occupied in excavating the ground to prepare store-houses for the preservation of their grain in the winter—some in removing the dirt from the streets that nothing may obstruct the progress of their various business—some in plastering the earth with a kind of clay, which they carefully prepare, that it may not fall in and destroy their populous city, while others again are preparing cells for the reception of their eggs.

Thus we see all is bustle, all is activity; like mortals, some are laying up wealth they are fated never to enjoy, or planning schemes of grandeur which will never come to pass. The ploughshare passes over, and where are those busy troops? Eurus blows his blast in the fierceness of his anger, and the whole colony is scattered, the swarming multitude is no more. Thus it is with man: placed by his Creator in so beautiful a world, endowed, perhaps, with health, and riches, and honours, surrounded by a circle of friends and flatterers, enjoying all the pomps and luxuries of this life, he drinks deeply of the intoxicating cup of Circe, and forgets that he is but a child of clay, "a stranger and a sojourner as all his fathers were."

I have been led into these reflections from the fact, that the people whose history I have been narrating are entirely exterminated from Antigua and the adjoining islands; that of all those swarming hosts who were gathered upon the beach to resist the landing of the Spaniards, who first visited this island, not one of their descendants is left. And now, in concluding this chapter, all that remains for me to do is, to crave the pardon and indulgence of my readers for so often leaving "Antigua and the Antiguans," and wandering in another pathway; but according to an old saying, "Our thoughts are not always under our own control;" or, as it is said in more modern language, "Woman is an Eolian harp, the strings of which are moved by every wind that blows."

---

[1] This was done, by allowing one of his veins to be opened for the purpose.

[2] The real name of this pirate was Edward Toutch, a native of Spanish Town, in Jamaica. Of all pirates, this man was the most ferocious; the deeds he committed being more like those of a demon than a man. He was at length attacked by a lieutenant of an English man-of-war, off the coast of Virginia, and taken prisoner. He was afterwards executed, and his head stuck upon a pole erected upon that coast, as a warning to other lawless rovers.

CHAPTER XXX

Negroes: Their introduction into the New World—Bartholomew Las Casas—His intercessions in favour of the Indians—Cardinal Ximenes—Origin of the slave trade—Its adoption by the English government—Character of slavery—Mental degeneracy—Instances of superior faculties among the Negro race—Juan Parega—Phillis Wheatley—Ignatius Sancho—His letter to the Rev. L. Sterne—Slavery in its early days—Punishment of the negroes in 1736.

In furtherance of my plan, of commencing from the earliest period the history of this small but important colony, it also devolves upon me to give some account of the first introduction of negroes into this quarter of the globe, particularly as they form so large a bulk of the population of Antigua.

The negroes, as perhaps many of my readers may be aware, were first introduced generally into the West Indies, as labourers, in 1515, although some few had been sent there a short time before. Bartholomew Las Casas, an eminent Spanish divine, was one of those who proposed this measure, and spent both time and money in its completion. Las Casas was born at Seville, in the year 1474; and at the age of nineteen, accompanied his father to the West Indies.

At this period, Rodrigo Albuquerque, the confidential minister of Ferdinand V. of Spain, had succeeded Don Diego, the son of Christopher Columbus, in the government of Hispaniola, which the Spaniards still considered as their principal colony. Albuquerque was a man of violent passions, and rapacious in the acquisition of wealth; and under his government the poor Indians led but a miserable life; and with hard labour and ill-treatment they were almost exterminated. The cruel and arbitrary proceedings adopted towards them excited compassion in the minds of all who had the least particle of commiseration in their natures. The missionaries had early expressed their abhorrence of the system of parting the Indians among the settlers, by which means they became the slaves of their conquerors. The Dominicans, in particular, had strongly protested against the "*repartimientos*" (or sharing) as it was termed; and not content with remonstrating in private, made the pulpit the theatre of action, and denounced curses upon the heads of those who followed that plan.

Bartholomew Las Casas early became a convert to their opinions upon this head. He not only gave up all the Indians which had fallen to his share, but tried all means in his power to persuade his countrymen to do so likewise. He remonstrated with Albuquerque upon the unlawfulness of his conduct; but he found that tyrant too much engrossed with the sordid love of acquiring gold for his remonstrances to be of any effect. When Las Casas found this to be the case, he determined to depart for Spain, and lay his complaint at the feet of Ferdinand.

After a protracted voyage of many weeks, Las Casas arrived safe at Cadiz, and quickly obtained an interview with his sovereign, whom he found to be in a very languishing state of health. Ferdinand listened with deep attention to Las Casas' representation of the sufferings endured by the unfortunate natives of the West Indies; and expressed deep compunction for his guilt in having authorized this measure of sharing, which had brought destruction upon so many innocent people; and finally, he promised to take into consideration the means of redressing the grievances he had occasioned. Death, however, put an end to all his resolves; and Charles V. of Germany, who succeeded him, being then in Austria, appointed the celebrated Cardinal Ximenes his regent.

Las Casas was not wearied with his undertaking, or disheartened with his disappointment; he obtained an interview with the regent, and argued his cause with so much feeling and eloquence, that Ximenes appointed a commission of monks from St. Jerome to go to the West Indies and make every inquiry into the situation of the wretched inhabitants, directing Las Casas to accompany them, with the title of "Protector of the Indians." Upon their arrival, the monks proceeded with caution to investigate the matter; and after some time spent in this way, gave it as their opinion, that the Spaniards must either give up their American conquests, or be satisfied with very little gain, unless the system of slavery was tolerated; at the same time, expressing their determination to try all endeavours in their power to secure to the Indians a milder and a better treatment.

All but Las Casas were satisfied with these proceedings, but he argued for total exemption; and so strenuously did he urge his plea, that the planters' anger was aroused, and he was obliged to retire into a convent to preserve his life. But Las Casas was not the man to give up a favourite project for a trifle. Finding how ill he succeeded in the New World, he determined once more to sail for Spain, and employ every means and exert every energy to accomplish his plans, and never to give up his labours until death or the accomplishment of his wishes ended them.

By the time he arrived at home, the Cardinal Ximenes had resigned the regency, and Charles had assumed the reins of government, and to this monarch Las Casas carried his complaints. The emperor listened to him, and appointed another commission of monks to inquire into the business; but Las Casas knew the opposition this measure would meet with, and the little good it would effect; he therefore set his wits to work to find out some other expedient, and at last thought of introducing other labourers into the West Indies in lieu of the Indians.

The use the Portuguese made of their African discoveries was to ensnare the inhabitants and sell them as slaves; and Las Casas thought that if these wretched people could be transported in numbers to America, they would, from their stronger constitutions and hardy frames, answer better than the natives themselves. This plan was laid before the council in Spain, and although strongly resisted by Cardinal Ximenes, who saw the impropriety of condemning an innocent nation to perpetual slavery to save another, the measure was carried by a majority of voices, and Charles granted to a favourite courtier a patent, empowering him to purchase slaves in Africa, and ship them to the West Indies.

This patent was purchased by some Genoese merchants, who immediately put it into execution, and thus that detestable traffic, the "slave trade," was introduced by men calling themselves *Christians*, and professing to follow the doctrines of their divine Master, while they deliberately set at nought his great precept—"Do unto others as you would have others do unto you." It is not within the plan of the present work to inquire how much the situation of the Indians was improved by this arrangement, but will merely observe, that while Las Casas spent his time, his money, and his health, in trying to benefit his favourite people, he forgot all other classes, and completely shut the door of mercy upon the unoffending Africans; and for no other cause than it had pleased their Creator to bestow upon them greater strength than upon the natives of the West, they were torn from their country, their friends, and home, and, to "increase a stranger's treasures," consigned to hopeless misery.

To the Portuguese and Genoese the slave-trade exclusively belonged for many years; at length, the Dutch, seeing the gainfulness of it, engaged in it; and in 1564, during the reign of Queen Elizabeth, Sir John, then Mr. Hawkins, introduced this bloodstained commerce (for so it may justly be termed) into the English trade, and thus tarnished the bright name he had acquired by his many naval victories.

Oh, that England, so famous for her spirit of liberty, should have ever imbrued her hands in this inhuman traffic!—that she, the "empress of the waves," should have lent her power to crush these unfortunate beings!—that that nation by whom the sweets of domestic ties are so peculiarly felt and appreciated, should have been among the first to rend husband from wife, the babe from its mother, the daughter from her old parent, and condemn them to

"Plough the winter's wave, and reap despair!"

that Britons, free-born Britons, such advocates for liberty! should have acted thus for so many years, even when the dark clouds of ignorance had been dispersed, and "knowledge to their eyes" had unfolded "her ample page," is almost beyond credence. But, alas! it proves how much "the clink of Mammon's box" charms the ear and deadens the nobler feelings of the soul. In 1592, two years before he died, Sir John Hawkins was so impressed with horror at what he had done in introducing the slave-trade to the notice of his countrymen, who had eagerly pursued it, that he built a hospital at Rochester, to atone, in some measure, for his violation of the laws of humanity.

Draco's laws were said to be written with a pen of iron, in letters of blood; and surely, so also have the annals of slavery been described. "Disguise thyself as thou wilt," says Sterne, "still, slavery—still thou art a bitter draught!" And, bitter as it is, our poor West Indian slaves have, in former years, drained the cup to the very dregs. But, thank God, the cry— "Am I not a man and a brother!" has been heard and acknowledged. The names of Sharpe, Wilberforce, and Fox, with many others, are engraved deep in the hearts of all true lovers of humanity, for their strenuous endeavours, year after year, in procuring the abolition of this infernal traffic; and universal gratitude is due to Buxton, Lushington, and their right worthy fellow-labourers of the present day, for their share in effecting the final measure of emancipation. And in this place, I must beg to proffer my thanks to the many kind hearts which beat in Antigua, *slave-owners* as they were, for their joint exertions with our English philanthropists in bringing this glorious freedom about; and for their cheerful acquiescence, when accomplished, in giving their slaves immediate freedom. They asked for no apprenticeship—they would not even accept it; but they trusted to their negroes, and set them free at once. Yet England did not behave to the Antiguans as she ought to have done. Instead of rewarding them for their disinterested conduct, by allotting to them a larger share of the compensation-money, their portion was *smaller* than that of any of the other islands. The excuse for this was, that slaves were *less* valued in Antigua. But what caused them to be less valuable? Did our English government ask that question? Do our friends "at home" know the answer? The Antiguans had become sensible of the inhumanity of dealing in human flesh; and although they were obliged to employ their slaves to till their fields, it was very few persons who thought of purchasing negroes. This was the reason, and not because her slaves were worse than those of other islands, or less competent for labour.[3]

Slavery is not only revolting for the cruelties it has occasioned, but it is debasing to the mind. How few, *very few slaves*, have we heard of, who have shewn any intellectual qualifications, or made any improvements in machinery or agriculture! Nor need we be surprised at this; for had a slave proposed anything of the kind, his master would have probably considered it as a suggestion of indolence, or a desire to save himself from toil at the expense of others.

Some authors have asserted, that negroes are an unimprovable race, incapable of receiving instruction, or having sufficient reason to discern right from wrong. But I am not at all inclined to assent to such a doctrine, but attribute the fact, that greater talents have not been shewn by them, as before remarked, to the degradation of slavery. Indeed, we have had some few instances of *considerable* display of abilities among this sable people; one or two instances of which it may not be amiss to introduce.

One of these *clever negroes* was a slave, named Juan de Parega, who was sent from the West Indies as a present to Diego Valasquez, the celebrated Spanish painter, about the year 1600. Juan was very fond of painting, and his own natural talents enabled him to study it with great effect. This he did, however, secretly, for fear of giving offence to his master, who, he thought, might be angry with a slave for disgracing the art. Philip the Fourth of Spain was a great admirer of the fine arts, and a frequent visitor at Valasquez's study, where, if he met any pictures with their faces to the wall,[4] he was sure to request they might be turned. One day, when the monarch came to the house, during the absence of Valasquez, and before he proceeded to the study, Juan took one of his own pictures, hung it up in a prominent situation, with the painted side turned to the wall, and with trembling heart awaited the result. Philip's step was heard upon the stair—his finger was upon the lock—poor Juan's emotion almost stifled him!—the door opened, and his majesty entered. His quick eye immediately alighted upon the new picture, which he ordered Juan to turn. This was done; and after examining it for some time, Philip pronounced it beautiful! The gratified slave, his eyes beaming with delight, while he trembled at the thoughts of his audacity, fell upon his knees before his sovereign, acknowledged it to be his work, and prayed him to intercede with his master for him, that his presumption might be pardoned. Philip raised him from his knees, commended his talents, and; upon seeing Valasquez, told him he ought to free such a man. This was done; but Juan would never quit his kind master: he remained with him, studying and improving under his tuition, until eventually he became one of the first portrait-painters of his day.

Another instance we have in Phillis Wheatley; she was purchased by Mrs. F. Wheatley in Boston slave-market, (America,) when she was about seven or eight years old. Shewing great natural talents, her mistress had her taught reading, writing, &c. As she grew up to womanhood, she attracted the notice of many literary characters, who supplied her with books and directed her studies. When about fourteen years of age, she attempted compositions both in prose and verse; and between that and nineteen, all her works were published.[5]

While upon this subject, we must not forget Ignatius Sancho. Ignatius was born on board a slave-ship a few days after it had left Guinea, in 1729. The severities his mother met with put an end to her existence a short time after her arrival in the West Indies; and his father took it so much to heart that he committed suicide. This plainly proves that negroes are not so utterly devoid of natural affections as some would have us believe—

"Skins may differ, but affection
Dwells in black and white the same."

But to return to our hero. After some years, he was brought to England, through the kindness of the Duke of Montague, and obtained means of instruction. He wrote a great many letters, which were deemed worthy of being published; and a large subscription was raised. They were reckoned very well written; one of them, upon slavery, may not prove uninteresting to many of my readers. It was addressed to the Rev. L. Sterne, 1776.

"REV. SIR,—It would be an insult to your humanity (or perhaps look like it) to apologize for the liberty I am taking. The first part of my life was rather unlucky, as I was placed in a family who judged ignorance to be the best and only security for obedience; a little reading and writing I got by unwearied application. The latter part of my life has been, through God's blessing, truly fortunate, having spent it in the service of one of the best and greatest families in the kingdom: My chief pleasure has been books— philanthropy I adore. How much, very much, good sir, am I (among millions) indebted to you for the character of your amiable Uncle Toby. I declare I would walk ten miles in the dog-days to shake hands with the honest Corporal. Your sermons have touched me to the heart, and, I hope, have amended it, which brings me to the point.

"In your tenth discourse is this very affecting passage:—'Consider how great a part of our species, in all ages down to this, have been trod under the feet of cruel and capricious tyrants, who would neither hear their cries nor pity their distress. Consider slavery, what it is—how bitter a draught, and how many millions are made to drink of it!'

"Of all my favourite authors, not one has drawn a tear in favour of my miserable black brethren excepting yourself and the humane author of 'Sir George Ellison.' I think you will forgive me—I am sure you will applaud me—for beseeching you to give one half-hour to slavery as at this day practised in our West Indian colonies. That subject handled in your striking manner, would ease the yoke perhaps of many; but if only one—gracious God! what a feast to a benevolent heart. And I am sure you are an Epicurean in acts of charity; you, who are universally read, and as universally admired, you cannot fail.

"Dear Sir, think in me you behold the uplifted hands of thousands of my brethren Moors. Grief, you pathetically observe, is eloquent. Figure to yourself their attitudes; hear their supplicating addresses; alas! you cannot refuse—humanity must comply. In which hope I beg permission to subscribe myself,

"Rev. Sir, &c. &c."

This is the letter; all must know Sterne's beautiful piece on "Slavery," which it produced. At one time, Ignatius Sancho had an idea of going upon the stage, and actually offered himself to Mr. Garrick, to perform the character of Othello and Oronooko; but an irreparable defect in his articulation prevented him from putting his designs into execution. Ignatius died from a complication of disorders in the year 1780, aged fifty-one; he was much esteemed by his friends in England.

These examples before us, and others which might be added, prove that the negroes are not always the unintelligent beings they have been supposed; and I do hope, that now so much has been done for them, they will alter their character, and strive to suppress those vices which their life of servitude has produced among them. They are no longer treated as beasts of burden, but taught to consider themselves as men; they make it a constant boast, "Me free, me no b'longs to you!" I hope they may shew they deserve their freedom by their good conduct; then we may hope for better days; we may see virtues springing up among them; emanations of genius may arise and surprise the whole world.

I wish them well—I feel interested about them—I desire their good—and I am sorry, *very sorry*, that in the course of these remarks I may have so much to say about them. But when I have to touch upon the dark part of their character, for "lights and shadows" *must* be depicted, I beseech you, my kind readers, to remember how short has been their life of freedom; how few have been their advantages, comparatively speaking; and above all, remember evil is not to be returned for evil, but rather good.

There are many worthy industrious characters among this class of persons in Antigua; not famous, it is true, for any great display of abilities, or of superior talents, like Juan Parega, or our friend Sancho, but men of sound mind, well-behaved, and clever in producing little articles of native manufacture. A fancy sale was held in this island in January, 1837, and among the contributions was a miniature sugar-mill, with all its vanes &c.

complete, capable of grinding the canes when peeled. This pretty little article was the work and gift of one who, in 1834, was a slave belonging to the Hon. Bertie E. Jarvis. It was purchased by two American gentlemen, friends of liberty, who were residing for a short time in Antigua, to see how the free system worked, and who carried it with them to America, to shew what a free negro could do. Had slavery still existed, that man would never have exerted his talents with such success, for either he would not have had the time allowed, or he would not have had the spirit.

In this remark, I mean no disrespect to his late owner; far from it, for I have ever heard that the Hon. B. E. Jarvis ranked among those worthy characters, many, very many of whom I glory to say were to be found in Antigua, who, while they knew their slaves were their goods, their *chattels*, scorned to use unnecessary punishments, but treated them kindly, listened to their wants, and protected them when in need.

Truly grateful ought we to be that, in British colonies at least, slavery is no more; for it was a dark spot in the fair character of Britain, which no reasoning, however subtle, could hide. Interested persons might boast of the legal regulations for the protection of slaves; but in truth, those laws were either insufficient or not rigidly enforced; some way or the other, the laws which were made for the protection of the slave, generally turned out to the benefit of the master.

At the trial of a planter for the murder of his slave, one of the persons summoned as a juror begged to be excused from acting, giving as his reason "that he thought such a trial would be hurtful to the West Indian Islands, as it would make the slaves saucy!" What! then a man was to lacerate, to *kill* his poor slave, under circumstances of the most barbarous cruelty, and yet not to be brought to justice, not to be punished as he justly deserved—and for why? Oh! blush to hear it, my readers—*because it would make the slaves saucy!* Happy am I to state, that this *conscientious* juryman lived not in Antigua —that this horrible murder was not committed there.

I mean not to insinuate that this was the general opinion of residents in the West Indies; far from it; this was a solitary case. Murder is a crime generally detested; man must become an incarnate demon, or one from whom all reason has fled, before he can perpetrate such an act: and whoever may be the victim, all classes are anxious to bring the murderer to justice. But, and I feel confident I am not going beyond the truth, in many instances, crimes of less magnitude, where loss of life and limb has not ensued, have been passed over, or if noticed, and the form of trial complied with, Astræa has not equally balanced her scales, and the negro has not been righted *because he was only a negro*.

Oh! I have heard and read of deeds of blood which would chill the very soul—deeds which in other days have been practised in Antigua, noted as she was for the mildness of her slave laws. Those infernal instruments of torture have been used, even invented, by man in his most debased state—"the detestable, ever-to-be-detested cart-whip," the heavy chain, the dark loathsome dungeon, the thumb-screw, and the barbarous "mouth-piece," as it was termed, which was a plate of iron pressing upon the tongue, while bars of iron enclosed the head, and a padlock, fastened behind the victim's neck, prevented their agonizing cries from reaching mortal ears. But the Infinite from his bright throne saw and pitied these poor wretched sons of Ham, and sent men of milder mood—men whose hearts were touched with their miseries, whose ears were open to their cries—to labour and exert themselves in their behalf, and at last obtain their liberty.

Sometimes iron rings were fastened round their legs, which their kind and humane masters jocularly termed, "negro-boots;" at other times massy iron collars were fixed round their necks, to which was attached galling chains; and fearful these might give *too little pain*, or occasion *too little inconvenience*, half-hundred weights were hung to them. It used to be a method of punishment, it is said, in former times, when owners did not mind losing the value of a negro or two, to take an empty hogshead, and after driving plenty of nails into it, making the points to protrude in the inside, to put a slave or two into it, and heading it up, roll them down a steep hill; and thus leave them to expire. Some masters, when their slaves were *very ill*, or *very old*, and could be of no further service, used to bury them alive; and it is said, that upon being put into their graves, they have been heard to say, "Pray, massa, no bury me, me no dead yet; do, massa, let dem take me out;" and the master, with a curse upon his lips, has replied that he had plenty of money to buy more; he did not want an old, half-dead negro.

Gibbeting alive was another mode of punishment formerly in use; and when adopted, the sufferers have been known to live more than a week. That any one could deliberately condemn a fellow-creature to such intolerable anguish seems almost impossible; yet that such has been the case in Antigua, is remembered by some alive; I have heard of one instance in which a white man was the sufferer. I should not have noticed it in this place, was it not that it proves how much cruelty was practised even in those days. All will allow, or at least ought to do, that when a criminal suffers the extreme penalty of the law, it is done for the sake of example, not revenge; and consequently, the mildest and quickest kind of death should be practised. The circumstance alluded to, was as follows. A white man, known as Captain White, the owner of a small vessel, had for some length of time committed piracy upon the high seas; but at last was taken, and brought into Antigua. He was condemned to die, and that death to be by gibbeting. A gibbet was accordingly prepared; the wretched man was carried to a bay, near where St. James's Fort is now erected, and there, in the face of heaven, *he was hung up in chains, alive!* with a loaf of bread and a calabash of water almost within his reach; but which, like the waters of Tartarus to him of old, only mocked him with their approach, as the wind blew them backwards and forwards. The man lived nine days in this situation; and in the extremity of his hunger, actually ate the flesh from off his shoulders. The place where he was executed is well known to many in Antigua as White's Bay, and a few years ago, the remains of the gibbet was to be met with. How ought we to bless God, that we lived not in those days; that our feelings are now not outraged by any of those dreadful exhibitions: certainly, his crime (piracy) was a dreadful one, but who cannot but feel for his after-sufferings?

The following letter from a white inhabitant throws a further light upon the insurrection of the negroes, in 1736, which we have noticed in the "Legend of the Ravine;" and points out the particular punishment awarded to many of the actors in that tragedy:—

Antigua, Jan. 15th, 1736.

"Dear Friend,

"We are in a great deal of trouble in this island; the burning of negroes, hanging them up on gibbets alive, racking them upon the wheel, &c., takes up all our time; that from the 20th of October to this day, there have been destroyed *sixty-one* intelligent negroes, most of them tradesmen, as carpenters, coopers, and masons.

"I am almost dead with watching and working, as are many more. They were going to destroy all the white inhabitants of the island. 'Count,' the king of the negroes, 'Tomboy,' his general, and 'Hercules,' his lieutenant-general, who were all racked upon the wheel, died with obstinacy. Mr. Archibald Hamilton's 'Harry,' after he was condemned, stuck himself with a knife, in eighteen different places, four of which were mortal. Colonel Martin's 'Jemmy,' who was hung up alive from noon to eleven o'clock at night, was then taken down to give information. Colonel Morgan's 'Ned,' after he had been hung up seven days and seven nights, that his hands grew too small for his hand-cuffs, he got them out and raised himself, and fell down from a gibbet fifteen feet high; he was revived with cordials and broths, in hopes to bring him to confess, but he would not, and was hung up again, and in a day and a night expired. Mr. Yeaman's 'Quashy Coonah' jumped out of the fire half burnt, but was thrown in again; and Mr. Lyon's 'Fine,' jumped out of the fire, and promised to confess all, but it took no effect. In short, our island is in a poor, miserable condition, and I wish I could get any employment in England to do."

I mean not to sicken my readers by too minute details of what slavery was in its dark and fearful days; but it is proper that a few instances should be given, that the young in particular may rejoice they live in a day when "liberty, that thrice-sweet and gracious goddess," has so ample a domain; and while they delight in the freedom of British negroes, drop a tear of pity to the fate of those unfortunates who are torn every year from all the endearing ties of country, friends, and home, that they may obtain for their unfeeling masters a little more of the "honey of Hybla," which is so sweet, that even peace of mind is too often sacrificed for it.

The examples which I have already given may be said to have happened many years ago; but still, for long after that, the life of a slave was looked upon as of very little value, provided the master was reimbursed for the cash they cost. If brought before a magistrate one day, they were, perhaps, condemned and executed the day after; and should a condemned criminal accost a passer-by in these words—"Ah! buddy you no no me now; but p'raps you will," and such salutation be heard by the sentinel, that person, if even a stranger, and guiltless, perhaps, of all offence, was taken up on suspicion of having some dealing with the captive, and in some instances suffered death with him. The intrigues which were carried on between negroes in those days, rendered it, it is said, expedient to adopt these harsh measures.

I have heard it asserted, that the reason slaves first came to be tried by jury, in 1785, was this:—A black man was brought up before two magistrates, on suspicion of having committed some heinous crime; and after hearing the case, the culprit was condemned and executed. A week or two elapsed, and something transpired to lead to a suspicion that he was not the guilty party. Through the exertion of a Mr. Gunthorpe, the case was tried again; and the result was, that the man was pronounced innocent. After that it was ordained, that no slave should be condemned to *death*, without being first brought before a jury, consisting of six persons.

For the particulars of this case, I am indebted to an old man well known in Antigua. He bears the burthen of eighty-six years, and is still as active and strong as many a one only half that age. I heard him speak very highly of our late gracious majesty William IV., who, when he was in the navy, visited Antigua for some time. "Prince Henry was a good young gentleman, God bless his memory!" cried the old man. "I used to wait upon him, and have often heard him speak of what good he would do, should he ever come to the throne. He has spared many a black person a good flogging. And when we all heard he was king, every one said—God bless him!" Old Mascall, for that is his name, can tell many a tale of other days, and no doubt has seen many shocking sights in the course of his long life. I heard him tell of another gentleman, who used to treat his slaves in a most barbarous manner, giving them commonly fifty lashes at one time, and then calling for a lighted candle, drop melted sealing-wax upon the gashes. His cook used to be chained to a "fifty -six," (a weight of fifty-six pounds,) with a chain long enough to enable him to walk from the kitchen to the house; and his washer used also to be chained in like manner to her wash-tub, in which situation, my informant told me, one woman dropped down dead, with her chains around her.[6] With regard to this piece of cruelty, all that I can say, but which on no account do I offer as an excuse, is, that the negroes are very stubborn, and given to prevarication. They have so often represented themselves ill, when such has not been the case, that they might avoid their day's labour, that when really suffering from sickness, they have seldom met with any sympathy.

---

[3] Although the slave-trade had been abolished, yet it was still customary for the island slaves to change owners as a horse would; but the Antiguans becoming sensible of such inhuman practice, few purchasers could be found, consequently negroes were of less value in the way of traffic. As regards their labour, however, they were of equal value to their masters in Antigua, as the slaves of other colonies.

[4] A sign that they were new subjects.

[5] See Chambers' Edinburgh Journal.

[6] Old Mascall's information may be doubted by some, but it certainly agrees with the authenticated cruelties which were practised in former years, the details of which have been omitted from want of space.

CHAPTER XXXI

Negroes: Palliations, *but not excuses*, for former cruelties—A harsh planter—Crimes of slaves—The little negroes' dinner-hour—A character—Negroes' want of thought—Bartering their weekly provisions—Pilfering—The Rock Dungeon—A Tortolian slave-master—The murdered slave—Branding—Slave cargo—Remarks upon slavery—A good slave-master—A kind attorney—Negro gratitude.

When I undertook this work, I laid down for myself one uniform rule, the propriety of which my readers must admit, which was, to adhere strictly to facts without fear or favour. I mourn to think that any one, much more a Briton, should have practised those cruel deeds which were perpetrated even in this island, in former days. I am well aware how much patience it requires to deal with negroes, and also how strong the force of example is. We all of us are liable to err; those passions which it has pleased the Giver of all to ingraft in our bosoms, although not to be extirpated, as the disciples of Zeno would have us believe, require to be kept under strict restraint, or else how soon we may be led to commit acts we ourselves would be the first to condemn. Self-control is no easy matter; the wise man says—"He who ruleth his own spirit is greater than he who taketh a city." Nothing will enable us to overcome ourselves but a deep feeling of religion. In those early times of slavery there was no settled place of worship—no sound of the "church-going" bell in Antigua; and men who might have left England with the best of feelings, from living in this manner, and having to deal with stubborn and aggravating characters, in time grew callous.

The flowers which deck this beautiful world require the suns and dews of heaven to support their fragile forms; the birds which charm us with their melody look up to their Maker's hand for their daily food; can it be supposed, then, that man, a weak and sinful creature, can walk uprightly without a daily intercourse with his God? No; let philosophers boast as they will, man's greatest strength is in his weakness; and it is from the spread of Christianity in these parts, and Christian pastors taking the place of those "blind leaders of the blind," who, in former days, presumed to preach the gospel here, that people are enabled to bear with the negroes, and not give way to such violent acts of resentment again them. As I remarked in the conclusion of the former chapter, I cannot, *dare not* offer these remarks as an excuse for cruelty; but while I reprobate such conduct as I have been describing, I cannot help thinking how different the time was then to what it is now—how the bright day-spring has chased away the clouds of night.

But my melancholy subject is not yet ended; a few more acts remain to be exhibited before the curtain falls. There was some years ago an Antiguan planter who was of such a tyrannical disposition, that he was an object of dread to the whole negro population, until at length he made himself so hated by them, from his cruel punishment, that he fancied his life in danger, and therefore quitted the island, and remained absent for many years. It was customary for many persons at that time to send, or threaten to send, negroes who were refractory or lazy, to Mr. —— for punishment, and so dreaded was his name, that, in most cases, it procured good behaviour and declarations of amendment; for hard, indeed, was the fate of those who fell into his hands. It is said that Mr. —— has been known to order two drivers to stretch a slave, no matter whether male or female, upon the ground, and to flog them until he rode round his estate, (which was one of good extent,) and upon his return, if he did not think the gashes sufficiently open, he would make them continue their demoniac employment for a longer period. The operation of flogging was thus performed:—the unfortunate victims of their barbarity were stretched upon the earth their full-length, four men held them down, while one or more drivers, with their immense cart-whips, lacerated the flesh at every stroke. Sometimes after this violent discipline of the whip, more humane masters, if they can be termed so, have ordered their bleeding backs to be washed with pickle, in order to prevent mortification; but Mr. —— would not allow this to be done; he would not let them have any assistance; but chains have been put upon them, and they have been led back to their dungeon, and maggots have been known to breed in their flesh!

This is no tale of fiction, no "Castle of Udolpho," to horrify the mind with its ideal fancies; no, it is the plain, unvarnished tale of truth, of what our poor negroes once suffered in Christian countries from those who professed themselves Christian masters. I mean not to say that every slave-owner was a man of blood; God forbid they should have been, for then every breeze that blew would have been loaded with groans—every sun that rose would have witnessed mangled bodies. No; there were many, very many, in Antigua who treated their slaves with the utmost kindness, even in slavery's early days; but more particularly in this generation, when milder principles were inculcated, and milder punishments put into effect.

But, it may be inquired, what was the fault of negroes? Surely they must be crimes of great magnitude to call for so severe a use of the whip. In answer, we can only observe that these faults, or crimes, or errors, call them what you will, were various. For example: sometimes a mule or two strayed into a cane-field and cropped the young canes, or part of the herd of cattle broke away from the cattle-keepers when inattentive to them, and devoured, or trod down, a piece of yams. Some of the slaves ran away for a day or two, and others returned saucy answers, (which all negroes are very competent to do;) some were lazy, some did their work ill, and some again were behind the time in which they were required by law to commence their daily labour in the field; the list was called over by the overseer before they arrived, and they were reported "absent."

Another frequent crime was theft. In times of slavery, as already shewn, instead of giving money to the negroes as a recompence, every necessary was found them by their owners—their dress, their houses, their doctor, and their food. The common practice upon estates was, to distribute to the negroes dresses twice in the year, and their provisions once or twice in the week. This consisted (as mentioned in a former part of this work) of so many yards of cloth, shirting, flannel, and so many woollen caps, handkerchiefs, &c., for their wardrobes; and for their weekly provision so many pounds of yams, herrings, or mackerel, &c., for each grown person; and at Christmas time, a further supply of salt pork and wheat flour.

The little children had their own allowance, and upon those estates where the proprietor or manager cared for their welfare, an old woman was employed to boil it for them; and about noon they all marched up to the "great house" with their calabashes in their hands, which answered the purpose of plate and bason, to partake of the "savoury messes" not "which the *neat-handed* Phillis dresses," for these pic'ni'es cook was anything but neat-handed or clean.

I have often been amused, upon visiting an estate belonging to Sir Geo. Thomas, Bart., where the attorney was a kind and humane master, at seeing these little people eat their dinners. There was a large paved court before the door, around which the little *blackies* were seated, waiting in silence for their share. The old woman having seen them well arranged, returned for the pot, which was placed in the centre, and contained various ingredients, as yams, potatoes, corn-flour dumplings, herrings, with a good supply of water, &c., forming a kind of "*olla-podrida.*" How many little black sparkling eyes were fixed upon that pot and its contents, while the old woman took the important office of distributing it into the numerous attending calabashes. When the information "All done, massa," meaning that the pot was empty, was given, (for the master was present to see that these poor little children got their proper portion,) and Mr. ——, with an arch smile, asked, "No more herring left?" and the negative given, they all rose, one by one, and fetched their own share, when, without any spoon but what Dame Nature gave them in their fingers, it quickly found its way to their mouths, without a drop being wasted; the calabashes turned down, shewed the important business was over, and the old woman and her charge departed to their accustomed pursuits.

Years have passed since I witnessed those scenes, but I fancy I can see that old woman now. Age is not famous for loveliness, and I am sure none was there. She must have been in her youth very tall, but when I knew her, time had bent her form and grizzled her woolly hair. Her complexion was of a coal black, with a most sinister expression of countenance; her dull black eyes were never still; her face looked as if every moment added another wrinkle, while an immense pair of elephant legs completed the picture. She was very famous, I afterwards found out, for giving the children the liquid portion of the mess, and reserving the herrings for herself, which occasioned Mr. ——'s question.

But to resume the sadder part of my picture, (for the digression I have been led into may be termed one of the "lights" of slavery,) slaves' crimes and slaves' punishments. Upon the "allowance days," as they were called, the negroes were very flush of provisions; and having no thoughts of a "rainy day," or, in other words, putting by a portion for the other days of the week, they sold them for anything that took their fancy. The consequence of this was, that for the rest of the week they were in a state of starvation, and unless any friend ministered to their wants, they very likely entered their master's provision grounds, and stole part of the productions. This, of course, was discovered in the morning, the culprits generally detected, and they received their punishment, varying in degrees of severity, according to the disposition of their masters. At one time this system of bartering the food given them by their owners for indifferent articles was so prevalent, that complaints were laid before the house of assembly; and in the year 1814, an act passed which was intended as a preventive against this practice.

Another crime of slaves was to milk the cattle upon the estates, and sell the milk in town; and this again called for the use of the whip. Molasses and sugar were also stolen in great quantities, and sold to persons making ginger drink; sugar-cakes, as they are termed, which are composed of sugar, molasses, ginger, and cocoa-nut, boiled up together; and many other different sweets. Even persons who ought to have known better, encouraged slaves in stealing, by buying of them sugar for domestic purposes. This also called for the interposition of the law; and slaves so offending were to be whipped, and sent to work in the street-gang. I have mentioned the street-gang in a former chapter; but it may be well to remark, that the slaves comprising it were worked two and two together, by having an iron collar round their necks, and connected by a chain, not exactly the size and thickness of that formerly shewn in "Aldermanbury;"[2] but rather like those used upon the convicts in the different dockyards in England.

These were the most frequent offences of slaves. Those of a higher degree, such as murders, and running away for more than three months, were, as we have already seen, punished in a severer manner. Although the slave-owner had redress by the laws of the island, for all faults committed by his slaves, revolting as it is to think of, there were some masters who thought thirty-nine lashes[8] too mild a punishment for such crimes: they would rather take the law into their own hands, and flog their slaves by the hour. They liked to see mangled bodies,—to hear heart-rending groans, and have the supreme felicity of ordering them back to their dungeons, garnished, perhaps, with chains, as in the case of Mr. ——. I have laid before my readers, or at least endeavoured to do so, slaves' crimes and slaves' punishments; and it is for them to say whether they deserved such severe discipline. In another part I shall have to enlarge upon the vices of negroes, and their perverseness of disposition; but it now remains for me to give one or two more instances of cruelty; and I will then banish from these pages the melancholy subject.

A gentleman of this island, as I have been made to understand, had a female *mustee*[2] slave belonging to him. This slave committed some misdemeanor, whether great or small I am unable to say; but at all events, her master had her locked up for the night in a place of horrors, called the "Rock Dungeon." The woman was in the last stage of pregnancy; in that place, removed from all assistance, she was confined during the night; and when the morning came, and that den of misery was opened, her poor baby was found to be devoured by the rats! This deed was done by one of our great men, an honourable too. It may be said, he could not foresee the catastrophe, and the woman might have given him great provocation, which no doubt she did; but still, would any humane master have shut up a female in such a condition in such a place? By the advice of the magistrates, this woman and her remaining children were afterwards sold, as her master and herself could never agree. This is not the only instance in which his name has been brought before the public. Some strange reports were abroad of his shooting one of his negro boys; and of his killing another, and burying him in a pond. These circumstances were brought before the slavery committee of the House of Lords in 1832; and in an examination of a divine, the rector of the parish in which the gentleman resided, he was asked if he knew anything about them? The Rev. Mr. —— returned for answer—"Yes, I heard a report about them, but do not know if they were correct." And again—"I never heard of his killing a negro; but I heard of his burying a white matross in the sand; but that was only hearsay. I only heard of it from persons, perhaps, that were not his friends. With regard to shooting a negro, he went and gave himself up for that; and I believe he was acquitted, or the coroner's inquest brought in a verdict of 'accidental death.' There was some sort of a trial; but I believe there was a great deal said about it, that probably he did not deserve,—I think so." This was the rector's opinion: whether the gentleman alluded to was guilty, is more than

I can say; we can but hope he was not. The matter rests between himself and his God; but if he did act in this manner, if he was guilty of these deaths, conscience must at times give him some sharp twinges.[10]

I have in a former page referred to the trial of a planter for the murder of his slave. It did not occur in Antigua, I am happy to say; but as Antiguan barristers pleaded for and against the culprit, it may not be amiss to give a short account of it. The offender against justice was a member of the council at Tortola; and upon his estate in that island these horrible cruelties were perpetrated. I cannot go into the details of the case, which were most revolting in their circumstances; but will just give the heads. This man—this vampire he might be called—was found guilty, and executed upon the common gallows, for the murder of *one* of his slaves, a poor African; but there were eight other indictments for murder ready made out against the same individual, whose cruelty of disposition was proverbial.

"Prosper," the name of the murdered man, was, as before remarked, a poor African, one who, to use the words of the counsel for the crown, "was murdered by the man, to promote whose interests the strength of his youth was exhausted;" and his crime was, eating one mango, which fell off a tree he was watching. For this one fault, the poor fellow was whipped, until not one piece of black skin was left upon him, from his hip to his hand; afterwards ironed, and thrown into a loathsome dungeon. The next day he was brought out and whipped again, because he had not six shillings to pay his master, (the sum demanded for the eaten mango, that would cost about three farthings sterling,) until nature was exhausted, and he fainted. But he awoke to consciousness and agony; the dungeon was again his refuge, and chained to two other objects of misery, he passed that wretched night. Here he remained five days, suffering unspeakable tortures; but at the end of that time, these three miserable creatures contrived to make their escape. Poor "Prosper," however, was too near death to go far; he crawled into his own hut, which was near, and after lingering for a few days, expired,—a prey to the worms before the last sigh had left his lips. When discovered, his remains were so offensive, that a hole was dug at his hut door, he was shovelled in, a little dirt thrown over, and he was left to repose in his irons, until that great day, when master and slave must appear before one bar.[11] Who can read this account without a deep feeling of horror? What will my readers say when I further mention, that when this monster was brought up under a writ of habeas corpus, his lawyer, a barrister of Antigua, asserted, that "it was no greater offence, in law, for an owner to kill his slave, than it would be to kill his dog!"

Another cruel act of proprietors in those days was to brand the negroes with their owner's initials. This was done with a red-hot iron, upon young and old, male and female. Indeed, altogether, the negroes were treated more like cattle than human beings. Before the abolition of the slave-trade, cargoes of from 100 to 200, and upwards, used frequently to be brought to this island. When landed, they were generally in a state of nudity, with the exception of strings of beads tied round them; and in this state they remained until purchased. Upon the arrival of these cargoes of "livestock," the merchants sometimes made an offer for the whole, and then retailed them out, should their offer be accepted. At other times, the master or supercargo of the vessel had them sold at public auction, or disposed of a part, and carried the remainder to another market. Those merchants who dealt principally in this commodity used to provide themselves with a long room, for the reception of these poor creatures, where they were placed all together, like so many horses or mules—the floor being littered down with trash.[12] They were fed twice a-day with rice, horse-beans, or cornflour; and every morning and evening, they were placed in a rank, two and two together, and driven to a pond to water. When persons wanted negroes, they went to the slave-store, and had several brought out to look at—made them skip, jump, run, and dance, to see if they were strong, and their limbs in perfect order; and then, if approved of, their price was paid in "paltry gold," and they became the property of a new master, a being like themselves, only differing, perhaps, in the colour of their skin.

Montesquieu, an eminent French writer, speaking of the unlawfulness of thus entrapping and selling these poor Africans, says—"The strongest reason which can be given for using negroes like beasts of burden is their having black skins and flat noses." Our own immortal Cowper, when writing upon this subject, expresses himself in a similar manner:—

"He finds the fellow guilty of a skin
Not colour'd like his own; and, having power
T' enforce the wrong, for such a worthy cause
Dooms and devotes him as his lawful prey."

That men, fashioned by the hands of the same Creator, descended from the same common parent, could thus buy and sell their fellow-creatures just as they would a horse or a cow, seems almost incredible. Future generations will, no doubt, be inclined to discredit such a report, as the wild tale of some imaginary mind. Even in this day, in this island, it causes surprise to many to think they acted so; and the different paragraphs in an old Antigua newspaper, which now lies before me, would appear almost as strange to them as they do to me. Among the list of imports for the week, in this old paper, are "*seven negroes*, five casks of coffee, one bag of cotton, and an old copper kettle!" Thinking of slavery as I do, I could almost say, with the poet—

"No! dear as freedom is, and in my heart's
Just estimation prized above all price,
I had much rather be myself the slave,
And wear the bonds, than fasten them on him."

I am aware that many people, speaking of the propriety of slavery, argue in this manner—"Has it not existed since the days of Noah? And did not the Almighty appear to sanction it then? Can it be more unlawful now?" I grant, that it has existed since those early days:—"A servant of servants shall he be unto his brethren" was, I know, the curse of Canaan; but reasoners like these should study the laws which the All-wise made for the prevention of cruelty to the Hebrew slaves or servants. Let them compare what slavery is, or rather what it was, with the slavery of biblical history. "Rule not over him (the servant or slave) with *rigour* but fear thy God;" and again—"Harden not thine heart, nor shut thine hand, for remember, he is thy *brother*." These were the words of One who cannot err. In all ages of the world, man's pride has made him love to domineer over his fellows; and where it is allowed by law, there are many who would rather have slaves to do their orders, than be at the trouble of persuading their inferiors.

I am happy to say, I have never met with any ocular demonstration of the successive cruelties I have been describing. It has been my good fate to reside in Antigua when a milder spirit in general seemed to actuate men; or if, in some of their bosoms, the demon of persecution still kept his abode, shame prevented its making its appearance. I have, it is true, heard the sound of the driver's whip, when the gang have been working; but it seemed to be used as a kind of stimulant, like the crack of the carter's whip, when he drives his team, to urge on his horses.

I have seen a dungeon, but its only occupants were rats; I have met with stocks and shackles, but they were thrown about as useless lumber. Still, I have no doubt there have been cruelties perpetrated here since my residence; but, thank God, I never witnessed them. I have often heard the voice of childhood supplicating mercy; it has been in the town, among the lower classes, who have been chastising their little servant. I have felt for the little creatures, as they begged for pardon; but pity was all I could give them. But now, the case is altered: slavery is no more—the whip is banished; and even the little children will scarcely take a blow. I was amused the other day, with a scene which took place before our dwelling: the actors, a mother and her child. The mother had a small cane in her hand, as if about to chastise her daughter, a child of about six years old, who begged very hard for forgiveness. "Do, mammy, don't lick me; me beg your pardon, ma'am. Oh! don't lick me, mammy; me no do so no more." The mother relented, and let go the child's hands, who, turning round immediately the fear of coercion was removed, stamped her little foot upon the ground, and, raising her tiny fist, exclaimed—"War you lick me for? Me free—me no b'longs to you!"

I visited some few estates in this island during the latter years of slavery, and I was happy to find that they were conducted under a mild system, and the slaves appeared happy and contented. At one of these, the proprietor seemed to be very much beloved by his people; but he had an ear always open to their complaint; a hand ever ready to minister to their wants; and under the free system, his kindness as a slave-owner is not forgotten. This gentleman is a magistrate; and at the time I am speaking of, he had frequent complaints brought before him from the negroes of the adjoining estates, for all negroes are very litigious. I am sure he deserved credit for the patience with which he heard their tiresome stories; and so the negroes appeared to think too, for I have often heard them say to one another, when departing from the house, "Wen me free, me come lib with dis massa; for if eber dere one good massa in Antigua, he one."

An instance deserves to be recorded of another planter, with whom I have the honour to be acquainted; which proves there were slave-masters whose hearts were not of adamant; who could be kind to the poor creatures so entirely under their control; and that some marks of gratitude and affection could be shewn by a *slave*. In 1831, the island was in a very unsettled state, from abolishing the Sunday markets, and not appointing another day for the negroes to bring their provisions into town to sell. Constant fires occurred on different estates; no sooner was one extinguished, than another was discovered. The militia was on duty night and day; and serious alarm was abroad for the safety of the island.

The gentleman alluded to was attorney for several estates; the one he resided upon was a very large property, belonging to Sir George Thomas, and possessed a gang of about 250 negroes. His militia duty called him to a distance, and he was obliged to leave his wife and children, surrounded by all the slaves: how far the spirit of mutiny and disaffection had crept in among them, he was unable to say.

Whilst these thoughts were passing in his mind, and of course rendering him very uneasy, a few of the head slaves upon the plantation waited upon him. I cannot give the precise words they made use of, but they were to this effect: "Master, you have always been very kind to us, to our wives, and to our children; you have never given us harsh language, or cruel beatings; and while we did our work orderly and quietly, you have been most indulgent to us. Master, we thank you for it, we feel grateful, very grateful; and we here solemnly pledge ourselves to guard with our lives your wife, your children, and your property, as you have guarded us and ours." The attorney trusted the negroes; he left the estate; and he found them act as they had promised. Oh, if anything can gild the dark picture of slavery, such instances as these will; and in these days of freedom, such men can lay their heads upon their pillows with ease, and bless God, that in the day of power, they were kept from exercising undue severity upon their defenceless slaves.

---

[7] The office of the Anti-slavery Society.

[8] By the Mosaic law, criminals were not to receive more than forty stripes at one time, and for one offence; but that there might be no fear of breaking the commandment, the Jews were in the habit of giving one *less* than the allowed number. Their whips were made with three thongs, or tails, and with this instrument the criminals received thirteen stripes, making the number of blows thirty-nine. Now the implement used for whipping negroes was a *cat*, with *nine* tails; and as thirty-nine lashes were given with it, the poor slaves received altogether 351 stripes at one time—a humane punishment, it must be allowed!

[9] See Chapter XLIII.

[10] From Anti-slavery Reports.

[11] It was customary in those days to bury negroes upon the estate to which they belonged, the burying-ground being generally near their houses.

[12] Dry leaves of the sugar-cane.

CHAPTER XXXII

Negroes: The assertion that negroes are careless of all domestic ties confuted by anecdotes—"Shadows" of negro character—Excuses for them —Conversion to Christianity—Belief of the Africans that after death they shall return to Africa—Instance of it—Africans and Creoles—Superstitions —Obeah.

Since writing the preceding chapter, it has been represented to me, that I have painted slavery in too gloomy colours, particularly the parting of husband and wife, parent and children, by sale; that the negroes are an unfeeling race; that parental or connubial affections are seldom felt by them; or if experienced at all, it is but very partially. As a proof of this, it is said that in Africa husbands will sell their wives and children, brothers their sisters, mothers their daughters, for a mere trifle. I am aware that such has been the case, particularly in times of scarcity, when part of a family has been disposed of to provide food for the rest. The Capuchin friars, in their mission to Congo, mention, that one day hearing a man making a great outcry, and saying, "I have no wife, no child, no brother! Miserable wretch that I am! I once had all these, but I sold them;" they asked him the reason for his acting so. "To purchase drink," was the reply; "and if I had them again, I should do the same." But this is a single circumstance; possibly, such an utter want of feeling would not be found in the rest of the tribe. Why *should* not love pervade the breast of the black as well as the white? That it does do so, may be proved by many pathetic instances.

A master of slaves in Kingston, Jamaica, owned a negro who was the mother of two fine little boys. Being in want of cash, the master disposed of one. The poor mother, in the agony of maternal feeling at having her offspring thus turned from her, made a hideous lamentation; and for this crime, as it was termed, her owner commanded her to receive a severe flogging. She had still one, however, left, and she would sit for hours, holding it in her arms, and pouring upon its unconscious ear her tale of sorrow. But alas! the spoiler came again: her master wanted more money, and regardless of the heart-rending cries of the distracted mother, who begged him not to take her last, her best-beloved, the child was sold. This utter bereavement "turned her heart within her," and caused "the light of madness" to kindle in her eye.

A short time ago, I was speaking to an old woman whom I knew when she was a slave upon McKinnon's estate; and among other questions, I asked her, "Juncho," (her name,) "are you happier now than when you was a slave—are you better off now than you was then? or would you be satisfied to return to slavery, and become once more the property of your old master?" "Missis," returned the poor old creature, "me no going to tell 'tory, me 'peak de truth; me no better off now den me war den, nor no so well self; for den me hab house and garden, an me could raise 'tock, (meaning poultry, &c.,) an plant yam, an pittates, (potatoes,) an green, an ebery ting else; and now me free, me hab notting." "And where is your house now?" I asked, to hear what she would say. "Why, wen August com, massa call me, and he say, Me no want you to lib here no more; you no good to work, you must go, me want your house to gib to one oder somebody dats 'trong; no ole like you; and you garden me want. So you know, missis, me forced to go; so me come to town wid me daughter, and me lib wid she, for me can do but lilly work now." "Then you would rather be a slave again?" "Oh, no, missis, me no want to be slabe gen, me sure. God made me free—God put it in buckra heart to set me free, an me bless God for it; me no want to be slabe gen." "But I understood you, that you were better off in the time of slavery—that you had many comforts then that you cannot obtain now, and yet you tell me you do not want to be a slave again—tell me the reason." "Well, missis, it true me better off den dan me am now, for since me free, me no get much; sometimes me no eat bread all day, for me daughter hab so many pic'nees (children) she no able to gib me much; but den me no me free; me no God gib me free, and slabery is one bad something sometimes." I went on to ask her what she meant by a "bad something," for I was anxious to know what the negroes thought of slavery and freedom. "S'pose, den," said Juncho, "s'pose you hab one pic'nee, dat pic'nee sick; well, he put in de sick house; me 'bliged to go field, me want to go see me sick pic'nee, but me no must go, me hab to work till ebening 'praps; wen work done, me go see me poor sick pic'nee, but me must no 'top wid he. Me hab make haste go; den me pic'nee say, 'Mammy, 'top wid me, no go, mammy:' but me forced to go and leabe me poor pic'nee. Den 'gen, missis, 'praps me pic'nee do something bad, something he no ought to do, and massa take he and tie he two hands up to one tree, else he make two men 'tretch he upon de ground, an den de driber lick he so, an me cry to see him lick so, and me pic'nee bawl, but me no dare say, 'Don't do so, massa; let him go,' but me hab to go way and lebe he dere; so you see, missis, dat make me say me no lub slabery. Now wen me noung, me hab to work hard, hab dig cane hole, weed cane, pick grass, do ebery ting; but now me ole, and no able to work, dey take away me house, 'cause me no b'longs to dem, but den me no me free, and me bless God me am free." This was Juncho's tale: it proves negroes do feel for their relations when in trouble, or suffering from illness; but with regard to her being turned out of her house after freedom, I think is not quite correct, for I never heard of an Antiguan planter doing so. Perhaps all of her children who could be of any service to the estate, by working upon the property, quitted it, and the manager might have told her, that if they did not return, she must leave too.

Another instance, which illustrates the doctrine that negroes do feel affection towards each other, is related by one who used to frequent the slave markets. One day, going his rounds, he saw two fine intelligent-looking youths, with their arms clasped tightly round each other, and being pleased with their appearance, he went up, and asked the price of the eldest of the two. After some talk, the bargain was completed, and the negro became the property of his new master.

While this business was going on between the buyer and seller, the youths looked on with the deepest feeling of attention depicted upon their sable faces. When the younger perceived that his companion was about to be led away from him, he clung to him with almost supernatural strength. Suddenly he released his hold, sprang up, for he had thrown himself down upon his knees, commenced jumping with all his might, dancing, and putting himself into a thousand different attitudes, to shew his strength and the pliancy of his limbs, in hopes the purchaser would take him also. All, however, was of no avail, and his sorrowing friend in affliction was about to be led away; when the poor fellow, as if to try the last resort, flew up to the gentleman, threw his arms around him, and with the most expressive looks of agony, seemed to beseech his pity. Nature has not made every one insensible to the voice of woe; he saw and felt for the boy's grief, and he lightened the bands of slavery by buying them both.

Another anecdote is related by a resident of Nevis, who had occasion to purchase some slaves, and accordingly, upon the arrival of a Guinea ship with a cargo of negroes, he went to inspect them. As they appeared strong and active, Mr. —— made a bargain for a certain number. After the lapse of some months, finding that he wanted an increase of hands to carry on the work of the estate, and another cargo having arrived, he visited the capital, and purchased a further supply of negroes, which were also conducted to his plantation. Upon their arrival, the former lot came forward to welcome the new comers; and amongst the number a young negress, who, when she had looked upon a female of about the same age as herself, suddenly started, her lips quivered with emotion, her eyes glistened, and then, as if fully assured, she started forward, and threw her arms around the neck of the girl who had attracted her attention, and who had been similarly affected, and burst into a flood of tears. Tenderly and fervently did these children of nature embrace each other, long did their mutual tears flow, until, when they had partly regained their composure, their master asked if they had known each other in Africa. In a voice of joy which vibrated upon every heart, the one who had first arrived, and who had acquired a little English, replied—"Oh, massa, she me own dear sissy!"

In many instances the character of the negroes is very bad—sullen, obstinate, and revengeful, given to lying, stealing, and deceit. Still I do not so much attribute this to their pristine state, as I do to the way in which they have formerly been treated. The Africans, torn from their native country and all their former connexions, made to work beneath a broiling sun harder than they were ever accustomed to do, beaten for the slightest fault, and scorned as the meanest reptile, could form, it is to be supposed, no very favourable opinion of their masters. Memory would at times transport them home; again, in fancy, would they roam their native wilds, or with their well-known companions rouse the tawny lion from his lair, or chase the fleet-footed antelope. Once more would the song be heard, once more, in imagination, would they join the festive dance beneath the spreading branches of some noble mimosa; but in the midst of this joyous scene, the voice of the overseer would be heard, or the crack of the driver's whip dissolve their airy castles, and they would return to despondency and despair.

Ignorant of the God that made them, and of the mild doctrines of Christianity, no wonder the dark spirit of revenge took possession of their breasts. The feelings of the parents were naturally enough inculcated into the minds of their children, and this, strengthened, perhaps, by harsh treatment from their owners, has conspired to render the negro character, in great measure, what I am sorry to say it is.

But we ought now to look for brighter days: a great deal has been done for the negroes, much even before emancipation; schools have been erected in all parts of the island, and instruction proffered, both to young and old. The labours of the Moravian and Wesleyan missionaries have, without doubt, done a great deal of good to society at large by teaching the divine truths to the black population, and striving to make them learn the important fact that they have something else to look for besides the gratification of the present moment. As an episcopalian myself, I feel sorry that the church of England should have been less forward some years ago in their labour of love. True it is there has been, from the time these missionaries first came to the island, up to the present, a great number of churches and parsons. But of these, few, I am sorry to say, practised the pure doctrine they pretended to preach; indeed, many openly denied by their lives what they taught with their lips: their motto was—"Do as I say, not as I act;" which conduct, although it ought not to make religion less respected, has, in a great measure, a tendency to that effect among all classes. "For how," would many exclaim, "could they enforce the seventh commandment when they wilfully broke it?—or teach a proper respect to the ordinances of God, when (as some have been known to do) they have left a card-table to read the service at church, and then returned to finish their game?" But those days have passed away: Antigua now possesses another race of clergymen very different to those alluded to; men of pious lives, and of ardent desire to further the cause of Christianity. The rector of St. John's, the Rev. R. Holberton, is an evangelical preacher, and has proved a great acquisition to the island. This gentleman is one who does not preach for the sake of the *loaves and fishes* alone, but strives to do his duty as an humble follower of his divine Master. To his talents as an orator, he adds the more sterling quality of earnest zeal in his vocation, evinced by the bright example he sets, of joining practice to precept. His discourses are not in that flowery style which, working upon the feelings and imagination, produces but a transitory impression; he rather strives to speak to the heart than please the ear. Like a skilful surgeon, he probes the wound he hopes to heal, and then offers the "balm of Gilead," and binds it up with the essence of love. I once more beg pardon of my readers for my digressions; but I could not let the opportunity pass, without noticing the great difference between the former race of clergymen and those of the present day; I will now return to my more immediate subject—the outlines of the negro character.

Before their conversion to Christianity, the Africans firmly believed that after death they would return to Africa, and there enjoy uninterrupted felicity. Under this idea, suicide was very frequent among them, particularly when they fell to the share of an austere and cruel master. But now this imagination is almost lost sight of: they are taught so to live, that, after death, they may inherit a better land than Africa: still I have met with some of the old people who seemed to entertain the opinion.

A short time previous to emancipation, I remember talking with a negro who fostered this belief. He was rather a remarkable personage: when in the prime of manhood, he must have possessed great strength, if we may judge from height and breadth. His cheeks, arms, and back of his hands, were deeply tattooed with different devices; his complexion was of a clear black, and his countenance very intelligent; nor had he that remarkable flatness of nose and thickness of lips by which the natives of Guinea are so particularly distinguished. He told me he had been "long 'nough" in the West Indies, (which phrase I found, by inquiry, extended to about four and twenty years,) and that he was a prince in his own country—brother, I think I understood him, to the King of Benguela, or something he pronounced very much like it; that, during a war with a neighbouring tribe, he was taken prisoner, sold to some merchants at Calabar, from whom he was purchased, with several others, by the captain of a slaver, and brought to the West Indies. Several persons whom he knew were on board the same vessel, but that they all died, with the exception of one woman. I afterwards saw this female, who confirmed him in the report of being a great man among his countrymen, where, she said, she could not speak to him, from her inferior station in life. Poor fellow; aged, (for I suppose he must have been about seventy,) infirm, and miserable—brought from comparative affluence to poverty, from governing others, to be himself a slave;—the tear of pity would not be restrained.

The circumstances under which I became acquainted with him excited also my sympathy. The estate had been, for a long time, robbed of its ground provisions, and to discover, if possible, the offenders, the owner had given orders not to distribute to the negroes their usual share of salt food, until the guilty parties confessed their crime. This poor old man came up to the "great house"[13] one morning to beg the owner's lady to intercede with "his massa" for him, that he might have some herrings to eat with his potatoes; "For," said he, "me ole now, missis—me want something to 'trengthen me; do, missis, beg massa gib me lilly salt provision." His tremulous voice, as it broke upon my ear, called my attention to him, and thus caused the introduction.

Seeing that I pitied him, he continued, "But now me ole, me soon go hom—me no 'top much longer to trouble me massa!" I asked him what he meant, and where was his home. "To me own country—to Africa!" he replied, the "light of other days" beaming, for a moment, in his eyes.— "What! now you are so *old*? You have less chance of returning there than you ever had."—"Oh! missis, you no sabby, (understand.) Me mean me die soon, an' den me go home—den me happy, den me hab no mo' work, no sick no mo', no hungry no mo'; me ole bone no ache den, but me get 'trong den an' happy too!" Poor fellow! before this he must have gone "home;" a better home than even Africa I hope he may have found it, for

"Though earth has full many a beautiful spot,
As a poet or painter may shew;
Yet more lovely and beautiful, holy and bright,
To the hopes of the heart, and the spirit's delight,
Is the land that no mortal may know."

There are not many Africans now in Antigua who were brought there as slaves, they having principally died off, but there are a great many who have been captured in slavers, and brought here by some of her majesty's ships, who have been made free, after serving an apprenticeship of some years. These persons are termed by the Creole negroes *Willeyforce nagers*, (Wilberforce,) and between them are constant bickerings—the Creole blacks looking upon themselves as so far superior. Whenever they meet and enter into conversation, it generally terminates in a quarrel; and at such times, the actions they make with their hands, and the clamour of their tongues, would almost lead you to imagine murder was intended. The African has generally the advantage over the Creole in garrulity; but when this is perceived by the other party, he exerts all his energies, "works up each corporal agent to the terrible feat," elevates his voice to the pitch of a bagpipe, throws aloft his arms, and, with fire-flashing eyes and quivering lips, exclaims—"You, *you Willeyforce nager, you!*" This is decisive; the African is stunned; and, with crest-fallen brow, goes his way, and leaves the ground to the victor.

I am now about to enter upon my "shadows" of negro character; and as I have not screened the master, neither can I gloss over the faults of the servant, or slave. The most predominant trait in their character is superstition; indeed, there never was a race so universally inclined to this weakness. What is called *Obeah*, has existed since the first introduction of negroes into these islands; it is one of those dark and fearful practices which they brought with them from Africa, where the devil is still openly worshipped, and temples built to his honour. Few English people can have any idea of the dreadful extent to which the practice of Obeah was carried in the West Indies, in former days. It led the unhappy followers of it on, from one crime to another, until the gallows was too often their end. Many, and many a one, has sunk into a premature grave, from the awful dread of Obeah hanging over them. These Obeah men and women are supposed to have entered into a league with the spirit of darkness, and by his aid are enabled to bring hidden things to light, and do many other marvellous actions; and to offend one of these person was, they thought, to seal their doom.

At one time, poisoning was so frequent a crime among these followers of Obeah, that in the year 1809, it required the strong arm of the law to subdue it. The old people are acquainted with many of the wild plants indigenous in the country; and they often recommend them as specifics in certain diseases. They also appear equally familiar with those plants which yield poison. When irritated with denials of what they wished for, or suffering from jealousy, or any other strong passion, instances have been known of the negroes applying to these Obeah people, and, for a small sum, receiving from them one of their deadly draughts, so prepared as to render death either almost immediate, or, as was most common, lingering.

I heard of an instance of this nature occurring in Antigua during my stay there. I cannot take upon myself to vouch for its authenticity, as it does not appear there were sufficient grounds of complaint against the suspected parties, to warrant their apprehension; I will, however, give the report then current in the island. An English gentleman, a native of Huntingdonshire, resided upon a property about eight miles from the capital, of which he was the manager. Upon one occasion, he had the favour asked him, by a female belonging to the estate, to give her a bason of milk; which request, from some reason or the other, was refused. The matter passed off, and no more was thought about it by the manager. A short time afterwards, he received an anonymous scrawl, warning him to be careful of what he ate or drank. This production was treated, as most anonymous ones ought to be, with contempt. Another note was received, and met with no more attention than the former. At length, sorrow came within his door; his son, a boy of about fourteen, strong and full of life and joy, suddenly fell ill, death claimed his prey, and he was consigned to an early tomb. This melancholy duty was but just performed, when his sister, a laughter-loving girl of twelve years, fell a victim to that all-conquering monster; and but a few more revolving suns, and the younger sister also departed for "that bourne from whence no traveller returns." Whether any *post mortem* examination of the bodies took place I am unable to say, but report attributed their deaths to the milk they used being poisoned.

This terrible crime does not, it is true, rage to the extent it once did; but even in these days of freedom, Obeah men and women are still to be met with, and many negroes consult them when they have lost anything, are suffering from protracted pain, or when they wish to injure any one they may have quarrelled with. One of the Antiguan magistrates related to me the following circumstance, which had recently occurred. A man who had formerly lived with him as groom, but who for some time past had suffered severely from an ulcerated leg, brought a complaint before him, against another of his sex. It appeared the defendant was one who practised Obeah, to increase his worldly store; and the other poor fellow, ignorant, and depressed in spirit from the almost incurable state of his leg, was induced to apply to him for advice. The Obeah man agreed to cure him, provided he received ten dollars for his pains. This the infirm man was unable to do, but said he had a surtout and a pair of black trousers at home, and if he would take them in place of the money, he would go and fetch them. The offer was accepted by the conjuror, the surtout and trousers were put into his hands, and the ceremony commenced. The diseased man was ordered to seat himself upon the ground, while Mr. Conjuror took a calabash of some liquid, and poured it upon his head, rubbed it very hard, and then putting his mouth to that part called the "crown of the head," sucked it for some time, and producing a tooth, said he had extracted it by those means, and that his leg would soon get well. Some weeks having elapsed, and the limb still continuing in the same state, the man began to think he had been imposed upon, and consequently brought the case before the magistrate, in hopes of getting his surtout and trousers returned.

The negroes, with but few exceptions, firmly believe the Obeah people can insert different articles, such as pieces of glass bottles, old rags, nails, stones, &c., into the flesh of those they dislike, and that the afflicted are obliged to get one of the same craft to relieve them.

I once heard a servant of mine relating a circumstance to a group of sable listeners, which illustrates this subject. His wife had lost a gown for sometime, and could not account for its strange disappearance. Soon after she experienced very odd sensations, but was unable to say what was the matter with her. In her distress she applied to the negro doctress upon the estate, but could receive no relief from her, until at length one of her friends advised her to consult an old Obeah woman who resided near, and to her she accordingly went. As soon as this Obeah woman saw her, she informed her she had "enemies," and it was from their machinations all her illness proceeded; but that if she would come to her again on a certain day, she would consult "Obeah" about it, and, by his assistance, conjure the evil things out of her, provided she brought "all the money she could procure." At the appointed time the woman attended, and after many mysterious rites had been performed, the necromancer proceeded apparently to draw out of the sufferer's arms and legs, pieces of the gown she had lost, various sized pieces of glass, parts of an old shoe, and many other similar articles. This was related with the utmost seriousness of countenance, and no doubt firmly believed in by the reciter. One of the party asked if his wife derived any benefit. "Why," said John, "she say she do, but me no no; me no see she look much better; hab to pay plenty money tho'; Obeah no like it if yo no gib much."

Another practice of these Obeah people is to dig a hole before the door of a house where the resident is obnoxious to them, and in it place their favourite commodities—old rags and pieces of glass bottle. If the person for whose injury these articles are intended, unconsciously passes over, their health decays, or else they will never be better off in the world than they were at that day. This the negroes also firmly believe; and so true is the old proverb, "Fancy kills and fancy cures," that many, knowing such charm has been practised upon them, have taken it to heart, and in a short time died.

It has ever been customary, and in these days of freedom it is not discontinued, to give the negroes upon the different estates, a plot of ground to plant provisions in, independent of their wages. The "negro-ground," as it is called, is frequently situated at some distance from their houses, and consequently, when its different productions are ripe, it is extremely liable to be robbed. To prevent this as far as possible, it is customary to go to an Obeah person, and, for a certain sum, obtain from them a bottle, partly filled with some mysterious mixture,[14] or else a piece of charmed wood, which they hang up in their grounds over against where their provisions are growing. This generally has the desired effect, for daring indeed must be that person who would steal those articles under the protection of Obeah.

---

[13] Proprietor's residence.

[14] I have been lately favoured with the sight of an "Obeah bottle," which was picked up a few weeks ago by J. Fairclough, Esq., a gentleman of Antigua, at his residence, the grounds of which are washed by the sea. The bottle has evidently been immersed in the water for some period, from the number of barnacles formed upon it, as also from the appearance of the cork. Its principal contents are two large nails, a bent pin, a few minute shells, and a conglomeration of substances of which I can give no correct statement. It is filled with a dark liquid, which stains the bottle, and gives the idea of something deadly; but it may only arise from the action of acids upon the iron nails.

CHAPTER XXXIII

Negroes: Superstition—Trials by ordeal—Flower-fence—Bible and key
—A way to recover stolen property—Charm to prevent a scolding tongue
—Jumbies—A night's adventure—The soldier's last jump—Jumbies calls
—Betsey, the nurse—The haunted house—A cure—The drowning boys—
The murdered woman—The jumby's revenge.

In the former chapter I endeavoured to give some description of the doctrine of Obeah. There are also several mysterious rites current among the negroes on which they rely to find out a thief. One of these trials by ordeal is thus performed: they procure some of the leaves of the "flower-fence," or "Barbados' pride," (called by the negroes "doodle doo,") and lay them in a heap, in some peculiar manner, with a black dog (not a quadruped, but a small copper coin of about three farthings sterling, current in this island a few years ago) in the middle. They do not tie this bundle together, but by the manner in which it is placed they are enabled to raise it to the neck of the suspected person without its falling to pieces. The accused is then to say, (holding the bundle under their throat at the same time,) "Doodle doo, doodle doo, if me tief de four dog, (or what- ever it may be that is missing,) me wish me tongue may loll out of me mout." If nothing takes place, the person is innocent, and the charm is tried upon another, until the guilty one's turn comes, when immediately their tongue hangs out of their mouth against their will.

Another trial by ordeal (which, I believe, has formerly been practised in England, and has probably been taught them by the whites) is thus performed:—A door-key is placed between the leaves of the Bible, upon the 18th and 19th verses of the 50th Psalm, and the book is then bound tightly round so that the key cannot fall out; care must be taken at the same time that the key is sufficiently large, that after being placed upon the verses mentioned, part of the handle or bole may be left out. Two persons, the accused and accuser, balance the bound book by placing the first finger of the right hand under the bole of the key, and in this situation make use of the following incantation, (as I suppose I must call it:) "By St. Peter, by St. Paul, you tief me hog," (or whatever else it may be that is stolen;) the accused answers, "By St. Peter, by St. Paul, me no tief you hog;" this is repeated thrice by both parties. If the accused is guilty, the key immediately turns, but if not, the charm is tried upon all who are suspected, until the event takes place. What St. Peter or St. Paul have to do with this, I could never learn, but to me it seems very shocking to make a conjuring book of the Bible. In respect to this part of superstition, the negroes are like the natives of the east, who never lose anything without trying some charm, either by balls of wax, grains of rice, or something similar.[15] There is another curious way by which the negroes endeavour to recover their stolen property. For example: If they lose a fowl or a pig, or indeed any other article, and they suspect it is stolen by their neighbours, they walk up and down the street, calling out, "Let go me fowl—let go me fowl! If you no let go me fowl, me tro grabe durtty upon you. Let go me fowl, me say!" If the person who stole the fowl hears this denunciation, he immediately looses it, in terror of the consequences; but if the threat is not attended to, the owner of the lost biped takes a dog (the same copper coin I have before mentioned) and an egg, and proceeds to a burial-ground. Here they look out for the grave of one of their friends, and depositing the dog and the egg, make use of an incantation, and taking up a little of the soft mould off the grave, depart. This mould, or *grabe durtty*, as they term it, they sprinkle all about in those streets where they think the suspected parties are more likely to walk, believing, that if the thief passes over it, it immediately causes his body to swell, and no medicine can give relief—death alone can end their misery. So terrible to the negroes is the denunciation, "Me tro grabe durtty upon you," that if possible, they will restore the goods pilfered to the last particle.

They have several other charms, all of which they deem infallible. When they fancy they are under the power of Obeah, they procure a snake, kill and skin it; when the skin is thoroughly dried, they bind it round their leg, and feel easier in mind, supposing the one charm will counteract the other. Again, if sent out of an errand, and they loiter about, to prevent any scolding from their employers, they pick a blade of a peculiar species of grass, and place it under their tongue, which they believe has the power of preventing any angry words. This also is done when they wish to escape punishment or detection.

I am aware that it is not the negroes alone who are given to superstition —to using charms and observing omens; the Greeks and Romans were famous for this practice; and in my own country, among the lower classes, most of the old women have a cramp-bone in their pockets, to drive away pains; the tip of a tongue, or a stone with a hole in it, for luck; and a horseshoe nailed to the door, to prevent the entrance of witches. Our seamen, too, are strict disciples of superstition, and rear her many an altar. I once heard a captain of a merchantman who trades to Antigua, speaking of this subject, and laughing at the generality of sailors for paying attention to this or that omen. "I don't believe in anything of the kind," said he. "What can a dolphin, or a Mother Cary's chicken, (the stormy petrel,) have to do with a gale of wind? It's nonsense,—altogether nonsense. Of course, though, it would be only a madman *who would whistle in a storm* or sail on a

Friday, if they could possibly help it!" I wished to ask what poor Friday[16] had done, or if Eolus disliked whistling.

All superstitious people, in every part of the world, are prone to believe in the existence of imaginary beings; and while the English have their ghosts, the Scotch their brownies, and the Irish their banshees, the negroes have their jumby.[17] These creatures, like all of their class, love to frequent churchyards, lonely roads, and the margin of ponds. They are represented by the believers in this creed to be very revengeful and malicious; strangling children, knocking down people, frightening old women into fits, and indeed, doing all the mischief they can. I have heard that "Spring Gardens," the part of the town we reside in, is a favourite spot for their ambulations; but I cannot say I have as yet formed any acquaintance with these *fleshless* beings. Many are the tales related of their exploits,—tales more terrible than that of the poor ghost in "Hamlet," whose "lightest word would harrow up the soul." But as I have too much love for my readers, to wish to "freeze their blood," and all those other dreadful threats his ghostship promised his hopeful son, I will merely relate a few little incidents about these night-loving people.

A servant who once lived with us had occasion to go a few miles into the country after dark. Upon his return the next day, he gave the following most frightful account of his night's adventure. He said, that after getting a little way out of the town, a string of jumbies met him, dressed all in white, who held up their bony fingers at him in a menacing manner. He was very much alarmed, he said, but determined to proceed as fast as he could, without looking behind him; for if by any chance he had happened to turn his head, they would have immediately strangled him. Finding they could not get this advantage over him, they went behind him, and "whispered soft and low"—"James! James!" Although not over-pleased at this salutation, he thought it best to bear it in silence, and hurry on as fast as he could.

At length he came to a pond, known by the name of "Tom Long's Pond," which is always reckoned a favourite resort for jumbies—a kind of Vauxhall of theirs, I suppose. Here he met with another troop, who joined their comrades in tormenting him, until our poor benighted traveller hardly knew what to do. Fear overcame him, the perspiration streamed from off his brow, and his excessive emotion caused "each particular hair to stand on end, like quills upon the fretful porcupine." In this awful situation, he remembered, that if he dispossessed himself of his upper garment, turned it before the jumbies' faces, and then put it on again, wrong side out, they could not hurt him. He tried this remedy; and as soon as his dress was altered, his unpleasant companions gave a loud scream, fled from him in every direction, and left him to prosecute his walk in silence and solitude.

This is James's version of the circumstance. I, who was an unknown, but attentive listener, could not help asking (so wishful was I of gaining information upon this *important* subject) if there was any great merit in turning his coat. "Oh, yes!" was the reply; "jumbies can never hurt you, if you can only have strength to turn your jacket." So, it appears, that whatever may be the character of jumbies in other respects, they shew their good sense in disliking *turncoats*.

During the first few weeks of my residence in this island, I was staying upon an estate a few miles from the capital. Having for some length of time seen nothing but the "sky above and the sea below," it may be imagined how happy I was once more to tread *terra firma*; and I lost no time in exploring this, to me, new world. In these rambles, I was attended by my servant, a rosy-cheeked English girl, who gave utterance to her surprise at tropical scenes and tropical customs, in like sentences to these: "Lawk, ma'am!" "Well, I never!" "Lawk-a-daisy-me!" One day we wandered far and wide; and after many devious routes, my attention was at last attracted by the appearance of a cluster of trees. I am very fond of these ornaments of the vegetable world; I love to watch the play of the sunbeams upon their leaves—to listen to the melody of the gentle gale, as it whispers among them; and when in this "far, far west," they greeted my eye with their verdant foliage, I was anxious to make their acquaintance. Upon a nearer approach, I found they formed a complete fringe to a kind of rivulet; they were mangroves, and very beautiful they looked. We walked by the side of them for some distance, and at length came upon the high-road, which crosses the rivulet. Here we fell in with a few larger trees, of a different species; and near to them was a spring of water. A soothing silence reigned around, occasionally broken by the murmuring of the breeze, the buzzing of those pigmies of the feathered race—the humming-birds, or the coo of the ground-doves, those constant frequenters of all sylvan spots. Now and then, the faint hum of human voices broke upon the ear, as the slaves were returning from the cane-fields, it being near the close of the day.

Altogether, I was quite pleased with the spot, and hardly knew how to leave it. As I was returning to the house, with "pensive steps and slow," I overtook the driver, one of the head slaves upon the property. With the native politeness which many negroes possess, he pulled off his hat, with "How d'ye, missis?" his black sparkling eyes, his white teeth glistening through his thick lips, his ebon complexion, and his large straw hat, rendered him quite a novelty to me. I remarked to him, what a pretty spot the spring was situated in, and thought it must be very serviceable to the estate. "Yes, missis," rejoined he; "it one pretty 'pring 'nough; but me no like to go dere much at night." I asked the reason; it brought the following tale:—"Some time aback, one soger buckra run away from de barracks. He

- 44 -

was gone long time, till at last sombody go tell upon he where he go hide. De soger cappen send two oder sogers to go look for he, an bring he to town; bery well, dey find he, an was going to fetch he back to town, when, just as he get to dis 'pring, 'fore de oder sogers no war he go do, he jump, bram! right into de 'pring; an by de time dey manage to get he out, he go dead; so eber since dat time, jumbies come see soger's jumby, an dey 'top here an make dance; so we no lub to come here much self."

A similar circumstance has been related to me by the attorney of the estate. A negro belonging to the property, who for several months had given way to idle, dissolute habits, at length so far forgot himself as to become a runaway. After being absent for some time, intelligence was brought to the attorney that he had been seen skulking about the capital; and accordingly, other negroes were despatched to endeavour to find him and bring him back to the estate. Their undertaking proved successful, the runaway was secured, and the party set out upon their journey home. Upon the road the man remarked—"He wished he could die, for he had no cause to run away, and he should be ashamed to meet his friends, for he knew not what excuse to make," and proceeded in this strain until gaining the "spring," at the entrance of the estate; he gave a sudden start, and before his companions were aware of his intentions, he had leaped into the water. By the time assistance could be procured, the man was dead; and his friends had the melancholy office of burying his swollen corpse.

The negroes have an idea, that if a jumby calls them, and they return an answer, they will very soon die. I have often called a servant by name at night, and could get no answer, when I was well aware they must have heard me; and upon asking them the reason have had the following reply given me—"Me no no, missis, it was you; me tink it one jumby calling me."

If a child is born with a caul it is preserved with religious veneration. My milk-woman came to see me one day with her two little babies; the little creatures had each a small black bag tied round their necks with a piece of black ribbon. I asked the mother what this was for; she said they were both born with cauls, and that if it was not always kept near them, the jumbies would strangle them the first time they were left alone; nor was this all, for if they did not wear it upon their persons, they would see the jumby (or spirit) of every one that died.

I mourned to think how superstition prevailed in these parts, what then was my surprise upon soon after taking up an English newspaper of late date, to see the, following advertisement:—"A child's caul to be disposed of, *a well-known preventive against drowning, &c. Price, ten guineas.* Address, post-paid, to A. B. C., to the care of Mr. Evans, Hyde Park newspaper-office, 42, Edgware Road!"

Had I not seen and read this myself, I could not have believed it. While we write and talk of the superstition of the negroes, although we mourn that its influence should extend so far, yet there is greater allowance to be made for them from want of education; but that such an enlightened people as the English should put such an advertisement in a public paper is almost incredible. A certain preventive against drowning!—why, superstition in her gala days could not have furnished a more striking instance of her power! That any rational creature should believe such an assurance is astonishing. I firmly hope, for the honour of my country people, that the *ten guinea* advertisement remains unanswered.

I had an old nurse living with me a few years ago, an African, but who had been brought to this island as a slave when she was about ten years of age. She is a firm believer in jumbles, and is one of those privileged people who, it is said, can talk to these gloomy beings, and, by some potent charm known only to themselves, hinder them from playing any mischievous trick. For this reason she was frequently called upon to use her art, when the jumbies troubled any of the little negroes. When this was the case, she went into a room by herself, and entered into a conversation with the invisibles, and by some means or the other, succeeded in drawing them away. No one else, who has not a similar power, dares to remain by; for they believe if they did, the jumbies would blow upon them, and throw them into a fit, or else cause their immediate death. Betsey, for that is her name, like most of her class, is very fond of talking to herself, and one day I remember hearing the following soliloquy. It was about some lady in the island who wore false hair and false teeth:—"Eh, eh! you eber hear such a ting as that tho', dat missis hab one sombody's hair, all curly curly, so tie it on he head, an say he b'longs to he; an den dat no all self, for he hab one sombody's teeth too! Eh, eh! me wonder how he like, me no go do so, war for? s'pose jumby cum an say, gib me me hair, gib me me teeth, war me go do den; jumby no like people com take der tings away." I ought here perhaps to remark, that when negroes are talking, they seldom use but one of the genders, and that the masculine, in direct opposition to Lindley Murray.

It is also a very prevalent opinion among the negroes that if they beg one of their dying friends to "trouble" any one they dislike, (that is, for his spirit or jumby to appear to him,) the jumby, which they expect to rise on the third day from death, will do their bidding, and that the person so haunted can never take rest until he himself dies. Their opinion respecting the immortality of the soul is, as far as I can understand it, this—that if a person die one day and is buried the next, during the succeeding night, the spirit, or as they term, it the "jumby," rises, and either goes to heaven, or, if during life they have committed any crime, or met with a violent death, wanders about the earth, until by prayers, fumigations, or something of the kind, it is laid to rest.[18]

When a jumby haunts a house, they get a coal-pot, upon which they place a quantity of pepper, salt, *nuno*, (the wild basil,) part of a horse's hoof, and a little brimstone. This coal-pot is set in the middle of the house, with the back and front doors open, and is allowed to burn until after midnight; at the same time, they stick over the doors and windows, and in the corners of the house, bunches of "milk-bush," another wild plant. This ceremony always takes place during the night, but they allow the bush to remain until it withers. Whilst these articles are burning, the friends who are assembled in the "haunted house," and the residents themselves, are employed in "cursing the jumby," telling it to "go where he com from," "that if he one good somebody he would hab been at rest," &c.; and just as the clock strikes twelve at midnight, the windows are opened, and a quantity of water thrown out to wet the "jumby" and send it away, for as long as the coal-pot continues burning, they believe the jumby cannot pass through the house, but is still lurking about the yard watching for an opportunity of getting in.[19] Strange as this may read, it is firmly believed in, and actually practised up to the present time, not only by negroes, but by many of the better sort of people.

When a negro wishes a jumby to hurt his enemies, he makes use of various charms to effect his purpose; one of which the following anecdote will illustrate. About two years ago, two black boys went to a pond at the head of the town, to water a horse. The one that was riding the animal carried it far into the pond, and by some mishap or the other, fell off. His friend viewed him struggling in the water; he saw him sink, and rise to the surface,—again he disappeared; and although the spectator of this melancholy scene was but a very little fellow, he leaped in to his assistance. But oh! the frenzied grasp of death! well may it be said, "What pain it is to drown!" or, in the words of the homely proverb, "A drowning man will catch at a straw,"—the dying boy saw the hand stretched to his aid; and grasping the proffered palm, both sank to rise no more. Some person residing near the pond gave the alarm, and by means of drags, the bodies were recovered.

A relation of one of these poor boys had an ill-feeling towards an acquaintance, with whom she had quarrelled, and she thought this a good opportunity of injuring her enemy. Under pretence of plaiting this woman's hair, (towards whom the ill-feeling existed,) she contrived to cut off a good portion of it, which she placed in the hand of the boy, just before the coffin was screwed down, at the same time pronouncing the word "remember." The consequence of this was, (as my negro informant related it,) "de pic'nee jumby trouble he so, (meaning, I suppose, the relation's adversary,) dat he no no war for do, till at last he go out of he head, an' he neber been no good since."

If any one is murdered, and the murderer is not discovered, the jumby of the victim cannot rest, but is continually roaming about the spot where the bloody deed was committed, or else tormenting the perpetrator of the crime, until they are obliged to confess the fault. I have heard an old woman talk of a murder, which was committed some time ago, where the spirit of the murdered woman pointed out to her friends the person of her destroyer. It occurred upon an estate called "Jonas's," and as "brother Jonathan" lately said of a most improbable tale, "is extraordinary, if true." A female slave upon the property was suddenly taken ill, and before medical aid could be procured, she died. There was strong suspicion that she met her death by swallowing some deleterious drug; but who tendered the "poisoned chalice," none could tell. The next day the body was to be consigned to the tomb. It was customary at that period to bury the slaves about the negro houses, and porters carried the coffin upon their shoulders to the grave. At the time appointed the company assembled; the porters took up the coffin, and the procession formed. But, lo! instead of going to the grave, the men commenced walking very fast in an opposite direction; the walk increased to a run; the company in amaze called after them to know the meaning; "It's the jumby in the coffin," was the reply of the porters. On, on they went, up to the "buff," (as the negroes call the proprietor's house,) down again,—round the negro houses, here and everywhere, the jumby carried them.

The two white overseers upon the estate came to inquire into this mysterious proceeding. Upon being told the circumstance, they laughed at it, and said it was the porters' nonsense; that if they would put the coffin down, they (the overseers) would take it up and prove it was no jumby running them. This proposition was joyfully agreed to, and the coffin shifted to the shoulders of the overseers. Once more the procession formed, and they started for the grave; but this time it was worse than ever; the jumby obliged the white men to run with their burden, until they nearly fainted with fatigue, and caused them most lustily to call out for the former bearers to relieve them.

Again the porters commenced their melancholy office of carrying to the grave a corpse that would not be buried. The same ground was again passed over, but no effort of theirs could lead them to gain the intended place of burial. At length, forced on by the jumby, they made up to a negro house, the door of which was shut; and before they could ask for admittance, the coffin was impelled through it, breaking it into pieces, and was dashing forwards against the face of a man, the only inmate, who, frightened and horrified at the encounter, was endeavouring to effect his escape. This at length he accomplished, but not before he bore upon his head and face the marks of a jumby's revenge. The open door gained, he fled as if ten thousand demons were hanging upon his steps, while the corpse, satisfied at having pointed out its murderer, bowed itself upon the bearers' shoulders, and then allowed them to carry it quietly to its last resting-place.

Time flew on, and no tidings of the murderer were heard, until about six months had elapsed, when a party of negroes went into a copse to cut wood. They had almost penetrated through its tangled mazes, when they thought they saw something lying under the brushwood; and upon a nearer approach, discovered it to be the man who had fled from the attack of the jumby. He was in a dying condition, and according to the old women who related the circumstance, "He face 'top most like one buckra, all *whitey whitey*, from de jumby licking he so;" a great compliment to us whites! But to return to our story. The negroes picked him up, and carried him home, where he lived long enough to confess, that a quarrel having arisen between himself and the deceased woman, he procured "something" from an Obeah man, which he put into some soup, and which caused her death.

Like everything else, my story has an end; and now let me ask my readers what they think of it? I am sure they will join with me in deploring that superstition has still so many votaries. Oh! that her reign was at an end! Yet there are some negroes who are getting over the dread of these things. An old woman remarked one day, "Missis, me hear of jumby, but me neber see dem; me can't go say dere non ob dem, but me say, if one sombody do good, God will neber let dem hurt you; an we ought to pray, dat wen we go dead, He will gib us some place ob rest."

---

[15] The manner in which these East Indian charms are tried is as follows:—When a trial by wax is agreed upon, a number of persons write their names upon scraps of paper, including those of the parties who may be suspected. These scraps are enclosed in balls of wax, and are thrown into a bason of water; those which float at the top are opened, and whatever name is written therein is believed to be the thief. When an ordeal of rice is tried, a few grains of that article are placed upon the tongue of the supposed culprit: if the party is innocent, the rice, when chewed, mixes with the saliva, and is expectorated of a milky consistence; but if, on the contrary, guilty, no power can moisten it, but it comes out a dry powder. I should not feel at all surprised at seeing this last charm turn out true, for of course the natives firmly believe the truth of it, and the guilty one's conscience must upbraid him, and his emotion probably parch his mouth. With regard to the *wax trial*, I cannot so readily account for it. Mr. Forbes,

in his "Oriental Memoirs," mentions seeing both of these charms, as well as many others, (being nine in number,) tried; some of which are sanctioned by the British authorities. He goes on further to state, that in *all cases* where he was present, they came true. I could not take upon myself to discredit what this clever and ingenious writer says; much, very much may be attributed to the effect of a strong imagination, which most Eastern nations possess.

[16] The dislike to this day is supposed to arise from the Crucifixion.

[17] The term "jumby" is applied to all supernatural beings.

[18] A similar idea to this still exists in the Department Indre, France. The inhabitants believe that after death the soul of the deceased flies about the apartment where the dissolution took place, seeking some cranny by which to escape to heaven. For this reason, as soon as any one is supposed to be near death, the friends of the dying person take care to remove every vessel that contains liquid, fearing the soul may fall in, and thus be lost. In Scotland, something of the sort seems to be believed in among the lower classes; for when a person is in the last agonies, the doors of the house are set open, that the soul may find no impediment in the way of its escape. The ancient Jews, according to Dr. Lightfoot, were of an opinion that the soul of the deceased hovered about its former tenement until after the lapse of three days, when it sought the regions of bliss or misery.

[19] This ceremony is performed nightly until the house is so thoroughly fumigated that the "jumby" quits in despair.

CHAPTER XXXIV

Seeming paradoxes explained—Negro suspicion—Instances of it—Stealing—Its various characters—Leasing—The dead canaries—Broken promises—Idleness—Negro wages—Their present lot—Domestics.

In continuing my "shadows" of negro character, methinks I hear my good readers cry out, "Why, here is nothing but paradoxes. In a former chapter the negroes were all and everything, but now it appears the tables are turning, and, Proteus-like, assume another shape." Stop a little, my kind friends; a word or two in my own defence, if you please. What may appear paradoxical at first, upon further research may not prove so; the sky we admire for its beautiful cerulean tint is not in *reality* blue. I have before remarked, that I should have to give the "shadows," as well as the "lights" of negro character. I am sorry to be obliged to do so, for I wish them well; but as, in describing the early days of slavery, I have not screened the master, so must I now give the real outlines of the negro. I ever did, and ever shall detest the name of slavery, and glad do I feel that it is done away with, at least in British colonies, if only for the honour of my dear native isle; and while I have to write of negro vices, I again repeat, that they do not so much result from the natural bias of their character, as from the effects of the bonds they have so long worn, which, degrading them in their own eyes, have conspired to render them what they are. Time can only correct their errors: let us, then, not despair, but hope for the best. Surely we ought to see some amendment in the rising generation, and we shall do so, I feel assured, if their old relations do not poison their minds, by telling them, because they are taught to read and write, it will be a degradation for them to work in a cane-field.

In the latter part of the preceding chapter, an account was given of their various superstitions; the next strong trait in their character is suspicion. They can seldom be brought to think you have an eye to their interest in any new arrangement you may make with them in their domestic concerns. If you address them with kindness, they suspect you have some motive for so doing, prejudicial to their welfare. Should you inquire after their living, the quantity of live-stock they keep, or any other little domestic comfort, or, indeed, ask them where they live, or who they work for, the same thoughts possess their mind.

It is strange, too, that they will hardly ever sell any of their poultry or meat, or, indeed, anything else they may have to dispose of, to the proprietor or manager residing upon the same estate as themselves. No! they prefer bringing it miles, perhaps, to town, and probably getting less for it, than if they had disposed of it to their masters. If asked to do so, they commonly find some excuse; it is too old or too young, or too fat or too lean, or they cannot catch it, or else they want it for themselves. This singular practice arises from suspicion; they are fearful of letting their masters know what their resources are, and what they do with their property. For this reason, they prefer going to a dark shop to purchase what they want. They do not like to be recognised by any one while thus employed; nor for any one to know how much money they lay out, or what they buy. There are some retail shops, or *stores*, as they are called in the West Indian idiom, which are scarcely six feet high, and which of course are very dark and uncomfortable; yet, as unpleasant as these stores or shops may look to the eye, they are for that very reason frequented by the negroes. I am, in this part of my subject, more particularly speaking of the state of affairs before emancipation, but I believe this mistrust of their employers still continues. In former days, so fearful were the slaves of letting their masters know how much money they possessed, that it was a common practice of theirs to bury it; and often death overtook them before they could tell their relations in what spot they had deposited it, and consequently it was lost. If "Daddy Whelan," the notorious "treasure-seeker," in Mrs. Hall's interesting tale of the "Crock of Gold," was here, he might be more fortunate than in his own country.

In receiving money they are equally suspicious; I have had opportunities of seeing this under the free system. It is customary upon estates to pay the labourers on the Friday, or early on the Saturday morning, and it is curious to see how they count and re-count their money, fearing the paymaster may have cheated them. In one or two instances brought beneath my own eye, a negro has returned his wages, with—"No right, massa, money no 'nough;" it has been counted again, the pay-book referred to, when instead of being *too little*, it has proved to be *too much*; the surplus deducted, and the right sum handed to the negro, he grumbles again, because he brought it back.

Another, and I am also sorry to say, very prevailing trait in the character of my black brethren is, stealing. This they appear to think no crime, so long as they are not found out; and when by any unforeseen occurrence they are, it is not for the criminality of the act they mourn, but for fear they may not have another so good an opportunity of repeating their exploit. In many instances, they are so adroit in purloining articles, that they are almost competent to give advice and instruction to the "light-fingered gentry" of "London and its vicinity." It seems impossible to break them of this habit of pilfering, so strong is it engrafted in them; people are never safe from their depredations. Upon estates they steal the sugar, molasses, cane-juice, (to make into vinegar, which they sell for a penny-halfpenny sterling a bottle;) cut down the canes, as soon as, or even before, they get ripe; milk the cattle; pick the cocoa-nuts; and, in a word, take all they can get.

The merchants suffer from their depredations in various ways. They not only take up goods they never intend to pay for, but they steal whatever they can lay their hands upon. Nothing comes amiss to them; and be you as clever and cunning as you may, they will be sure to outwit you, in one way or the other. Should you be the owner of a small craft, which you man with a few black sailors, and which you employ in trading between the different islands, you are sure to lose something in every voyage. Your rope and canvas is gone—*nobody* knows how; a cask of salt-fish is opened and robbed of its contents—*nobody* touched it. If dry goods form your cargo, pieces of shirting, bales of cotton, or something of the kind, generally take their departure—*nobody* saw them.

If you employ a carpenter, your nails and lumber are sure to commit suicide or something of the sort, I suppose, for they are gone, and *nobody* used them. A mason steals your lime; a cooper steals your staves and hoops; a painter steals your oil, your turpentine, and paint; and domestic servants steal all they can. Some negroes employ themselves in walking about from store to store, selecting various dresses, handkerchiefs, ribbons, gentlemen's coats and vests, or any similar article, which they carry, they say, to shew Mrs. this or Mr. that; but, somehow or other, these persons are generally very much afflicted with that malady, want of memory, and they forget to return the goods in question. The shopkeepers have suffered so much from this infirmity, that now they will not deliver anything to be looked at, unless the messenger brings a written order. But this resolution does not at all intimidate these clever thieves; they get a scrap of paper written in a lady's or gentleman's name, and unless some errors in orthography, or a particular specimen of bad writing, leads to a suspicion of their authenticity, they often succeed in getting a "pretty considerable deal of goods," as the Americans say.

Others, again, go to a store and ask to be shewn some shingles;[20] they take two or three as a sample, and if approved of, they are to return for so many bundles. About ten yards further, they meet with another store, and here they procure another sample; and so they go on, until, in time, enough is obtained to patch their houses. In the same manner, they get samples of tea, peas, rice, coffee, &c., which saves them having the very disagreeable necessity of paying for what they use.

Some of the country negroes fall upon another plan of levying contributions upon the public. They make love to a pig or a fowl, or some other article belonging to their neighbours, but which they will not steal upon any account; accordingly they entice or carry them to a convenient distance, and leave them there. After a little time has elapsed, they return by the same road, and as soon as they perceive the articles, whatever they may be, (although left there by themselves,) they exclaim, "Eh! eh! me lucky true to-day, me find dis fowl; well, me want it 'nough, me sure!" In this manner, they endeavour to stifle the "still small voice within us," while, should they be accused of this, they immediately cry out, "Well, me neber know if one somebody find one someting he call tief for it!"

I should have enlarged upon the thefts of our domestic servants, but really, upon thinking over it, the task appears too arduous. I might write and write and never finish,—it would, in truth, be "a story without an end;" for this system of stealing is so indelibly implanted in some of their minds, that no measures you can try will break them of it. You may use the greatest leniency towards them, argue with them in the kindest manner, point out to them the sinfulness of their ways, it makes no impression upon them—they only wait until you retire, or are off your guard, and the same theft will be repeated. Nor are coercive measures of more avail; you may take them before a magistrate, who will commit them to the house of correction; when the period of their punishment is expired, and they are again at liberty, they return to their illegal habits with redoubled avidity, as if to make up for lost time. I do not say this is the case with all; a few weeks spent in confinement has often the effect of restoring to society a reformed member. To thieving we must add lying, and in this accomplishment many of them are so well skilled, that Ferdinand Mendez Pinto must have hid his diminished head. It is really wonderful to hear to what extent they will carry their lying; for example, if you miss anything and inquire after it, they will deny peremptorily they ever saw it, when, at the same time, they know full well where it is, but do not want the trouble of fetching it. They will rather tell a story at any time than be forced to use the least exertion. While I am writing, I hear complaints of this. A servant of ours has just drawn a lucifer match, and knowing how careless all negroes are of throwing about fire, the question has been asked her, "Where did you put the match after using it?" —"Upon the table," was the reply.—"Are you sure of that, and that it was extinguished before you left it?"—"Yes, sir."—"Susan, go and look; I cannot believe her, I am sorry to say." Susan returns with the box of lucifers; the match, *still burning*, has been replaced in the box, and the lid put on, to the imminent hazard of setting the house on fire, had it not been fortunately discovered. My attention being drawn by this colloquy, I ask, "Grace, how can you use yourself to tell such stories?—are you not a Sunday-school scholar?"—"I forgot, ma'am." They never own they do tell a story; they always forget, or else they boldly stick to their first assertion, let the contrary be as plain as it may.

Another bad practice of theirs is, that if they have committed any error which might be remedied, or neglected to do anything which might afterwards be performed, they will never let you know, until it is too late. I had a very beautiful pair of canaries, who greeted me every morning with the sweetest of songs. I loved the little creatures—"for the bird that we nurse is the bird that we love;" and in this far distant land, away from all my kith and kin, with the exception of one for whom we are taught to forsake all other earthly ties, they were my constant companions. Months rolled on, and the fervour of a tropical sun fevered my blood, and parched my lips. I sighed for the pure breeze of my own dear land; and as my little birds warbled their sweet, clear song, memory carried me back to those pleasant fields, where, in my early days, I gathered the fragrant hawthorn, and listened to each "wood-note wild." But, alas! a wide, wide ocean rolled between me and them, which may be very easily crossed in imagination, but not so in reality; and consequently, I had to content myself with leaving the crowded town, and trying the country air. I left my little birds to the care of a domestic, with particular injunctions to give them daily fresh seed and water. From time to time, when I saw her, I inquired after her little charge; they were quite well, was always the answer, until at length, when I returned, I found my poor little favourites dead—dead from starvation; and when I spoke about it, and asked why such stories were told me, all the satisfaction I got was—"I forgot dem."

It has been remarked, in black workmen, that if they promise to come and complete a particular job on a certain day, and they conclude with "Please God, me come,"[21] they seldom keep to their word, for if they can procure another job which they think will pay them better, they consider it of no importance disappointing their first employer. In the same manner, they will engage to build a house, or indeed any other work, for a certain sum; if, after going partly through it, and drawing all the money they can, they find it will not pay them as well as they at first supposed, instead of representing it to the parties, and resting upon their generosity to enlarge the sum, or else putting up with the result, they immediately leave it, and you may get it done the best way you can. So, again, upon estates, a party of negroes will undertake to plant or hole a piece of canes for so much: if they find it will pay them very well, they keep on; but if, on the contrary, they think they have not made so good a bargain as they imagined, they shoulder their hoes, and away they start. This habit of not speaking the truth is so proverbial, that it gives rise to the vulgar adage—"a negro lies like a horse trotting." I have heard of a white emigrant from Anguilla saying, "that he would never again believe a negro, until he saw hair growing within the palm of his hand," so notorious is this propensity.

Idleness is another fault in many negroes: everything that is done by them is done lazily. If working upon an estate, as long as the master's eye is upon them, they get on pretty well; but as soon as he retires, down go their hoes. I should think this, in great measure, must be attributed to their having been so long used to working under a driver; for although they are free in body, they are far from free in mind. I am sure they ought not to do this; for, badly as they used to be treated some ninety or a hundred years ago, since they have been free, and, indeed, for many years before, only that they bore the name of slaves, they have had nothing to complain of. I am, and ever have been, a stanch advocate of anti-slavery doctrines; and, consequently, this assertion coming from me may be considered of some weight. It is said, that immediately after their emancipation, the wages of the negroes were rather low; but that, I am sure, cannot be said now. The common rate of wages is a shilling sterling per day; but then they often work "task-work," as they call it, and in that case frequently get from three to four shillings. Indeed, their earnings depend entirely upon their own exertions; for the estates upon which they work will always find employment for them.

Besides this actual sum, it must be remembered, that they enjoy various privileges, which our English labourers can never hope for. The negroes have their houses found them, a spot of ground to plant provisions in, a doctor and medicine when they are ill, and a certain quantity of molasses and rum when doing certain work. Besides all this, they have the liberty of picking what wood they please, of keeping what stock they like, provided they keep their pigs, sheep, and goats, confined or tied up, that they may not injure the young canes, which injunction they regularly break. Then, again, they pick the grass, sheep and goat meat, growing upon the property, which they bring into the capital of an evening, and generally sell for three bits, another shilling sterling. And not only this; but as West Indian property is but seldom enclosed, they think it but fair to gather what fruit they choose from the several trees growing about the estates, and which they also bring into town, and sell in the market. Would that many of our poor English peasantry were as well off as the negroes now are, instead of suffering, as they often do, from cold and hunger. What Englishman would let them help themselves to the produce of their orchards! I have often before remarked how much I detest the name of slavery—there is something so revolting in the idea of men selling and buying their fellow-creatures; but I cannot hear the West Indian negroes *pitied* for their hard lot, when I know that in *these days* it is so much the contrary, without trying to put my English friends in possession of the real state of things.

It is observable, that but few negroes are to be met with who do not possess some money; and, in dress, they deny themselves nothing that pleases them, or, as they say, "fills their eye." Many, since emancipation, have purchased many spots of land, built houses, and appear to have many comforts, and almost every head negro keeps his pony or his horse, while others run their stanhopes. As I have already observed at the beginning of this chapter, many may think I am writing paradoxes; but such is not the case, and any one intimate with West Indian affairs will confirm my statements. The fact is, great changes have taken place in this island as well as everywhere else; in former days, when those dreadful acts of cruelty which I have recorded used to be practised, religion was held in very slight regard. That the negroes are a very provoking race all must allow who have any dealings with them; and men with strong passions, uninfluenced by Christian feelings, possessed of wealth, and having their slaves entirely under their control, were apt to give way to resentment against them when in error, and commit those deeds at which their descendants blush.

But now the case is very different; the negro has been freed, and his rights as a man acknowledged. Still his interests are so inseparably connected with those of his employers, that the subversion of the one must end in the ruin of the other. What would any one think, who has the interest of these important colonies at heart, of the introduction of slave-made sugar into England at any rate of duty, and leaving the West Indian planter (after having cheerfully acquiesced in emancipation) to bear the burden of this high rate of wages. Although no one can deny that most of the Antiguan planters have benefited by emancipation, in the way of cultivating their estates, yet free labour, generally speaking, and from what has fallen beneath my own observation, cannot cope with slavery. No! it is the whip, and the whip alone, which can give to England the cheap sugar she is promised. Who, then, would not rather give a penny a pound more for their sugar, than, after having freed the British negro, eat that which is seasoned with the tears and groans of foreign slaves.

It is among the domestic servants that negro idleness is most severely felt, for there are ways of making the others work, although the whip is banished, by checking their pay. In the case of our house-servants, however, it is not so easy; they seem to have no wish to please their employers. If left to themselves, they care not how the day passes, so long as they get through it; one English servant will do twice the work two Creoles will. Probably this arises in great measure from the practice of having so many servants to do the work that two or three at furthest ought to do. I have frequently seen six or seven domestics lounging upon the floor of an anteroom, amusing themselves with stringing "jumby-beads," as a pretty little red and black seed is called, sucking sugar-canes, or telling *nancy stories*,[22] or else singing one of their favourite songs; perfectly at their ease, it is immaterial to them whether their daily business is completed or not. If their mistress calls, it is often unheeded; or else it is, "Bro' James call see Agnes to tell aunty Jenny missis call he," (Anglicised, "Brother James, call sister Agnes to tell aunt Jenny," &c.) Thus they loiter away the day; whilst their *missis*, after in vain endeavouring to be heard, or at least attended to, resigns her fair form to the couch, and that listlessness which many Creole ladies like to indulge in during the heat of the day.

---

[20] Used instead of tiles for the tops of houses.

[21] A by-word with the negroes when making appointments.

[22] Tales of *diablerie.*

CHAPTER XXXV

Negroes: "Shadows" continued—The crime of murder—Instances of it
—Hon. Sam. Martin—Giles Blizard—Adam Ogilvie.

The next crime I have to mention, in this continuation of dark tints, is
murder. This dreadful act, however, I am happy to say, is not very common
now; in these days they seldom embrue their hands in human blood; but in
former years, years of moral darkness, the negroes used frequently to suffer
death for the Obeah practice of poisoning, or in some other way taking the
lives of their fellow-creatures, particularly those who had authority over
them, and who, in the exercise of that authority, made use of harsh
measures. Perhaps it may not be uninteresting to some of my readers to
narrate a few instances of the most remarkable murders which have been
committed in Antigua; for, strange as it may appear, almost every one likes
to hear of deeds of blood.

In 1701, a dreadful murder occurred, the details of which are as
follows:—The speaker of the house of assembly, the Hon. Samuel Martin,
the owner of that beautiful and romantic property "Green Castle," had for
some reason or the other refused his slaves their usual Christmas holiday,
and compelled them to work throughout the day. This infraction upon what
they considered their right so exasperated his negroes, that on the 25th of
December, 1701, they with one accord rose upon their master, determined
to take sure revenge. Accordingly, at the dead hour of the night, they broke
open the doors of his mansion, and rushing to the chamber of Major
Martin, fell upon him, and actually hacked him to death, with the hoes they
had been using in the cultivation of his sugar-canes.

Shocked at the dreadful fate of her husband, and fearing the same
terrible death from the infuriated slaves, should they discover her, Mrs.
Martin fled from the scene of horror, and with her frightened children,
sought safety within the precincts of a neighbouring cane-field. Here she
remained throughout the remainder of that awful night; until when the
morning came, and the bright sun arose and chased away the clouds of
darkness, she summoned courage to leave her place of concealment, and
throw herself and children upon the protection of her friends. The body of
the unfortunate Major Martin (after an inquest had been held upon it) was
interred in the churchyard of St. John's; and the chief actors in the tragical
affair were afterwards brought to condign punishment. Mrs. Martin lived
for many years after this sad event, and married for her second husband
Governor Byam, (vide Appendix, Byam Lineage.) The father of Major
Martin was the first of the name who emigrated to the West Indies, and the

ancestor of the present Sir Henry Martin, who traces his descent from thence.[23]

About seventy years ago, a gentleman of the name of Giles Blizard owned an estate in that part of Antigua called Pope's Head, which estate at the present day is added to another, and the whole is in possession of the Hon. Bertie E. Jarvis. Giles Blizard was a true planter of the olden time. He resided in an old roomy mansion upon his estate, where wealth and meanness were strongly contrasted,—where the silver flagons and costly salvers glittered amid the coarse earthenware of England, like a proud and high-born beauty, who by some strange chance has been mixed with the common herd,—where the polished surface of the mahogany furniture mocked the unwashed walls and darkened roof of the apartments, whose protruding beams afforded safe protection to innumerable hordes of insects. Surrounded by his numerous slaves, the old gentleman exercised the power of a prince, and gave no bad idea of the Saxon Thane, or more haughty feudal baron. Everything in his dwelling was conducted upon a scale of heavy munificence; his table groaned beneath the weight of its various viands; but there was no order, no delicacy observed in the arrangement of them. Like the generality of Antiguan planters, he was hospitable in the extreme; his doors were ever open, and every visiter was sure of a hearty welcome. A stranger would have been surprised at having wines of the choicest vintage handed to him by a bare-footed butler, or his every movement attended to by a host of half-naked negroes; but such was the domestic arrangement of the old Antiguan mansions. Giles Blizard was supposed to be exceedingly rich, and to keep by him a noble portion of hard cash, which in *those golden days* was generally in the form of doubloons and joes.[24] He was fond of boasting of his ample share of this world's wealth; and this exciting the rapacity of two of his slaves, prompted them to murder him, that they might become possessed of his store. A convenient opportunity for perpetrating this foul deed had long been waited for, and was at length obtained.

At the close of a gloomy day, in the last month of the year, the old gentleman seated himself upon a sofa, and prepared to take his evening nap, attended only by a black boy of the name of Diamond. The evening was tempestuous; and between the pauses of the storm, the inmates of the apartment listened once or twice, as they thought they heard approaching footsteps; but the wind shook the ill secured shutters with such violence as to drown all other sounds, until at length they supposed that it was nothing but fancy, or the hollow moaning of the blast.

Giles Blizard was at that period of life when to many the pleasures and luxuries of this world seem sweeter from the certainty that they are drawing near their close, for often, very often, is it that—

"Aged men, full loth and slow,
The vanities of life forego;
And count their youthful follies o'er,
Till mem'ry lends her light no more."

Thoughts similar to these might float through the brain of the old gentleman, for Giles Blizard was a lover of conviviality, and many a festive scene had those old walls witnessed; but the hands of an antique clock, painted in various devices, pointed to the hour of midnight, and once more adjusting his head, the planter sank to sleep.

The two slaves, the intended murderers, who, through a crack in the shutter, had been watching the movement of their master and his youthful attendant, perceiving by his unaltered position and deep breathing that he slept, and having full proof of the other's being in that oblivious state from the sound of his nasal organs, quietly took off the shutter, and entered the apartment, armed with a blunderbuss. Placing their hands upon the shoulders of the old gentleman, and holding the deadly weapon to his ear, they demanded where he kept his cash. In vain their victim prayed for mercy—in vain solicited the boon of one short hour to collect his scattered thoughts; the murderers were not to be turned from their fell purpose; the finger was pressed upon the fatal trigger, and the deed was done; the soul of Giles Blizard winged its way to the vast shores of eternity, and the sofa where he laid him down in full confidence of safety was covered with his brains, and blood, and silver hairs.

Shocking as it is to humanity to relate, one of the criminals was the natural son of the old man, who, although he was not the actual murderer, was the instigator of the dreadful act; for when, at his master's earnest prayer for mercy, the black man seemed to relent, Geoffry (the name of Mr. Blizard's coloured son) told him to do it at once, and make sure of it, or else he would himself. After the perpetration of this atrocious crime, the murderers placed the blunderbuss upon a table, close to the side of their victim, with a glass of brandy and water near it, supposing that, when discovered, it would be surmised that it was an act of self-destruction; but murder is an offence "that's rank, it smells to heaven," and, in most instances, the slayer is discovered. The boy, who really slept upon the entrance of the men, was awakened by the noise; but perceiving the blunderbuss, and hearing the conversation which ensued between his master and his murderers, he became alarmed, and, to ensure his own safety, counterfeited sleep. Upon the morrow's dawn he hastened to relate the circumstance, and by these means the offenders were brought to justice. They were carried before a magistrate, and condemned to suffer death by decapitation on the following day, which was Christmas-day; but Mr. Rose, the then marshal, got it postponed until the day after, thinking that a greater number of spectators would be present, to whom it would act as a warning. The culprits were taken down to a spot where such scenes were generally performed, and which still goes by the name of Gallows Bay, and there, after being blindfolded, they were bound to the upright post of the gallows, their right hands first struck off, and then their heads. The heads, after being dipped in pitch, were stuck upon spikes, and the hands nailed under them, while their bodies were carried down to the water's edge, and there burned in a lime-kiln. This, I think, was the last time decapitation was practised in Antigua, although in former years that mode of execution was very frequent; it may be said, perhaps, that it is more dreadful to the sight than pain to the culprit, for a skilful executioner at one stroke would sever the head from the body; but I must say I am very happy that now no whitened skull or distorted features are likely to meet my sight in an evening walk.

The next most remarkable murder committed in Antigua was one in which a young man of good extraction was the unfortunate victim. About the year 1800, Mr. Adam Ogilvie, son to Sir John Ogilvie, arrived in Antigua, to take charge of his father's property in that island. Young Ogilvie was in the spring of life, for he had not numbered more than twenty years, and all things glittered around him, and presented to his eye a fair and pleasing prospect. But, alas! for man "nought ministers delight but what the glowing passions can engage;" drawn by that alluring goddess, Pleasure, who hides beneath a smiling mask her haggard and distorted visage, Mr. Ogilvie was led into a train of debauchery, and, among other excesses, formed an illicit connexion with a female named Molly belonging to the property. To this female might justly be applied the hackneyed sentence, "Frailty, thy name is woman!" for during this intercourse with her master, she proved *enceinte* by one of the servants, a boy of the name of "Martin;" and fearing a disclosure of her infamy, and not willing to give up her favoured suitor, she, in conjunction with him and two other slaves upon the property, planned the murder of her unfortunate master. During the residence of Mr. Ogilvie upon the estate, he thought proper to have some of the negroes punished for various offences committed by them, among whom were the accomplices of Martin and Molly, and this was one cause of their so readily joining them in their diabolical scheme.

On the night chosen for the execution of their design, Mr. Ogilvie retired early to-bed, and soon tasted that sweet restorer—balmy sleep. His murderers, after waiting a sufficient time to assure themselves of the fact, proceeded in a body to his apartment, attended by the wicked, heartless Molly, bearing a candle and lanthorn in her hand, for the purpose of giving light to the men while in performance of their demoniacal office of strangling Mr. Ogilvie. Upon gaining the bedside of their sleeping victim, who, unconscious of his fate, perhaps some

"Fantastic measure trod o'er fairy fields,"

or else dreamt of health, long life and honours, all alas! fated to exist but in the brain—the murderous party sprang upon him, and as a refinement in cruelty, awoke him, and with many imprecations, informed him that for his ill conduct, they were come for the purpose of taking his life. Death is common to all; but then to die by violent hands in the midst of health and vigour; to be so rudely awakened from an earthly slumber, so soon to be consigned to that last long sleep, which all must do,

"When we have shuffled off this mortal coil;"

how hard to bear! What "tempest to the soul!" Oh! how that victim begged! how promised to be all they wished, would they but give him that one boon—life, which, when once taken, can never be restored. All was of no avail! To each agonized entreaty, no answer was returned, but a firmer grasp upon his throat. Mr. Ogilvie had ever been in the practice of sleeping with loaded pistols under his pillow, and in this moment of danger, one of his first cares was to possess himself of those weapons. But here again Molly stepped in as his evil genius; for to carry fully into effect her murderous intentions, she had, during the preceding day, contrived to take out the flints. The tragedy hastened to a close; disappointed in his hopes of defence, and pinioned by his murderers, Mr. Ogilvie's struggles became fainter and fainter—his sighs burst thicker from his lips—the blood gushed in torrents to his head and face, as his deadly enemies pressed more tightly the heaving throat—his blood-shot eyes started from their sockets—and with one sharp pang, one choking frenzied cry, his spirit winged its flight to another sphere, and his body sank on the pillow a blackened corpse.

The dreadful deed completed, no feeling of contrition, no twinge of conscience haunted the murderers; but taking the key of the cellar, they hastened to convey to the chamber of the dead, a bottle of wine, and another of shrub. After enjoying themselves with a portion of these liquors, they placed the remainder upon the bed, at the feet of their inanimate victim, thinking that as Mr. Ogilvie had lately given way to excessive inebriety, an indulgence in that vice would be considered as the cause of his death, when the body should be discovered.

Long did the overseer upon the property wait the following morning for the appearance of his employer; anxiously did he watch the door, as hour after hour rolled away; but the door still remained closed, and his patience becoming exhausted, and fearful of some misfortune, he at length determined to burst it open. This effected, the dreadful truth quickly forced itself upon his conviction; there lay Mr. Ogilvie stiff and cold, who only the day before exulted in all the glow and strength of youth. As no information could be obtained from either of the servants, as to whether Mr. Ogilvie had complained of indisposition during the night, it was thought necessary to call a coroner's inquest to sit upon the body; and consequently, Martin, on account of his being the deceased's most constant attendant, was despatched to convey the necessary information to the coroner.

Mr. Ogilvie's estate was situated at the extreme west end of the island, and at that period, the person who exercised the office of coroner resided at the extreme east end. Martin, who knew too well the cause of his unfortunate master's death, found his interest lay in retarding, rather than urging on his journey, and from this cause, the coroner did not reach Mr. Ogilvie's residence until the following day, when the body was found to be in such a decomposed state, that the coroner's jury could form no correct opinion as to the cause of his death, and therefore returned a verdict of "Died by the visitation of God."[25]

So far all was well with Martin and his associates; no hand pointed to them, no eye watched their movements. Suspicion was at rest; and no "foul whisperings" were abroad which would tend to urge further inquiry into the tragic event. In this manner, three years rolled away; but murder will out; sooner or later, such deeds are published in the broad front of heaven. Like the savage tiger, who, having once tasted human blood, longs for more, Martin and his accomplices, finding how well they got through their first murder, resolved to attempt the life of the manager, Mr. David Simon.

Mr. Simon had been living upon another estate belonging to the Ogilvie family and for some time before had been suffering from severe indisposition. When in a convalescent state, he was invited by Dr. Ogilvie (who had taken charge of the estates, after the demise of Mr. Adam Ogilvie) to spend some time with him, for change of air. The room appropriated for his reception was the one in which Mr. Adam Ogilvie met his fate: and here it was that Martin and his party determined to strangle him, as they had formerly done their master. Night, "sable goddess," from her ebon throne, "stretched her leaden sceptre o'er a slumbering world," and Mr. Simon retired to rest; but before he courted the embrace of sleep, his thoughts dwelt upon that kind Power who had so graciously supported him throughout a severe fit of illness, and at length brought him to that state of convalescence when he could again enjoy those things which make life sweet. Whilst ruminating upon these subjects, his attention was drawn to a slight rustle in his apartment, and listening more intently, he heard a whispering voice exclaim, "Hold him!" His first plan was to spring from his bed, but in the act of doing so, he was grappled by one or two of his assassins. Fearful was the struggle which ensued—the one striving for his life, the others for their safety, which they well knew would be lost did their intended victim escape. At length, wonderfully renewed with a sufficient degree of strength, Mr. Simon was enabled to jump to the back of the bed, which fortunately happened to be distant two or three feet from the partition—a place not calculated for the murderers following up their attack. Here, keeping his assassins at bay, Mr. Simon redoubled his cries of murder, which at length were fortunately heard by Dr. Ogilvie, who occupied a distant chamber, and who quickly coming to his assistance, the culprits became alarmed, and endeavoured to make their escape by the windows. This they finally succeeded in doing, but not before Martin (the individual who, it will be remembered, was sent to call the coroner on the occasion of Mr. Ogilvie's untimely death) was fully recognised by the manager and Dr. Ogilvie. The next morning, it was discovered that Martin and his accomplices had absconded, upon which, search was made, and in the course of a short time, they were apprehended and brought up for trial. Molly, the faithless paramour of Mr. Ogilvie, turned king's evidence; and in the course of her examination, admitted the facts of that gentleman's murder, and her own share in that shocking deed. It may be necessary to observe, that when the murder of Mr. Ogilvie was determined, the ranger upon the estate, a man of the name of Jacob, was fully sensible of their intentions, although he would not aid them in the completion; he was therefore found guilty as an accessary before the fact, and with Martin and the others, condemned and executed; his body hung in chains upon the property as a warning to others. Molly and her child are still alive, and reside upon the estate where she played so shameful a part; whether a prey to remorse, I am unable to say; but we hope she has truly repented, and sought pardon where it is only to be found—at the throne of Heaven.

The family annals of Sir John Ogilvie present little but a series of disasters. Out of nine sons, two died prematurely in the East Indies, one was killed in Egypt, another fell in the capture of Martinique, while, as we have already seen, young Adam was murdered in Antigua.

---

[23] For the genealogy of the Martin family, see Appendix.

[24] A gold coin, of about the value of 3*l.* 4*s.*. sterling. The joe was a gold coin worth about 36*s.*. sterling.

[25] Decomposition takes place so soon in this warm country, that interment is necessary within twenty-four hours after dissolution.

CHAPTER XXXVI

Negroes: The crime of poisoning—Instance of it—Murder of Mr. Brown—Love and jealousy—The end of unlawful love—Infanticide—Incendiarism—A late instance of it—Polygamy—Disregard of marriage vows.

After having given a short sketch of the murder of Mr. Blizard and Mr. Ogilvie by their slaves, it was my intention to have entered more fully into the cases of poisoning which in days gone by have occurred in this country. But in looking over the dreadful catalogue of such crimes, I find them so frequent, and the manner in which they were carried into effect so similar, that one instance will suffice.

About twenty years ago, a woman of the name of Betsey, belonging to a highly respectable family, had a dispute with her mistress. With the feeling of revenge burning at her heart, she carried her complaint to a friend, who advised her to consult an Obeah man, and get him to give her *something*. Not having an opportunity of going herself, or else not wishful of being known, she sent an old woman of the name of Jenny, an *attachée* of the yard, to obtain the deadly potion, the mysterious *something*, as the negroes generally termed it. The old woman accordingly visited an Obeah man of the name of John, who gave her a liquid which was to be administered to her mistress in some of her nourishment, and which he said would kill her in one minute. This obtained by Betsey, who, like most of her tribe, was the slave of her passions, she resolved to lose no time in carrying her plan of revenge into execution; accordingly, she handed it to the butler, with whom, it appears, she had formed a *liaison*, and who was concerned with her in her plot, with injunctions to put it into whatever liquid her mistress might order. By some means or the other, a suspicion that all was not right was raised; certain circumstances were inquired into, and the result was that Betsey and her accomplices were tried and executed. Old Jenny, the messenger employed in their dealings with the Obeah man, was sentenced to work in the street-gang for a certain period. From her statement at her trial, that the Obeah man, John, told her the draught would kill her mistress in "one minute," she ever after obtained that cognomen from the negroes about the streets.

In the year 1820-30, another murder was committed, the details of which are as follows:—A person of the name of Brown was living as overseer upon an estate called Big Deurs, now in possession of Messrs. Manning and Anderdon. The negroes upon this property had been for a long time in the habit of pilfering, and in many instances Mr. Brown had discovered the offenders, which caused him to be disliked, and determined one among them, more heartless, perhaps, than the rest, to undertake his destruction. On Christmas day, Mr. Brown rode to La Roche's, a neighbouring estate, and upon his return in the evening, between the hours of six and seven, he met with his untimely death.

The slave to whom Mr. Brown had rendered himself particularly obnoxious was named Cambridge, and this man had long lain in wait for an opportunity of completing his crime, and for the purpose had sharpened an old copper skimmer, (used in boiling sugar,) which he thought would prove an effective weapon.

Mr. Brown, like too many other white men in this island, carried on an amour with a woman belonging to the property, named Christiana, and it was the first intention of Cambridge to murder her as well as the overseer, supposing it was through her communications that so many discoveries of thefts had been made. On the Christmas day, Cambridge dressed himself in his best suit, and proceeded with many of his fellow slaves to the Methodist chapel at Parham, intending upon his return home to waylay and murder the woman, who had also visited the same place of worship. In pursuance of his plan, he hurried out of chapel immediately after service, and took up his stand in a part of the road which he knew Christiana must pass. After waiting in vain for a long time, a group of negroes at length hastened by, when Cambridge, whose stock of patience was exhausted, joined them, and asked if they knew where Christiana was? In answer to his query, they informed him she had visited a neighbouring estate, and after remaining there for a short time had proceeded home by another path. Thus thwarted in his views of obtaining revenge, his designs upon Mr. Brown gained double hold of him; and hastening home, he disrobed himself, put on his working-dress, and first telling his wife, *"That he had lost one opportunity, but he would take good care he did not lose the next,"* quitted the house, taking the old copper skimmer with him.

It was a beautiful evening; the moon shone in all her splendour, and every star that twinkled in the heavens glittered around that murderer's step. Oh, that such dreadful thoughts should have possessed that man's mind in the midst of such a lovely scene upon the evening of that very day when angels proclaimed "Good will towards man!" But, alas!—

"Nor grateful evening mild, nor silent night,
——————————— nor walk by moon,
Or glittering starlight,"

had any effect upon his hardened heart—

"His soul was dark within;
He lived but in the sound
Of shamelessness and sin."

Many a minute stole away, and Cambridge (who had concealed himself in a cane-piece, bordering the road his intended victim must necessarily pass) kept his fatal stand. Not a sound was heard, save the evening breeze as it whispered among the long leaves of the sugar-cane, or the occasional croaking of some night reptile. At length, the tread of a horse's foot was heard, and warned the murderer to be upon his guard. Unconscious of the dreadful fate hanging over him, Mr. Brown rode slowly on, accompanied by a black boy, when, as he was passing between two cane-pieces, just where the canes grew thick and high, with one bound the murderer was upon him. A heavy blow from the sharpened skimmer upon his head, stunned him; and ere a prayer could rise to his lips, his soul flew to meet his God, and his murderer was left standing alone, with the stain of human blood upon him.[26]

The boy who accompanied his unfortunate master was the nephew of the culprit; but as he was unperceived by Cambridge, he was enabled to make his escape into the cane-field, where he remained an unknown observer of the dreadful event. As soon as the murderer had quitted the spot, the boy hastened to the overseer's house (not far distant) and related to the inmates the fate of his master, and the name of his destroyer. An immediate alarm was given, and, guided by the boy, they quickly reached the scene of murder, where they discovered the unfortunate overseer, bereft of life, and presenting an appearance too horrible for description. They then proceeded in quest of Cambridge, whom they found at his hut, with his blood-stained garments still upon him, and in the act of washing his unhallowed hands.

After a coroner's inquest upon the body, and a verdict (according to the circumstances of the case) returned, Cambridge was conveyed to the capital, where he took his trial for murder. He was found guilty, and condemned to suffer death by hanging; and to make the punishment more impressive to others, he was ordered to be carried to Osborn's Pasture, in the vicinity of the spot where the murder was committed, and there to be hung and gibbeted.

Long did his whitened bones glisten in the moonbeams; and as the wind shook the chains which held the body, many a little negro who had strayed that way in search of guavas, fled from the spot, for fear of the "dead man's jumby."

About ten years ago, murder again stained the annals of Antigua. The slayer was one of the softer sex, and jealousy prompted her to the act. She broke into the house where her rival lived, and in her passion at finding her husband an inmate of the dwelling, stabbed her who had destroyed her peace. The husband escaped by the window; and after the perpetration of the deed, the murderess obtained the assistance of some of her friends, and between them they dragged the body of the murdered woman to the beach, and threw it into the sea. Weights were attached to the feet of the corpse to make it sink; but they were either insufficient, or they became detached, and the body floated. A negro belonging to a neighbouring estate, who was out searching for stray cattle, discovered it among some mangrove trees, and gave the alarm, the deed was traced to the woman, and she was condemned to follow her victim to the "tribunal of the Just."

Since then, this offence has rarely been repeated; but some instances there have been since my residence in this country, where the demon Revenge has sealed and stamped them for his own, and instigated them to perpetrate crimes at which the soul revolts. A circumstance of this kind occurred in the year 1840. A black man, of the name of Joseph Gould, formerly belonging to the Rev. Mr. Gilbert, the descendant of the founder of Methodism in Antigua, was living in an unlawful state with a coloured girl, of whom he became jealous, and in consequence resolved to end her existence. The unfortunate woman was murdered in a very brutal manner, by means of a thick stick, which completely shattered the head, and scattered the brains; her fingers and part of her ears were then cut off, to secure the rings and earrings which she was too fond of wearing, and the body then flung into a cane-piece.

The dreadful effluvia first attracted notice; and after some search, the body was found. A woman came forward and related some circumstances which occurred upon the last evening the unfortunate girl was seen alive, which led to the apprehension of Gould. He was brought to trial,—the evidence was all circumstantial,—and after a patient investigation of the case, he was sentenced to transportation for life. It appears, however, that no opportunity has occurred of putting the sentence into effect, as he still remains an inmate of the gaol, where it is said he suffers the stings of a guilty conscience, which conjures up the shade of the murdered girl before him, soon as "evening gray" sets in. This is the last case of particular note which has stained the domestic pages of this pretty little island; and I do hope, that now education is so liberally tendered, the minds of all classes may become enlightened, and this horrible crime become extinct.

Infanticide has also been too often perpetrated in Antigua, particularly since emancipation; although, it is true, it does not prevail to the extent it does in that "emporium of the world"—London. It is one of those unnatural offences which shews too clearly our fallen state. "Can a woman forget her sucking child?" is asked by the inspired Book; and then, as if the sad reality of what human nature is capable of is remembered, it is added, yes, "She may forget!" And, alas! those words have indeed proved true: the mother has indeed forgotten to have compassion upon the helpless little being which has derived its existence from herself.

In the days of slavery, the negroes were not allowed by law to marry; the union between them in most cases lasting only so long as agreeable to themselves. From this cause, it was frequent to find a family of eight or nine children, who all owned, perhaps, different fathers. This the woman considered no disgrace, and consequently had no incentive to disguise the fact by destroying the child. The case, however, is now different with many. Since schools have been established in this country for the benefit of the negroes, it has been the constant aim of the parents, in most cases, to avail themselves of the privilege, by sending their children to receive instruction. So far all is well; I am a great advocate for the spread of education among the lower classes, and think not, with some, that the withholding knowledge from them is the only security for obedience. "If ignorance is bliss, 'tis folly to be wise," says one, whose name stands high in the rolls of literary fame; and those who would wish to debar the poor from receiving the instruction tendered at the different free-schools &c. are apt to take this sentence as their motto, without answering the question it undoubtedly implies, "where *is* ignorance bliss?" It is good when the labourer feels his want of learning, and strives to obtain for his children the boon which has been denied his own youth. But the great evil which is likely to ensue in this island, from this liberal gift of education, until the negroes become more wise, is in this —when they send their children, particularly their daughters, to a school where they are taught to read and write, &c., they fancy that any kind of servitude will be a degradation to them; and consequently every means in their power are tried to bring them up as *ladies*, that is, to sit in the house all day, although, for a remuneration, they will condescend to do a certain portion of needlework for any one who may require it; or else to get them appointed teacher in some of the infant schools upon the several estates. These "young ladies" of course lay aside the ancient fashion of tying their heads with many-coloured handkerchiefs, and wear bonnets instead; and that everything may appear in a proper light, whatever follies or errors they may commit, they endeavour to screen as far as lies in their power. It is principally among this class of persons, then, that the crime of infanticide is to be found: to preserve their own character in the eyes of the world, they add to their former error the heavier guilt of murder; and without one pang of remorse, expose to the hungry dogs the little innocent they ought to have guarded with double care, as they had already deeply injured it by denying it a father's protection. Several instances of this kind have lately occurred within a short period; but the subject is so revolting to the sensitive mind, that we will banish any further mention of it from these pages.

In the list of higher offences, incendiarism must be noticed, which has been frequently practised by the negroes to carry out their plans of revenge. Before emancipation, as well as at the present period, the horizon has been frequently illuminated with the glare of an incendiary fire. We have already seen, in the year 1831, how much the negroes resented the abolition of their Sunday markets, by scattering abroad that devastating element; and within a few weeks ago, a case of arson occurred in the capital, which might have proved very fatal in its consequence.

A highly respectable inhabitant of Antigua, had, with his family, retired for the night, perfectly unconscious of harm. Who would not think himself safe within the precincts of his own home?—where but in that fortress would we look for rest? Alas! that human depravity should rage to such an extent that, even in our own domestic circle, revenge, that deadly "upas," should spring up, to destroy, with its poisonous exhalation, that great blessing, family peace! A few words between the servants of the establishment and their employer led, it is supposed, to the event, which, had it not been fortunately discovered, might have hurried a whole family into eternity by one of the most dreadful deaths.

On the night in question, a female inmate of his house was unable to sleep, and after tossing about for some time with a degree of feverish irritation, her sense of smelling was considerably annoyed by what appeared to be the smouldering of burning cloth. Awaking the rest of the family, she communicated to them her alarm, and on proceeding to the staircase to ascertain the cause, it was found to be completely enveloped in smoke. Making their way down with precipitation, a sofa was discovered to be in flames, which, with some difficulty, was extinguished, and once more the family prepared to seek their respective chambers. As, however, they proceeded to the staircase for that purpose, a lambent line of light was perceived to issue from a small closet under the stairs, and upon opening the door, it was found to be in a blaze, and small billets of wood, coals, and other combustibles, heaped together amid the pile of table-linen, silver, &c., which the place contained. A reward of one hundred pounds sterling has been offered by the owner for the purpose of discovering the offender, but nothing has been elicited which could lead to the apprehension of the miscreant, who, for the gratification of an evil passion, would have so heartlessly injured those who never offended. It appears strange that the legislature should have taken no notice of this wilful deed (which might once more have spread the horrors of a conflagration throughout the town) by increasing the reward offered; it must have been a great oversight on their part, as their own safety might depend upon it; for if the perpetrators of the deed remain unknown, and consequently unpunished, who can say where the evil may end?

From taking a short glance at incendiarism, the next point to be considered is polygamy—and here, again, we see the demoralizing effects of slavery. It has been before remarked that there was no legal marriage rite for slaves, such unions being merely transitory. It is true by what has been called the "Melioration Act," rewards were held out to such slaves who should preserve their fidelity in such contracts; and those persons who had the management of negroes were forbidden to encourage immorality among the women by their own example. But, alas for Antigua! when were these regulations put in force? No European can imagine to what extent such vices were carried in former days, vices which will still be painfully felt by society for many, many years to come—at any rate, until this generation shall have passed away; and, even then, the plague-spot will, perhaps, shew its taint. When the light of day began to dawn upon this benighted part of the globe by the introduction of Christianity among the negroes, they were encouraged by the Moravians and Methodists to choose a partner from among the other sex, and, in the face of the congregation, vow to each other fidelity and love. Although, of course, such marriages were not held binding by law, it was hoped that it would in some measure check the increase of immorality; and, in some instances, it might have done so, but the greater part violated those vows without compunction, or held them only until a fresh object gained their attention. It has been frequently known for a man thus married to maintain his wife and his mistress in the same house, which arrangement occasioned frequent domestic broils; and in such cases, the man, being applied to as umpire, has settled the dispute by remarking to his mistress, "That she must not quarrel with her companion, who was *his wife*, and that if she did, he would turn her away;" and then, addressing the aggrieved wife, tell her, for her consolation, "That she must not mind, because she was his *wife already!*"

After the negroes were freed from the thrall of slavery in 1834, and the same privileges open to them as to the rest of the British subjects, it was their pride to be married at the established church. In many instances, they had been already joined by the Moravian or Methodist preachers, but wishing to get rid of their partners, who had borne with them the brunt of slavery, they privately paid their addresses to some of the young ladies already mentioned, carried them to the altar, and there married in direct opposition to their former vows, which were as binding and sacred in the eyes of God as if his grace the Archbishop of Canterbury had pronounced the nuptial benediction. Among such an immense number of negroes, it is almost impossible to discover the offenders in this respect against common decency, although the clergymen are generally indefatigable in their exertions to discover the truth. Still, vigilant as they are, they have been deceived; and instances are known, where parties have been twice married, even in the episcopal church. In some cases, a wedding-party have assembled within the sacred walls, the intended bride and bridegroom waiting at the altar until the lips of the presiding minister shall have made them one; when, as that solemn charge has been given, "If either of you know any impediment why ye may not be lawfully joined together in matrimony, ye do now confess it," those important words, "I do," have been suddenly heard, and (as in most cases) a female has come forward declaring that herself and the guilty beau had been long ago married at the chapel. When such circumstances have occurred, and the clergyman refused to re-marry them, it has been no unfrequent practice for the parties to embark on board a small vessel, and proceeding to Monserrat, or some other island, there to procure the completion of their unhallowed purpose.

Another evil to be deplored is, that even when parties are lawfully joined in the bands of wedlock, they pay such little regard to the solemnity of the act. The smart dresses, (for which often they commit an unlawful deed,) the plentiful breakfast, or lunch, the gilded cake, and the driving about in borrowed gigs, is much more thought of by them than the serious, the important promise of loving one another in sickness and in health, and, forsaking all others, cleave only unto them who, by the ordinances of God and man, are made one flesh. From this want of regard to the serious part of the ceremony, great mischief ensues. As soon as the novelty has worn off, the husband forgets the wife he ought to cherish, and the wife forgets his honour which she is bound to protect. The old leaven cleaves about them, and throwing off all shame, they follow the bad example of their parents, (who indeed are less faulty than themselves, not having had such means of instruction;) and by these means, give to the country, instead of an honest peasantry, a race of idle illegitimate children. I would by no means take upon myself to state, that of the many weddings which weekly take place among this "sober-hued" people, none remember to keep their marriage-vows unstained; on the contrary, no doubt many find it what it should be—a state "ordained for the mutual society, help, and comfort, that the one ought to have of the other, both in prosperity and adversity."

---

[26] The negroes say that no grass has ever grown in the spot where the blood dropped since the time of the murder.

CHAPTER XXXVII

Negroes: A little change for the better—"Shadows nursed by night retire"—Respect to age—Filial affection—Generosity—Their kindness to the poorer class of whites—Cleanliness—the opposite vice—Behaviour at church—A black exhorter—Reading and writing—An anecdote.

I am happy to find that at length I have got over the most prominent vices of the negroes. I must say I have a great love for my species, of whatever shade they may be, and I would at any time rather have to paint their virtues than their vices. But, alas for human nature! the latter are by far the most numerous, or else "men's *evil* manners live in *brass*, their *virtues* we write in *water*." To relieve ourselves for a little from the dreadful deeds of blood which have so lately engaged our attention, let us turn from the "shadows," and try to pick out of the negro character something a little pleasanter—something which, if we are forbidden to term virtues, we may, at least, give them the appellation of good qualities.

In pursuance of our plan, I think we may mention filial affection, and the respect they pay it. It is but seldom that a child will behave ill to its parent; on the contrary, they generally do for them whatever lies in their power. Age, too, is particularly venerated; and the noisy little negroes at their sport will stop while one of their old people are passing, with "How d'ye, marm?" and "How d'ye, me pic'nee?" is the courteous reply. Generosity may also be mentioned among the "lights" of their character. When they see one of their own class in distress, they generally relieve them to the extent of their ability, and to their sorrows turn a listening ear. When any of their friends or relatives die, they commonly have some little offering to make to assist in defraying the expenses of the funeral. Sometimes they will carry a bottle of wine or porter—sometimes bread and cheese, or a few biscuits, &c.; but however small the article is, it is always gratefully received, for this feasting at a funeral is as necessary to their idea of etiquette as giving the corpse a shroud or a coffin.

Nor do negroes always confine their generosity to their own colour, of which I can give a striking example. It is true, it does not much concern either "Antigua" or "the Antiguans," but I have already apologized for wandering out of my path, and this comes so *apropos*, that I cannot refrain from mentioning it. In the course of my peregrinations through different parts of the world, it has been my fate to meet with many deplorable objects—the half-starved diseased negroes—the dirty emaciated North American Indians, and their miserable squaws, (as they term their wives,) suffering from the effects of the alcohol they purchase from their white brethren at the expense of their domestic joys—the ragged, quarrelsome "wild Irish," "the finest *pisantry* in the world," in their own estimation—the deformed and almost naked beggars of England; but in all my travels I never saw so truly wretched a class, taking them altogether, as the poor white inhabitants of Barbados. I never shall forget the appearance they presented to my eyes upon my first visit to "Little England," as the Barbadians in their pride call their pleasant little island. From the intense heat of the sun, and their constant exposure to its rays, their complexions are changed from a natural white to a fiery red. The women allow their long hair to float all down their backs, and be blown about by every zephyr. This may sound very pretty in poetry, but it is anything but pretty in *real life*, particularly when we take into consideration the colour and state of these locks; the fervent kisses of the "great luminary" has changed them into the appearance of dirty flax, while their disordered and matted condition brings the idea forcibly to your mind, that they have seldom, if ever, undergone the ordeal of "brush and comb." With respect to their persons, they are, generally, almost in a state of nudity, or their dress is put on in such a manner that it leaves you with that impression; no shoes or stockings envelope their feet, while their meagre, attenuated forms altogether produce an effect which no pen can accurately describe.

The men look even worse than the women, for to their squalid appearance they add the air of a "Regent-street lounger." Their castors stand in great want of "Rowland's Macassar," as well as Dr. Winn's "true anticardiam," which engages to make *old* articles look like *new*; the original size has gradually diminished until it is almost insufficient to cover their pericranium, while the form beats in distortion those to be daily seen in the shop-windows of "Lloyd." This *elegant* article of dress is placed upon *one side* of the head, while on the other protrudes a huge mass of disordered hair. With regard to the other articles of clothing, they bear anything but the marks of taste, their coats being generally "out at elbows," and partly devoid of collars, their trousers reaching about half down their legs, and the use of shoes and stockings dispensed with; a short stick denominated a "two *foot* two" swings from their hands, and then the costume is complete. Their houses are as dirty as their persons, and from their incurable habits of idleness, starvation is often their fate. To these poor unfortunates, the Barbadian negroes are known to step forth as their guardian angels; they will work for them, feed them, clothe them, and often shelter them from the weather, and all this is done without the slightest wish or prospect of receiving remuneration; their generosity in some instances knows no bounds, and they will attend to their every want with the kindness and affection of a parent. Although we have no such miserable objects in Antigua, still I am persuaded that, were it the case, the negroes of this island would not be behind their Barbadian brethren in these acts of charity; for whenever any European sailors get out of employ, and wander about the streets in a state of misery, (although brought on by their own misdemeanour in most instances,) the Antiguan negroes extend to them their bounty, taking them to their houses and giving them food, and not unfrequently small sums of money.

Next to generosity, cleanliness (in most instances) may be ranked among their good qualities. Those who have any regard to appearance make frequent use of water, which, in this climate, is particularly conducive to good health; and they are careful to make their children follow their example in this particular. In their houses they are also very cleanly, and their culinary articles are kept with the greatest care. They are very fond of sending presents of eatables to their acquaintance, (such as portions of their breakfast or dinner, &c., particularly house-servants;) and when this is the case, they always pay some regard to appearance. A clean white towel is wrapt round it, whatever the viands may be; and if soup forms a part, it is sure to be sent in a smart-coloured cup, with a cover. Sundays are the principal days on which such presents are sent; and an observer may often catch the little messengers peeping into the utensil which contains the savoury mess, or tasting it, by inserting one or more of their fingers, at the hazard of receiving a flogging, should the tidings reach the donor's ears.

It must, however, be allowed, that all negroes are not celebrated for their purity of habits; on the contrary, there are many exceptions among the indolent, and these present an appearance painful to behold. Among the men, all the money they can procure is spent upon that plague of the West Indies, "new rum;" consequently, what they wear is of no importance to them. They are, indeed, in a state bordering upon nakedness; and the filthy manner in which they keep their persons renders them disgusting in the extreme. A small insect, which is called a *chegoe*, or, as the negroes express it, "jigger," gets into their feet; and if not extracted in time, makes its nest and breeds in the flesh. The dirty and indolent beings I am now describing allow these insects to breed so fast, and remain until they attain to such a size, that it is impossible for them to be taken out; and the consequence is, they feed upon the flesh, until the feet are in such a state, that they are often obliged to suffer amputation as far as the knee. Again—the dirt which they allow to remain upon them for so long a time, produces various horrible complaints, which, in the end, also call for the knife of the surgeon. This latter class of persons meet with the abhorrence of all their tribe, who never fail to express their contempt whenever they meet; and was it not for the humane conduct of the Rev. R. Holberton, (whose name must often occur in "Antigua and the Antiguans,") by seeking them out, and getting them admitted into the lazaretto, (which owes its origin to his exertions,) many must expire in the open roads.

But to return to the good qualities of the negroes. Another thing worthy of remark is, the quiet and decorous manner in which they behave in a place of worship. Upon my first arrival in this country, I was particularly pleased with the conduct of the black congregation at the episcopal church. Not the least noise was to be heard—only the voice of the preacher, and the deep, and apparently heartfelt responses of the people; and during the sermon, the dropping of a pin upon the floor could have been heard, so silent and motionless were they. At particular parts of the service, all were kneeling, with the *appearance* of the deepest humility. Nearly all the negroes belong to one sect or the other, and keep the outward ordinances of religion with exactness. They all talk of the goodness of God, of their own unworthiness, and their hopes of salvation, &c.; but, alas! among many of them, these are words *only*, as far as their general conduct leads us to conclude. There are others, however, who appear to have benefited by the instructions of their pastors, conducting themselves in a praiseworthy manner, thus giving encouragement to the missionaries,[27] who must feel richly rewarded for their exertions in behalf of this benighted class, and for being made, under the hand of the Almighty, the honoured instruments of snatching them as so many "brands from the burning."

Among the higher order of negroes who have joined respective sects are many who at times officiate as *parsons* when those of the "cloth" are absent. They bury the dead, (that is, when such event takes place in the country,) read prayers to the sick, or pray extemporaneously, (which is most frequent,) and sometimes preach in the country chapels. I have heard an anecdote related of one of these kind of parsons, who used to be very fond of giving an oration at the grave; or, to shew forth his skill in reading to the astonished multitude, favoured them with a portion from some of his favourite authors. On one occasion, when a minister was about to inter a friend of this black preacher, he asked permission to read an exhortation after the funeral service was performed. This request was immediately granted; and, accordingly, he proceeded to his house, which was near the place of burial, for his books. It took him some time to collect them together, so extensive was his library; at length this important exploit was effected, and he left his house, armed with folios, quartos, and octavos, and proceeded to the grave. To his great surprise, upon his arrival, he found the funeral over, the minister gone, and the mourners dispersed; so, like poor Dominie Sampson, he had to shoulder his volumes and return also.

Perhaps it may afford matter of surprise to some of my readers to hear that the negroes of former days could read or write; but although slave-owners in general opposed the system of opening the book of knowledge to their slaves, it is to the honour of Antigua that she has been the most forward in pursuing a contrary line of conduct, and allowing her negroes the privilege of being taught those necessary qualifications. I am again referring to those dark days of slavery when the negroes were looked upon as little better than cattle; but in this part of my subject, I cannot help remarking what a difference a few years has made with regard to the instruction of the blacks. In former days, as above alluded to, the negroes were purposely kept in ignorance both of spiritual and worldly knowledge; all attempts to inform them were decidedly against the wishes of the proprietors, (I am now speaking of the West Indies generally,) who thought it one step towards insurrection. From this state of darkness and bad policy Antigua was about the first to awake; her efforts were at first but very slow, and her plans but half formed. But now the case is very different: schools abound in all parts of the island, both for young people and adults; there is not a negro who cannot obtain instruction if he wishes, and among the young there are none but the very worthless who cannot read. In the statistical part of this work will be found the number of schools, what sects they belong to, and also the number of children; but besides these, there are a great many private schools where the little black boys and girls who attend are taught reading, writing, and arithmetic. The Wesleyans were the first who instituted these schools; they were followed by the Moravians; and upon the appointment of a bishop to this diocese, the church followed their example.

Among the children who are instructed in these various schools, many of them can read fluently, write a good hand, and cast up an account with correctness; but with regard to those who gained their learning at an earlier date, very much cannot be said for their chirography. I have seen some of their writing, however, which is very passable, while others, again, presented the appearance of complete hieroglyphics, and which I should as soon think of interpreting as the characters on the tomb of "Cheops," or a Chinese manuscript. An anecdote is related of a person whose name was Mac Namara; he was considered a superior kind of man for his line, but was not much of a penman, his writing being chiefly confined to the signing his own name. One day, his signature was required in some haste, and taking the pen in hand, he commenced "Macnamamamama," till at length, turning to some person who stood near him, "Brother," says he, "tell me when me done; here, don't you think it looks long enough?." It was his custom, it appears, when signing his name, to look more to the *length* than the spelling, but being rather flurried on this day, he exceeded his usual limit.

---

[27] I include under this term the very zealous and worthy preachers of the Wesleyan sect, and the kind-hearted Moravians, as well as the established clergy.

CHAPTER XXXVIII

Negroes: Their amusements—Natural ear for music—Singing—Dancing—Subscription routs—Christmas balls—The ball-room decorations—Ball dresses—Gentlemen's appearance—Ladies'—Politeness—Supper, and the supper-table—The morning after a ball—Cards of invitation—The "good night."

We have now to mention the amusements of the negroes, and their conduct in their hours of recreation. The blacks have a remarkable ear for music, and consequently are particularly fond of singing. Indeed, they can hardly do anything without "forming their voice to melody." The sailors, when heaving an anchor, have a peculiar song which they sing in chorus, pulling the cable at the same time. When moving their houses, (which it is customary to do in this part of the world,[28]) another ditty is requisite; and even if you get them to lift any article which obliges them to use a little exertion, a song must accompany the action. Most of these songs are extempore, and are sung to some favourite tune, the poetry being generally a species of parody, or else a ludicrous composition upon some person who may have attracted their attention, either by a peculiarity in dress or manners; and it is surprising how soon the whole tribe learn it. Some negroes have a clear, sweet, and powerful voice, while others again resemble the screech of a pair of bagpipes, or give the idea of a parrot warbling an Italian air. The black boys are nearly all good whistlers, and some of them will go through, with correctness, many of our best airs, with variations. They are also great psalm-singers, the streets often resounding with this peculiar species of harmony.

Next to singing, their favourite pastime is, to "trip the light fantastic toe," and at this sport they are indefatigable. These dancing parties are differently conducted; at some are danced quadrilles! (I am not aware if the gallopades and Mazurka have found their way into these *coteries* at present, but as all negroes are great sticklers for fashion, I suppose they have,) at others only country dances and reels are introduced; while the Africans are content with their own native dance, and their music of the *Bangoe* and *Tum-tum*. Christmas is the principal season for these assemblies, although there are subscription balls held once or twice a week in some of the small houses at the back of the town. These meetings may be very agreeable to the negroes, but they are anything but agreeable to those unfortunates who may chance to inhabit houses in the vicinity. Little or no sleep will visit their eyes upon those nights dedicated to gay Terpsichore, and they may be led to misquote Shakspeare, and say, "*Dancing* murders sleep." The music generally consists of a squeaking fiddle, a tamborine, (upon which they have a peculiar way of performing,) and a triangle, played without any regard to time or melody. The worst characters frequent these houses, and the refreshments are always levied by contributions upon the public.

Some of the Christmas balls (or as it is the fashion now to term them, "quadrille parties") are, however, conducted upon a very grand scale. The ball-room is decorated with branches of the cocoa-nut, interspersed with the many beautiful flowers which, in these sunny climes, grow in such wild profusion, while boughs of the Pimento (or "Christmas bush," as it is generally called in this country) and the orange tree, loaded with its tempting fruit, impart a pleasing fragrance throughout the apartment. Around the walls, brackets of deal are nailed to support the innumerable tapers which serve to light up this "temple of mirth," and throw a radiance upon the countenances of the ebon beaux and belles. The orchestra generally occupies one end of the apartment; and the company is arranged, in two lines, the ladies upon one side, and the gentlemen upon the other. The glittering throng at "Almacks" cannot outvie in dress with the *glittering throng* at an Antiguan negro ball. Fashion exerts her power, and seldom finds more devoted votaries than among these dark damsels and their loving swains.

The dress of the gentlemen consists of a blue, brown, or purple coat, (not *quite* equal in make to one of Stultz,) with velvet collar, and shining brass buttons; pantaloons, which would rival in whiteness the snows of great St. Bernard; a many coloured vest, a very smart cravat, silk stockings, and well-polished pumps or fancy boots, with tassels, &c., in the most approved fashion. In the folds of the cravat are deposited one or two brooches, (not quite equalling in splendour and dimensions the celebrated "brooch of Lorn," but no doubt thought by the wearers to be very tasteful;) a glittering brass chain, which after performing countless figures and evolutions around the neck, is deposited with its accompanying quizzing-glass (set in the same *precious* metal) in the waistcoat pocket; sundry brass rings upon the fingers; a box to contain that fashionable dust, called by mortals—snuff, ornamented with a *correct* likeness of "Her Majesty Queen Victoria," or "Prince Albert," with cheeks of the colour of red ochre, and eyes "like two full moons;" these, together with a voluminous silk handkerchief, plentifully besprinkled with *new rum*, sold under the approved name of "*Eau de Cologne*," and then the costume is complete.

Smart as these beaux are, the fair sex make a much greater display. Their favourite colours are pink, blue, and bright yellow, and of these their dresses are generally composed; but the manner in which these several shades are arranged defies all description. For example—a dress of white gauze or net, over a yellow slip, is profusely decorated with quillings of blue ribbon, interspersed with red flowers; or perhaps a blue dress is ornamented with green trimmings. Of course these dresses are made in the height of the fashion, very long skirts with flounces, and tight sleeves, with lace ruffles, and streamers of varied tints, while the long kid or lace gloves, are drawn up the arm to the exact point at which such articles are worn. Among the bijouterie displayed upon these *gala* nights, may be distinguished a diversity of brass bracelets, two or three encircling the same arm; numberless rings, in which the "lively diamond," the ruby's "deepening glow," the sapphire's "solid ether," the "purple amethyst," the yellow topaz, and the green emerald, are wonderfully imitated in coloured *glass*; these *choice gems* are liberally bestowed upon every finger, and I am not quite sure that the *thumb* is exempted. Splendid brass chains also encircle their (not) *swan-like* necks, long pendants gleam from their ears, and very pink silk stockings, with red, blue, or yellow shoes, are called in, to astonish with their brilliancy of hue, the eyes of their attendant youths. But notwithstanding all this finery, it is upon the adornment of their heads that these ladies lavish the most time and pains. This may surprise some, when they consider how devoid the negroes are of that great natural ornament which Rowland, by the aid of his incomparable "Macassar," so kindly and bountifully offers to dispense; but still it is no less true, for what Dame Nature denies, art bestows in the shape of a false set of curls, or a complete *toupée*. These ringlets are cleverly fastened on by bands of different coloured cotton-velvet, and the back of the head is covered with wreaths of flowers and bunches of ribbons. Those whose natural hair is long enough, wear it in what they term "French curls;" but they never fail to have a sufficient quantity of flowers intermixed with them.

The gentlemen are particularly polite to the ladies, attending to their little wants with the greatest assiduity, and watching their every movement, to anticipate, if possible, their wishes. The ladies are also quite graceful in their manners, and forget not to practise those pretty little airs of affection which some of their white sisters so ably perform.

When the tuning of instruments is over, and the musicians, by stamping their feet and drawing up their persons to their full height, give notice that they are ready, and have full confidence in their own powers of drawing from wood and catgut "a concord of sweet sounds," the ball commences. A gentleman advances with smirk and bow—"Oh, Miss, will you dance wid me?" "I'se must be excuse, Mr. Charles Edward, 'cause I'se got to dance wid Mr. Albert" "Oh, Miss, den me be too late." Another lady is therefore sought and won—"Wid much pleasure, Mr. Charles Edward." At the end of the set, refreshments are handed about, and again the gentlemen vie with each other in shewing forth their gallantry—"Miss, will you hab a glass of drink?" "I'se feel much obliged to you, sir, if you please." The "drink" is composed of ginger, water, molasses, and "Christmas bush," drank in a fermented state.

While the dancing is going on in one room, another apartment, (or, if the house contains not such a desideratum,) a neighbouring domicile is being prepared for the supper. Here, again, their taste is shewn in the arrangement of the flowers &c. with which the table is decorated, and in the disposal of the many viands which are prepared for the occasion. They generally employ a gentleman's servant to superintend, so that this is often performed in the first style. Among the multitudinous supply of eatables may be found baked mutton, legs of pork, turkeys, ducks, fowls, and guinea-birds; hams, tongues, salt-beef, and cheese; cakes, tarts, and fruits, flanked by no inconsiderable quantities of yams, sweet potatoes, *Irish* potatoes, (as the Creoles always term them, whether they come from England, Ireland, Scotland, France, or America,) boiled rice, and bread. Nor must it be supposed these *solids* want the accompaniment of liquids—rum, brandy, wines, and brown stout, are as liberally provided, and as liberally partaken of.

Perhaps it may be asked, how do the negroes obtain these different articles specified,—where find the *cash* to meet these heavy demands? In the first place, it must be taken into consideration, that nearly all the negroes who reside in the country, upon the different estates, keep a great deal of stock; they have their patch of ground, in which they raise vegetables; and living as they do nearly all the rest of the year upon less expensive dishes, they have money enough by them to procure the above luxuries. Then again, it must be remarked, that it is not *one* family which gives these routs, but almost in every instance it is a joint concern. The company pay a proportion, by the gentlemen procuring tickets to admit themselves and ladies for half-a-dollar, about 2*s*. 3*d*. sterling, which of itself affords sufficient means to provide all those sumptuous viands and costly liquids with which they regale themselves when fatigued with dancing. The competition for opening the ball is generally very great, and from one to five dollars is demanded for that honour; but such has been the contest at times that a doubloon, or 3*l*. 4*s*. sterling, has been offered for obtaining the enviable post; and this of course further adds to their resources.

When these grand balls are held in the country, the servants feel no reluctance in riding their masters' horses to and from the place of entertainment; and consequently it is nothing uncommon for great complaints to be made the next morning by different gentlemen, when they visit their stables. "Why, Thomas, what's the matter with this horse? how jaded he looks," says the gent, addressing his groom; "I hope it's not ill!" "Me no no, massa; me quite sick meself, dat de trute," replies one of the *beaux* of the preceding night. "And this one," continues his master, "his legs are quite swollen, and he's all over mud; I hope you have not been riding them last night, sirrah! I know you are full of tricks!" "Eh, eh! massa, me no say, me quite sick; war for me go ride de poor dumb brute for, dat's all?"

While this dialogue passes in the stable between the injured master and his faulty groom, respecting the state of "de poor dumb brute," who, had he the power of speech, could, like Hamlet's ghost, "a tale unfold," a similar conversation takes place in the house between the mistress and her confidential(!) domestic. "Celestina, what is the matter with you this morning? you don't seem to know what you are doing,— are you ill?" "No, ma'am." "Then what do you look so heavy and dull about?" "Me no able to sleep last night, missis," is the answer of the fatigued belle.

When the family meet around the breakfast table, "My dear," says the lady, addressing her *cara sposa*, "do you know where John (the butler) is gone?" "No, my dear," returns her better half, sipping his mocha; "is he not in the house?" "No; he has not been seen since last night." "Very strange," rejoins the gentleman. "I must make inquiries about it as soon as I have looked over the 'Weekly Register;' the fellow gets too bad." At this moment the door opens, and John enters, his head tied up in a handkerchief and a quantity of plantain leaves;[22] his countenance, deprived of its naturally deep black, displays a sickly-looking hue; his heavy blood-shot eyes, turning from one member of the family to the other, as if to inquire what they had been saying about him, and presenting altogether a most rueful appearance. "Why, John," cries his master, elevating his eyebrows, and wiping his spectacles, to be certain it is really the lost butler,—"Why, John, where have you been, and what have you been doing with yourself?" "Quite sick, massa," returns poor John, in a very doleful tone; "hab feber all last night, neber sleep 'tall a 'tall; head really hurt me; 'bleive me go get *hager*," &c. The real fact of the case, John was one of the party the night before, who had paid their devoirs too zealously to the "rosy god," "jolly Bacchus," and the consequence was, headache and all its accompanying et-ceteras, without the benefit of "soda water" or "Morison's pills of health."

When these "grand balls" are in contemplation, great is the flurry and fluster of the conductors; cards of invitation are issued about eight or ten days before; glasses, lamps, dishes, &c., are borrowed from managers or overseers upon the estate where the rout is given, or if in town, from any "buckra" who they may live with; flowers are begged, or gardens robbed; and many other necessary deeds achieved. I have several of these "cards of invite" lying before me, and for the edification of my readers, I will transcribe one or two of them *verbatim*:—"Mr. James Hammilton Compliments to Mr. James, and invite him to a Quadrille party on Tuesday next week, with lady;" addressed, "Mr. James Hammilton to Mr. James, Spring Gardens." This is written upon paper, which had once been white, but, alas! too many touches have tarnished its fair character. The next which comes to hand is traced upon that particular kind of green paper which we commonly see wrapped round quills in the stationers' shop windows, in far-famed London, and is expressed as follows:—"Mr. James will be happy of Mr. Brown and Lady Company on Saturday the 2nd Quarter of the Moon. Price 4*s.* 6*d.* Lower Form."[30] The direction to this last-named note is, I think, very unique—

"Mr. Brown,
"Town!"

meaning, of course, that the gentleman resided in St. John's, the capital of Antigua.

Having given two specimens of their written invitations, perhaps some of my readers may call out, "Enough!" but there is still one before me, which looks so very dashing that I cannot pass it by with any propriety. It is written upon a *red* card, (placed in a *blue* envelope,) in the following manner:—

"Mr. Edward and Sam will happy of Mr. Hues Company on the 25th instant, &c. Quadrilles in Bishopsgate Street.

"G. PRIDDEYS,
"G. SILISES. Stewards.

(Direction) "MR. HUES, ESQ."

The ball generally breaks up between four and five, and then there is great cloaking-up with the ladies, the gentlemen lending all the assistance. "'Tanky, Mr. *Theopolus*, you're bery kind, I'se sure." "Miss, anything dat *lays* in my power for a lady like you." "Oh, sir! you're very purlite." "Miss Eleanora, does dis shawl 'blongs to you?" "I'se 'bleive it do, Mr. Frederick." "Well, I do declare, I thought so, 'cause it's handsome, like its owner," &c. &c. The *Good nights* are then repeated, and the ladies move off, accompanied by their *beaux*, and the late gay ball-room is left to the smell of expiring tallow-candles, and lamp-oil; drooping flowers, and broken bottles; sleeping musicians, and half-starved dogs, who creep in with the hopes of picking up a stray bone or two; until the bright sun arises, and bids the inmates bestir themselves to clear away the relics of their midnight orgies.

---

[28] For mode of moving houses, see page 132.

[29] A negro's specific for the head-ache.

[30] I am not quite certain what is meant by this expression; but suppose it relates to the arrangement of the forms, or benches.

CHAPTER XXXIX

Negroes: Fondness for "Nancy stories"—Negro loquacity—Their signification of the word "cursing"—Markets—Confusion of tongues—Weddings—The drive to church—Wedding banquet—Blushing brides—Funerals—"Wake nights"—Funeral procession—Christening—High-sounding names.

After dancing, I think the next favourite pastime of the negroes, particularly among the younger ones, is to collect together upon a fine moonlight night, and talk "Nancy stories," (which, as before remarked, generally consist of tales of *diablerie*,) and the far-famed "Scheherazade" of the "Arabian Nights" could scarcely invent more marvellous ones. Some tell of a wondrous bird, (equalling in magnitude Sinbad's roc,[31]) which in other days appeared, and completely covered Antigua for some time, obliging the good people to "light candle all de day, so dat dey neber no when night come self;" others tell of men turning into monkeys, (no uncommon thing now-a-days;) some of demons, and their deeds; and others, again, of golden houses, and streets of silver, flying dragons, and talking birds. These "Nancy stories" are generally given in a species of recitativo; but the conclusion to them all is the same—"I was dere, an see it well done, and I get a glass of wine for me pains!" The relater of these tales is held in great repute, and to obtain instruction in the art, many a little negro will give their dinners, and go hungry to-bed.

The negroes are indefatigable talkers, at all times, and in all seasons. Whether in joy or grief, they ever find full employment for that little member, the tongue. If none of their acquaintance are near at hand to enter into conversation with, they talk to themselves, maintaining different characters, and answering their own questions. I have often thought two persons were conversing, but upon inquiry, have found it to be only one. One peculiarity of expression among the negroes is, that if you have to find fault with them, and you express your dislike of what they have been doing in the mildest terms, they immediately say you have been *cursing* them. When speaking, their tongues are very vociferous, and prove extremely disagreeable to a stranger. Upon my first arrival in this island, I was one day seated in a back apartment, and wandering with Milton through the blissful shades of Paradise, when I was aroused by hearing one of our domestics speaking in a most clamorous manner. I bore it patiently for some time, until finding it appeared to have no *terminus*, I exclaimed—"My good Sarah, I should feel particularly obliged if you would not speak *quite* so loud." How was I surprised, a few moments after, to hear the same servant calling, in a still louder tone, to one of her companions—"Sissy, (*Ang.*, sister,) war for you 'peak so loud? Me 'bleive you no hear how missis *curse* me just now for doing dat 'ting!"

But the market is the place, where the chattering is the loudest and longest; it is a complete Babel—a scene of confusion almost unimaginable. Black, brown, and yellow—indeed, almost every tint which "sober autumn" wears—may be met with in the crowds of men and women, boys and girls, who frequent the busy spot. The women scream—men shout—the boys and girls, clad *à la nature*, laugh—the little pic'nees, (as the negroes call their babies,) clinging round their mothers' hips, squall. In this warm country, where meat is obliged to be dressed soon after it is killed, most of the stock is brought to market alive; so to this tumult of human voices is added the cry of goats, squeaking of pigs, cackling of poultry, &c. To increase the noise, the venders call out the different articles they have for sale:—"Want any corn *poon?*" (*Ang.*, pudding)—"Want any green corn *duckana, ladies?*" (a similar production)—"Want any *yam* and *pitaters?*" (potatoes)—"Here's your peas and pork!" Another party cries—"Bargain, ladies! Bargain here!"— "Here's your 'trong cloth! Here's your nice handkerchief! tie your head smart as eber! Here aw you see de last an de bery best, aw you cum buy um —only a bit and a half," (about 6*d.* sterling.) One cries out—"Pine tarts and pickled peppers!" while another vociferates—"Nice fat chickens, ladies, and castor oil!" rather heterogeneous articles, it must be allowed.

Evening brings no silence with it; for then the *cries* increase. "Candles here, ladies! Candles here! hard, like stones—burn like wax, (in plain English, *soft as butter*,) two for a half-a-bit!" (2¼*d.* sterling.) "Here your nice crackers! (small American biscuits,) seven for a dog! Here your fine coffee! Cigars here! Cigars here! only cum see, make you buy! Here your nice cakes! —Fish! fish!! fish!!! just come out of the sea, ladies! ladies! make haste, an buy dem!"—"Sugar-cakes here! Bread here! Salt fish here! Cum an look, only cum an see!"—"Goat-meat here, ladies! Sheep-meat! Vine here! (the vine of the sweet potato, used for fattening stock.)" "Want any grass? Want any wood? Want any pies? Sweet *oranger* here! Ripe pear, really nice!" besides a thousand other announcements, fill the air, and deafen the hearers. Talk of *London cries!* oh! they are mere *whispers* to the *West Indian ones!* The "dustman's bell," or the "watchman's rattle," would, I verily believe, pass unnoticed amid their stormy tongues.

At the principal market, which is held upon a Saturday, (the Sunday markets having been abolished, by orders of the legislature, in 1831,) all kinds of articles may be met with. Beef, mutton, pork, and goat's flesh; live pigs, sheep, goats, and lambs; ducks, fowls, turkeys, geese, and guinea-birds; potatoes, yams, eddoes, peas, &c.; and fruits of every description, including the luscious pine-apple, the cooling melon, the fragrant guava, and the delicious "jelly cocoa-nut." The market is also plentifully supplied with varieties of fish; some of which are very delicious fare. Besides these enumerated articles, hot soups, boiled horse-beans, boiled peas, and Indian corn, "fungy and pepperpot," (a standing Creole dish,) "fried fish and dumplings," souse, pigs' heads, and black puddings, with all kinds of cakes, bread, "drink," spruce-beer, Dyer drink, (made from a peculiar bark,) and different varieties of sugar-cakes, are exhibited, to allure the eye, and charm the taste of the sable beauties who attend this mart. Many other wares are also sold in this place of bustle, which, according to the Antigua black bellman, would be "to *tedus* to *'numerate*."

It was formerly the custom to ring a market-bell at six in the morning, and the same hour in the evening, and also to have a clerk of the market, whose duty it was to see that the street where the market is held was properly swept, and that the people dispersed upon the ringing of the bell. For his services he received the sum of 200*l.* currency per annum; but the legislature at last thought it a waste of the public money, and within these few years the office has been disannulled. There is no markethouse at present, the principal market being held in a long street running from the court-house to one of the gates of the churchyard. It was under consideration of the house of assembly, some time ago, to erect a covered market, but the proposition was overruled.

From a visit to the market, we will take another turn, and accompany the bridal party in their attendance at the altar. In former days, during the existence of slavery, the ceremony of marriage was but seldom performed, consequently the nuptial feasts were "few and far between." The case, however, is now very different; for, since the "glorious 1st of August," (1834,) weddings are very frequent, and many a grand fête is given in honour of the "saffron-crowned god." The first step upon this eventful occasion is, of course, to get the bans of marriage published—or, as they term it, "to hab dere name call out"—unless they can afford to purchase a licence, which is the case with some. Then comes the purchasing of that "small and holy round," the wedding ring, the bridal dresses, and the wedding breakfast. When all these preliminaries are arranged with satisfaction to themselves, the next grand point is to borrow, from different gentlemen, horses, gigs, and phaetons. Not being their own property, and not often having the *chance* of shewing off their knowledge of the "whip," no mercy is shewn to the unfortunate animal they that day guide. To give *éclat* to the wedding-day by astonishing the inhabitants of the town, the gentlemen drive as violently as they can up one street, down another, turn the corners like wildfire, and then, after running over a chicken or two, or disturbing the ruminations of a few quiet ducks, deposit their female companion at the church doors, and start away, in the same random manner, to fetch another fair dame from her homage at a sixpenny "looking-glass." It is impossible to describe the noise and confusion which ensues on mornings when such deeds are done,—Virgil's chariot-race was nothing to the speed with which these aspiring youths urge on the foaming steeds. The consequence of this is, that the horse is very often returned to his owner broken-kneed, or else killed upon the spot, by the shaft of another gig penetrating its chest; and the carriage left minus a shaft or a wheel.

At length the company assemble in the church, the clergyman arrives, and the ceremony begins. The "blushing bride" has frequently to snuff up the fumes of her "eau de Cologne," to support her trembling frame in that moment of excitement, and many a rent is made in the white kid gloves, as such articles are drawn off to sign the marriage X, when, as it frequently happens, the art of writing has been dispensed with in their education. The ceremony over, the party again enter the different vehicles, and after driving in the manner before described, re-assemble at the house where the nuptial banquet has been prepared. This is conducted in similar style to the "ball supper," already mentioned; great mirth and jollity prevail at it; the health of the bride and bridegroom is drunk in "full goblets;" many a loyal and willing toast, no doubt, given, and then the company separate. I must not forget to mention that a wedding-cake of approved dimensions, and splendidly arrayed in gold and silver leaf is placed in the centre of the table, and calls for many a sidelong glance from those damsels who, as yet, are doomed to remain in single blessedness. Sometimes these wedding breakfasts, or whatever else they choose to term them, are held in the country; at other times, the company remain in town, and the bride and bridegroom retire there by themselves to spend a part of the "honeymoon," and then return to the capital to receive the complimentary congratulations of their friends, and make their appearance at church in their wedding attire.

The dress of the gentlemen upon this eventful occasion is similar to that worn by them at their balls: brass chains and rings are rubbed up with chalk in order to restore their pristine brightness; silk stockings, dyed with the flowers of the Hybiscus to the colour of a pigeon's legs; and shops and stores ransacked, to procure waistcoats and stocks of the brightest dyes. The bride is generally arrayed in white: if they can raise sufficient *cash*, white silk, satin, or figured "challis" is the material; but if the funds are rather *low*, white muslin suffices them. The bonnets are either white satin, or tuscans trimmed with white ribbon, and wreaths of white flowers are fashionably arranged on the left side. Veils are sometimes worn upon these occasions, (to hide their "*blushes*,") and "parasols and sandals," and then the lady's dressed. The morning after the wedding, the "bride's cake" is sent round to their numerous acquaintance; and then they return to their usual business and their dishabille, until the sound of the "Sabbath bell" bids them open their chests of cedar-wood,[32] and put on their gala-dress. It may be remarked that the greater part of these *"blushing brides,"* these "nervous fine ladies," have been living several years in a state of concubinage with different persons, and are perhaps the mothers of several children; but still marriage is a state which "calls up all our hopes and fears," and the black buckras[33] (as these dashing black people are called in this country) think the ceremony would be incomplete did they not shew forth some emotion, or call up from their source some of those

"_____ drops that fall,
When the young bride goes from her father's hall."

We now come to take a view of their burials. I have in a former chapter made some mention of these ceremonies; but still there is a great deal to be said, for be it known, a negro funeral is a matter of no small importance.

When the intelligence reaches them that one of their friends has departed to another world, many of them immediately flock to the residence of the defunct, and are very ready to assist in the melancholy but necessary offices which are required to be performed. The first consideration of the relatives is to procure a coffin, a decent shroud, and a suit of apparel to inter the corpse in. The coffin is made of deal boards, *not over thick*, and is covered with black or white cotton cloth, according to the age or state of the individual; those persons who cannot afford to purchase cotton for this purpose have the coffin painted black or white. Among the higher class of negroes the shroud is made of white mull muslin, but those of less means purchase cotton cambric, while the *very poor ones* are enveloped in a sheet. If the deceased has a pretty good stock of clothes, the best amongst them are selected for the occasion. Should it be a man who is dead, he is arrayed in his "Sunday clothes," with the exception of coat, shoes, and hat; but if it is a female, her best white dress is used, a cap trimmed with white ribbon is placed upon her head, a white band round her waist, silk stockings, and white gloves. The warmth of the climate necessarily obliges the interment to take place soon after dissolution; for example, if a person dies one day, he is buried the next. The intervening night is called by the negroes "wake night;" and about seven or eight in the evening a great number of persons of both sexes meet at the house of death to assist in keeping the "wake." This is understood to mean, the singing of psalms and hymns over the corpse; but, in most cases, while the females are so employed in one part of the house, the young men are laughing, talking, or playing off practical jokes upon some one whom they deem not quite so wise as themselves. It sounds very melancholy, should you chance to be awake at the solemn hour of midnight, to hear these persons chanting forth their sacred lays, and as the breeze sweeps its strain to and from your ear, memory "starts up alarmed, and o'er life's narrow verge looks down" upon a "fathomless abyss." But in the midst of these thoughts the heartless laugh breaks upon your ear, like the voice of some scoffing demon; and "so dies in human hearts the thoughts of death," for "all men think all men mortal *but themselves!*"

About five o'clock in the morning, coffee, bread, biscuits, and cheese, are handed round, and then the company depart, until such hour as the funeral is arranged to take place. Some of the nearest friends or relations, however, remain all the time, and of course partake of the different meals provided; for there is one thing worthy of note in these negro-funerals— grief never spoils their appetites. If the person dies in the country, it is sometimes the practice to bring them into town during the night; at other times, the funeral takes place in whatever part of the island they may chance to reside in. The company assemble to a town-funeral about four o'clock, and (a multiplicity of chairs having been borrowed from the neighbours for the occasion) seat themselves, the women in the house, and the men on the shady side of the street; but as for thinking of *death*, and its important consequences, it is as far from them as if they were at a ball or a play. They laugh, they joke, they make bargains, and they discuss the news of the day, and think no more of the inanimate corpse within, than if it had been a waxen figure, or an ideal form. I am sorry to add, that it is not the negroes alone who exhibit this utter thoughtlessness of heart upon these melancholy occurrences, as I shall have further to mention when I come to speak of the superior grades of society. But to resume our subject: about the time the company are assembled, and the bearers arrayed in white or black cotton scarfs and hat-bands, according to the age of the deceased, the hearse arrives; for, it is to be remarked, it is but seldom that a funeral takes place in Antigua without the attendance of one of those "carriages for the dead." The hearses are rather differently constructed from those used in England, having more the appearance of a van painted black. There is a top to them in a kind of half-pyramidal form, mounted by a few brown-black or dirty white feathers; the body of the hearse is partly railed round, so that the coffin can be seen, and a door opens behind. They are drawn by two sorry horses, one perhaps white and the other brown; or, as is often the case, one a horse about twelve hands high, its companion a Canadian poney, rough and shaggy as one of the Shetland breed. Another observable fact is, that these animals are generally as opposite in tempers as they are in appearance, so that while one is wishful of going to the east, the other has an incontrollable desire of proceeding in the opposite direction. This, as may be supposed, leads to a violent contention between them and the driver keeps the company standing in the streets and often endangers even the safety of the vehicle. A stranger could not fail to notice all these particularities, and also the indecent manner in which the hearse is driven to the house where the corpse is, and upon its return from the place of interment—namely, as fast as the two horses can possibly be urged.

Another matter of surprise to a stranger is to see the prodigious number of persons which attend these funerals, often consisting of from four to five hundred, and very seldom less than from two to three. These persons are arranged as follows:—The nearest members of the family walk immediately after the hearse; if the deceased is a man, then follow a number of that sex, then a number of women, after them men again, and so on until the procession is complete. On the contrary, should the corpse be that of a female, the women precede the men; the train is sometimes so long, that it reaches the entire length of a street. Of course it is not to be supposed that all this multitude is habited in black; from the short time which intervenes between the demise and the interment, even the family are unable to procure mourning, unless, as it sometimes happens, they may chance to have those sable garments by them; the consequence of this is, that the procession presents a most motley group. Some of the followers are indeed habited in black; some in white, with a little black ribbon and a coloured bonnet; but the greater part appear in the various hues of the rainbow. As before remarked, at these funerals almost all their friends give something, if it is but a bottle of wine, or a small quantity of tobacco, and so universal is this practice, that I knew a servant who refused to attend the funeral of his father, because he had not money enough to give. It used to be the custom in former times, to hand round to the company cake, wine, rum and water, porter and "drink," but this is now dispensed with; the greater part of the assemblage follow the corpse to the place of burial, and then disperse. When a funeral takes place in the country, however, a grand dinner is generally provided for the company after the ceremony is over; and on these occasions all is mirth and joy, and the cup and the glass is so often replenished, that many of the party return home in a state of intoxication. It is among the Moravian congregations the largest funeral processions are seen, the reason of which is as follows:—As is the case in the established church, and with the Methodists, the Moravians have formed a society among their own people, in which every member throws in a certain sum monthly, and when attacked by illness a doctor is found them and so much per week allowed until they recover. When any of these members of the Moravian society die, it is incumbent upon the rest to follow the deceased to the grave, or if they fail in so doing, a fine of 2s. currency is imposed upon them; the consequence is, that, as few like to pay this penalty, they endeavour upon all occasions to be present.

A christening sometimes gives rise to another entertainment, although, of course, not so grand as a wedding or a ball; fruit, cakes, and wine forming the principal repast. The baby is very smartly dressed in a long white robe, smart cap or bonnet, and is carried in the arms of one who acts for the day as an attendant, with a parasol held over it to screen it from the sun's rays, although at other times it is exposed to every change of temperature with scarcely anything to cover it. In former times, the negroes were generally known by the names of "Sambo," "Pompey," "Quashy," "Quasheba," &c., &c., but those days have long ago passed. The "march of intellect" has marched into the West Indies, and we now have "Arabella Christiana," "Adeline Floretta," "Rosalind Monimia," &c., for the girls; and "Augustus Henry," "Alonzo Frederick," "Octavius Edward," and similar *high-sounding* names for the boys. "What's in a name?" is a query. I think a great deal; but really it is perfectly ridiculous to hear such aristocratic appellations applied to your servants. The parents are not always satisfied with even two names, but are unconscionable enough to add a *third*. To hear them accosted by these lengthy names brings to recollection "Miss Carolina Wilhelmina Amelia Skeggs," whom Goldsmith has immortalized.

----

[31] A large bird mentioned in the travels of Sinbad the Sailor, a tale in the "Arabian Nights."

[32] A chest made of cedar, for the purpose of containing their wearing apparel, is looked upon by the negroes as quite indispensable; and consequently, there are but few among them who do not lay by part of their earnings, that they may be enabled to procure one.

[33] It may be necessary to remark, that the word *buckra*, in the negro tongue, signifies "a white person;" but as the smart people I have been describing imitate in everything *fairer brethren*, they are ironically termed "black buckras."

CHAPTER XL

Negroes: Further sentences upon "dress"—Sunday transformations—
The black cook and his metamorphosis—Christmas waits—Negro houses
—The mode of building upon estates—Town negro houses—Architecture
—The mode of moving houses.

I have in so many places made reference to the style of dress adopted
by the negroes, that to bring it under a particular head may be deemed
superfluous. And yet I cannot let it pass without saying something more
upon this subject.

I must own I was very much surprised, on first arriving in Antigua, at
the style of dress adopted by these people. That the negroes were very fond
of adorning themselves I was well aware, but I thought it consisted in a
display of what we should term *trumpery*, such as the worn-out garments of
their superiors which had once been smart; but I was soon undeceived. It
was during the jovial season of Christmas I first made my appearance in this
island, a time of all others devoted by the negroes to the purpose of
exhibiting the contents of their wardrobes. Christmas-day, and the two
succeeding days, are, in this country, exclusively termed "Christmas;" and
poor indeed must be the negro who does not sport a new dress upon that
occasion, even if they have to wear nothing but rags for the rest of the year.
Those of the *fair sex* who can afford it, generally purchase three dresses; one
to wear each day, and formed of various materials, such as silks, (figured
and plain,) satins, mousseline de laines, challis, crapes of different names
and textures, or handsome white muslin robes variously embroidered. The
fashion now in vogue among these *ladies* is, to have the skirt of their dresses
dropping on the ground for about a quarter of a yard in length, the bottom
terminated by two rows of flounces, *demi-bishop* sleeves, and pointed
corsages. But the great novelty is in the arrangement of the different tints,
most of them thinking they are not sufficiently well-dressed if they leave
out any of the prismatic colours. The bonnets are worn just at the back of
their heads, and often present a singular appearance. A negress lately
presented herself to my notice, whose dress deserves particular attention.
Her daily business is to work in the cane-field, and for some time past I had
been used to see her bringing grass for the use of our horses in a state
approximating to nudity. Upon the Sunday she honoured me with a call the
case was, however, very different. Her dress of figured white muslin was
profusely ornamented with pink ribbon and fringe of the same gay tint, her
silk stockings were "ditto to match," and her shoes yellow, with white
sandals. But her bonnet struck me as most particular; it was formed of that

material called "Tuscan," lined with green, trimmed with pink, and further decorated with a prodigy among flowers, a blue rose with silver leaves!

Another very favourite article of dress amongst these black belles, is what they term "a Victoria cloak," which is nothing more or less than a square of coarse net, tamboured, in the commonest manner, in large flowers; but which, like everything else of the present day, is named after the queen. I am sure, did her majesty but know how her name is applied to all kinds of articles, from a steam-coach in England, to a lap-dog here, she must think herself greatly honoured! I have already spoken of their splendid jewellery, and therefore it only remains for me to mention, that elaborately worked collars, with three rows of cotton lace round them, fancy reticules, coloured boots and shoes, and parasols, are to be found composing a part of their attire. The latter mentioned articles are unfurled, and twirled about by the young ladies with peculiar grace; but those who are less modish in their manners generally close them, and carry them over the right shoulder, with the end sticking up like the point of a bayonet. A few years ago, the negroes were accustomed to tie their heads with Madras handkerchiefs of the brightest dyes, or else wear large leghorn or silk hats, covered with flowers and ribands; but since emancipation, bonnets are most generally worn, particularly among the young, although some still prefer the use of the hat.

The gentlemen negroes present also a most *dandified* appearance. Surtouts or coats of different colour, with velvet collars, splendid waistcoats, white or coloured trousers, with very high-heeled boots, are most in vogue. It is customary with these beaux, when they order a pair of boots, to give particular injunctions to the cordwainer, to make them in such a manner that they may "stamp and creak well," when they wear them. To these specified articles of dress, must be added broad-brimmed hats, silk umbrellas, (if they can get them, if not, cotton suffices; but a negro never thinks himself well arrayed without this article,) and pocket handkerchiefs, one end making its appearance from the coat pocket. The persons who dress in this manner are generally coblers, tinkers, carpenters, bricklayers, and servants. It is almost impossible to know your own domestics, so great are their metamorphoses.

In the ship which conveyed us hither, was a black man, who officiated as cook. Our first place of destination, after leaving England, was British America, where we arrived in the beginning of a very severe winter. Sincerely did I pity this poor man, for his scant and tattered clothing was no protection from the pitiless blast, and excessive cold of that hyperborean clime. Being a native of so warm a country as the West Indies, and having never before experienced the rigours of winter, it was with some difficulty he could bear up against this (to him) accumulation of ills. His custom was to remain in the steerage of the ship, and when any of his messmates tried to arouse him, and invite him to visit the deck, his only answer was, "I brought all my fingers and toes from Antigua, and please God, I must try and carry them back again." After remaining in America for some time, (suffering *hot aches*, and I know not what beside,) until the ship had discharged her cargo of *interesting* emigrants, and re-loaded with that necessary article "lumber," (*alias* timber,) we took our departure, with many a favour of "King Frost's" hanging about our vessel, in the shape of huge blocks of ice. A pretty fair wind soon carried us into warmer latitudes, and I used frequently to remark, how delighted that *poor half-clothed* man must be. "Oh! oh!" was the answer, "that poor half-clothed man, as you call him, is a very respectable and dashing fellow, I do assure you, in his own country." I thought this assertion bordering upon the burlesque, but I made no reply, wisely remembering the old saying, "Time will shew all things."

At length, after encountering, as every other mortal must, calms as well as storms, one bright morning brought us to the shores of fair Antigua. This, as I have before remarked, was during the season of Christmas, the time for fun and dress among the negroes. The morning after we landed, I early shook off "tired nature's sweet restorer, balmy sleep," and hurried over the duties of the toilet in order that I might look about me, and see what kind of *bipeds* I had fallen in with. I had not long left my apartment when I saw a very dashing-looking gentleman enter the back gate, and approach the door near which I was standing, admiring the bright sun and blue sky of this December morning. It certainly struck me as rather surprising, that a gentleman of his appearance should enter by that part of the house usually appropriated to the servants, but I supposed it was one of "the customs" of the country. Not wishing to be in that disagreeable situation of having to introduce myself, I retired into an inner apartment; but ere long I learnt, to my great surprise, that the "*exquisite*," whose appearance caused my sudden departure, was no less a personage than the black cook from on board the ship.

Christmas is also the season here, as in England, for roast-beef, plum-pudding, and plum-cake; most of the negroes endeavour to get *one* of these articles, should they not be able to procure them all; but if their pockets are too low to do this, they purchase a few raisins to treat their friends with. "Christmas day" is ushered in with the sound of fiddles and drums; parties of negroes going round the town about four o'clock in the morning, playing upon these instruments for the purpose of breaking people's rest, (for I am sure it cannot amuse;) and then they have the assurance to call at the different houses during the day for payment. At the conclusion of this serenade, or *waits*, or whatever else they choose to term it, the musicians generally raise their voices to the highest pitch, and call out, "Good morning to you, massa; good morning to you, missis; good morning to you, ladies and gentlemen *all!*" a flourish is then given with fiddle and drum, and they march off to disturb another quiet household.

The next point to be considered is the dwellings of the negroes. The generality of negro houses upon estates contain two apartments, and are built of stone, cemented by a rough mortar. The roofs are composed of *trash* (the dry leaves of the sugar-cane), loosely piled on, which gives them an untidy appearance. Some of the industrious people, however, greatly add to the look of the interior, by neatly ceiling them with the split boughs of the cocoa-nut, formed into a kind of basket-work. The best huts have the hall, or sitting-room, paved with bricks, or a kind of smooth cement, and the sleeping-apartment boarded. Among the articles of furniture may be found sofas, sideboards of manchineel, (or some other species of native wood,) mahogany and deal tables, and a large cedar chest. Besides these articles, some of them possess decanters, tumblers, wine-glasses, and a large bowl to make their punch in, with plates and dishes, tea-cups, and various other kinds of gaudy crockeryware. These are the residences of the head negroes; the next kind have their stone-houses unceiled, and only the bare earth for their floor; they contain but little furniture, two or three chairs of the country make, a deal table, and a wooden box or two being their principal stock. Some estates have fallen into a plan of building their negro-houses entirely of wood, as it has been found that the negroes prefer hiring themselves where such dwellings have been provided for them.

Since emancipation, many proprietors have disposed of part of their uncultivated lands to the negroes, which are divided into lots, measuring 30 feet one way, and 40 the other, at 30 dollars, or 6*l.* sterling per lot. Upon these spots of ground, the purchasers have erected houses, some of them very neatly finished, and containing two rooms, a hall, and chamber; and here they reside, supporting themselves by working upon different estates, (where they obtain higher wages than the resident labourers, on account of not being provided with houses or negro grounds;) huckstering, or else working their own land. In some parts of the island, whole villages are formed in this manner; and from the similarity of the dwellings, and their several little patches of ground, laid out in rows of different luxuriant edibles, present, altogether, a very pleasing appearance. Some of the poorer negroes build their houses in the following manner. A sufficient number of stakes are firmly driven into the ground at regular distances; these are interwoven with the branches of the "black cherry," (a native wood,) stript of their leaves, and the interstices filled up with clay. The roofs are composed of a species of coarse grass (called by the negroes, "hurricane grass," on account of its wild growth,) fastened on with the bark of the "soursop tree." I cannot speak much for the apparent comfort of these last-mentioned dwellings; there is one thing, however, to be considered, warmth is not necessary in this climate, yet, I should think, the heavy rains which fall at times must penetrate them, and render their clayey floors still more unpleasant. The fire with which the negroes cook their victuals is always made in the open air, unless they fence in a small portion of ground, and loosely throw a bundle of dry cane-leaves on the top, in which case it frequently answers for stable and kitchen.

Those negroes who reside in the capital invariably have their houses built of wood; they seldom consist of more than one room, in which a whole family, of perhaps six or eight persons, eat, sleep, and live; and from whence issue, upon a Sunday, those *ladies* and *gentlemen* who equal in splendour of dress the habitants of princely halls. The form of architecture is very simple; four sides, of equal length, breadth, and height, are first erected, and the whole surmounted by what is called a *pitched* roof, which also consists of four uniform sides, meeting at the top in a pyramidical form. For further protection from the weather, this roof is covered thickly over with "shingles," (flat pieces of board, manufactured in America, for that purpose, from the wood of the cypress, or cedar,) which are put on in the same manner as slates. Some of these dwellings have doors facing to each of the cardinal points, besides a window or two; so that, when agreeable, they can have a free circulation of air. When I speak of windows, it must not be understood I mean such as contain any portion of glass; but simply what Dr. Johnson calls them, "an opening in a house for light and air." These houses are generally left destitute of any outward colouring, except what they acquire from exposure to the weather, but when paint is made use of, the favourite tints are yellow for the sides, and red for the roof and doors. As I have before hinted, many of these small houses are built by pilfering a board or a plank at a time, or now and then a few shingles. It often happens, that dwellings which are erected upon this plan, take some time before they are completed. To assure myself of this assertion, I need only raise my eyes from my paper, and one of these *contributory* edifices greets my view. It was commenced before I came to the island; and after remaining here for about two years, and returning to England for near the same period, upon my second visit to Antigua, I found the house not quite finished. I could not help observing this house during its tardy erection; a stroke or two of the hammer now and then broke upon the silent ear of night, and in the morning it might be perceived that another board had been added to the side, or a few more shingles nailed upon the roof. It most frequently happens, that the possessors of these small tenements have no land of their own, but pay a small ground-rent for the space occupied by their habitations. When they are wishful of removing to another part of the town, like the snail, they carry their houses with them, which, from the manner of construction, is no difficult matter. These buildings are always raised a little way from the ground, and have a step or two at the principal entrance. Sometimes the space between the ground and the house is entirely filled up with loose bricks or stones; others have only an empty barrel, or a few stones piled up at each corner, just sufficient to support the fabric.

When a removal is agreed upon, their first care is to hire a few porters, and an accompaniment of trucks. These "four-wheeled" carriages are firmly fastened together, and placed under the house, the slight foundation pulled away, and strong ropes being attached to the first truck, the porters (with the assistance of other men, women, and children) commence pulling with all their might, and the house moves off to the song and chorus adapted to the occasion. To preserve its equilibrium, two men march on each side of the house with long poles, which they place against the side; one of these commences the song, (which is of their own composition,) and the whole tribe join in the chorus of "Pull away, my hearties," or similar phrases. In former times, when the negroes had only the Sunday allowed them to perform any of their own work, that day was used to execute these removals; but the noise it occasioned during the period of Divine service was such, that the legislature found it necessary to prohibit this practice at the same time they abolished the Sunday markets.

It is particularly disagreeable to be in the vicinity of these houses when their owners take it into their heads to remove them. The negroes are always noisy; but when such deeds are in contemplation, they are more so than ever; the songs they sing, the quarrels they have, and the language they use, would tire the patience of the most stoical. Sometimes a sudden crash is heard, and the whole edifice comes tumbling to the ground; this leads to another "wordy war,"—the goddess Discord again waves aloft her arm,— the whole neighbourhood is in commotion,—and poor I (who, alas! am a most *unwilling*, but compulsory listener) cannot help exclaiming—"Oh! that I were in dear old England, where at least the houses are not moved."

CHAPTER XLI

Negroes: Occupations—Agricultural labourers—Black sailors—Their excessive gormandizing—The hungry captain's disappointment—Black cooks—"Melted butter"—A receipt for a cookery book—The obtrusive fish—Grooms and "house boys"—An old planter's opinion—Concluding remarks.

After mentioning the recreations, dress, and general habits of the negroes, it may be necessary to give some account of their principal occupations. By far the greater part of the black population, as will be seen in the statistical portion of this work, are employed in the cultivation of the sugar-cane, which, although very laborious, pays them better than any other work. When engaged in this pursuit, the hours of labour are as follows:—the bell rings at six o'clock in the morning, and the negroes proceed to the field, and remain there until nine, when the bell again rings, and they go to their breakfast; an hour being allowed for that purpose, they enter the field at ten, and remain until twelve, when they leave for their dinners; at two they resume their labours, which continue until six, when their daily work is finished. It must be remarked, that during the short days, they scarcely reach the field until near eight; and just as the sun begins to sink, they confidently assert it is after six, and refuse to work any longer, let the hour be what it may. During the time of slavery, such women as were nursing did not commence working until seven o'clock; but in these days of freedom, they do not resume the hoe until their children are nine or ten months old. Some of the negroes gain a very plentiful subsistence, by buying a horse and cart, and carting manure to the different estates; others again will agree with a planter to do a certain portion of work; they procure other labourers, and when the work is finished, they divide the profits; but let them do whatever they will, they contrive to make such bargains, that they never fail in obtaining a *good supply* of that necessary evil—money.

Besides agricultural labourers, there are a great many artisans, fishermen, and sailors. With regard to these last, I cannot say whether they are very *firm* in times of *danger*; but from ocular demonstration, I can assert, that when the sky and sea looks fair, they are very careless, although, from July to October, the West Indian seas are very liable to sudden squalls. These black sailors generally confine themselves to the navigation of the Caribbean Sea, making voyages in small vessels to the different islands. Very few of them know all the points of the compass, some of them not any—their manner of steering being more after the manner of the ancients. They see the sun when he rises, and they know that is the east; they observe him when he sets, and that, they are aware, is the west. Their mode of proceeding when upon these voyages is, to keep within sight of land as much as they can; and in most parts, the channels between the different islands are so narrow, that this is not difficult; but to make a bold stretch across, so as to lose all landmarks, they seldom or never think of. The greatest peculiarity among these black sailors is their extreme voracity— never were there greater eaters. In my frequent voyages in these small vessels to the other islands, I have had numberless opportunities of observing this; for from the confinement of the cabins, and the great heat of the climate, the deck is the only supportable part of the vessel, and there it is the sailors partake of their dinners. Such piggins of *fungy*, with accompaniments of rice or potatoes, salt fish, or beef, as I have then seen consumed, and in such a short period, is really marvellous! Even when at the helm, they are occupied in eating biscuit, of which they generally manage to have their pockets full.

Upon one occasion, I was coming from St. Kitts to Antigua, on board one of these small craft. The second day from our leaving, the sailors caught a very large sucking-fish, (*remora,*) which was scarcely pulled upon the deck, before they commenced the operation of cooking it. The "captain," as he termed himself, was that day unfortunately tormented by a violent headache; and after seeing their prize safely deposited in a huge kettle of water, laid himself down to sleep, in hopes of getting rid of his unwelcome visitant. "Soft slumber" sealed his eye for many an hour; but when at length he awoke, his first demand was for some of the tempting dish, whose early stage of cookery he had so ably inspected. "All eat," was the consoling reply to a hungry man. It was certainly provoking, and so he seemed to think; for he put himself into a violent passion immediately. "War for you eat aw dat fish for, eh? fish big so to. War for you go do so? You aw too much greedy—you aw reg'lar nagers." And with much growling and grumbling, he was obliged to solace his unappeasable appetite with a hard biscuit, instead of his favourite fare.

This *penchant* for eating among the negro sailors is universally known. I have heard it remarked, by a gentleman of Antigua, (in answer to some query upon the subject,)—"Oh! have nothing to do with small vessels; or, if you *have*, on no account provision them, but rather pay them so much a week to find themselves; for those black sailors are never satisfied—they will be eating eleven hours in the day, and on the twelfth they are, or rather *pretend* to be, hungry. This, I am sure, is the fault of their mothers during infancy; for their common cry to them is—'Eat, me pic'nee, eat; fill youself, an den go sleep;' so that the custom grows upon them to that degree, that when they become men, they cannot break themselves of it." So much for the remark; those who are acquainted with the subject will, I think, readily assent to the truth of it.

In times of slavery, it was customary, among some owners or managers of slaves, to allow such negroes as were not employed in the cane-field the privilege of hiring themselves out to strangers, providing they regularly paid to their masters a certain sum weekly from the wages they received. Many of them acquired a good sum by this permission; while others, again, although they earned high wages, had to pay so large a proportion to their proprietors, that they were not so well off in pecuniary matters as those negroes who remained upon the property. Still, they were comparatively more their own masters; and so dear to every breast is freedom, that they preferred doing so, and gaining less.

Another large body of negroes are to be met with as domestic servants. That there are some good servants among them none can deny; but I am sorry to say, they are seldom met with. In general, the men make better domestics than the females. Some of those who hire themselves as cooks are very clever in their profession, and will dress turtle in various delectable forms, equal, if not superior, to the vaunted cooks at "Cornhill," or the celebrated "M. de Barre" (late cook to Louis XVIII.) himself. This is to be the more wondered at, as they have not half the conveniences in the culinary departments as their brother cooks on the other side of the water; on the contrary, many an invention has to issue from their teeming brain, before they can arrange these matters to their satisfaction. But one precaution must be carefully observed, in order to insure success: in cookery, they must be left entirely to their own discretion—no improvement proposed; for either they are obstinately bent on following their own plan, and will not adopt any other, or else they do not fully understand their instructions; and what was intended as an improvement will result in failure.

It is the practice in Antiguan cookery, when "melted butter" is used, merely to oil it, and send it to table in that state, which to many strangers proves disagreeable. Soon after my arrival in this country, I begged the cook to adopt some other plan, explaining at the same time, to the best of my abilities, how it was commonly done in England. The next day, at dinner, there was something "in such a" *very* "questionable shape" upon the table, that I was fain to summon Mr. Cook from his tenement, to ask what it might be. "Melted butter, missis," quoth the knight of pots and kettles. "*Melted butter!*—impossible! it has more the appearance of pudding, boiled like the French cook's, without a cloth." "Eh, eh, missis, war for you go call him pudding? you no tell me put flower in de butter—it *dat* make him 'top so!" I was confounded. After my learned dissertation upon melted butter the day before, (which, by-the-bye, I borrowed from the worthy Dr.

Kitchener himself,) to be served in this manner was too bad; however, it taught me never for the future to interfere with his department.

They have some peculiarities in dressing different meats in Antigua which I have never heard of being practised in other countries, although it must be owned my knowledge in such matters is very limited, not having devoted much of my time to studying the "Cook's Oracle;" indeed, (the truth must be spoken,) I am better pleased to form an acquaintance with ragouts, or any other dainties, when they are upon the table, than I am to inspect their various formations, or become versed in their different modes of cookery. But as some of my readers may, with Peter Pindar, be fond of peeping into pots and pans, I will, for their benefit, try to elucidate kitchen mysteries for once in my life, and expound to them the method of *doving* meat, as the Antiguan cooks term such process. The first point to be achieved is, of course, to procure the meat, and then to see that the "igneous element," as Mr. Dryden learnedly calls fire, has attained a sufficient degree of heat. These preliminary matters being adjusted, an iron pot is made thoroughly hot, the meat placed in it without the aid of water, and the utensil carefully covered over. In this fiery durance it is allowed to remain until one side becomes of an approved brown; it is then turned to another, until at length it arrives at that state of superexcellence, that, like "Sancho Panza's cow's heel," it has only to cry "Come eat me, come eat me!"

The greatest fault to be found with these kitchen gentry, these black cooks of Antigua, is, that while from various meats and spices they are compounding ambrosial food for their masters, they forget the rules of equity, and, like the lordly lion of the forest, keep the largest share for themselves. This is done with impunity by all the class; they dread not even the "strong arm of the law," nor exempt the lawyers themselves from this exaction, if report speaks true. When discovered in these petty thefts, they use the greatest art to make you believe it is a mistake, a slip of (not the tongue, but) the fingers, and, consequently, not their fault; or else, that "*somebody*" did the deed, and laid the blame at their door.

A gentleman proprietor of this island had a servant living with him who was famed for practising this particular species of depredation, quite an adept in the art, and who at the same time possessed a tongue well versed in the doctrine of excuses. Many and oft have been the occasions when this sable offender has appropriated to his own share the eatables which ought to have graced his master's table, and yet escaped without reproof. But one day, (for so the Fates had willed it,) being pressed for time, "Lemon" was obliged to transfer to his *pocket*, instead of a place of more approved security, a fish he had adroitly managed to purloin, and hurry into the dining-room, (in his double capacity of cook and footman,) with the remainder properly dished up. "Truth," says the old proverb, "will pop out its head;" and although the stubborn fish did not exactly do that, it made amends by popping out its *tail*, and proved to the master's eye the undeniable fact of his servant's deviation. Unconscious that his silent but no less true accuser had betrayed him, the faulty cook kept his stand, until, at length, his master, pointing at the same time to the purloined luxury, inquired, "Lemon, what is that you have in your pocket?" His blushes, if he knew how to blush, were effectually concealed by the blackness of his skin, while, with the counterfeit surprise of innocence, he replied to this question by asking another: "Pocket, massa? war pocket?" And then, turning his eye to that particular part of his garment, and perceiving in a moment that the presence of the obtruding fish could not be denied, with ready cunning, he continued, "You see dat, massa? you see dat, missis? you eber see how 'de ebil' (witchcraft) follow me! Ebil come quite in me pocket, come put fish dere, so make you aw tink me go tief it!" Oh, worthy Lemon! oh, noble son of Ham! hadst thou lived in the days when Jupiter and his train peopled bright Olympus, undoubtedly thou wouldst have been turned into a constellation as a reward for thy ingenuity!

Among the grooms and "house-boys" (as the Antiguans call their domestic men-servants) there are also some to be met with who have a fair character for general good behaviour, but they are rare instances—seldom found. The greater part of the grooms are too fond of galloping their masters' horses, (a practice common with most negroes, who will ride almost as soon as they can walk;) and with respect to the latter-mentioned class, indolence and prevarication form (as we have already seen) too often the predominant traits in their character.

Another peculiarity among this tribe is the freedom with which they address their employers. This has even increased, if anything, since emancipation; for now they are free, they appear to think themselves upon an equality with the highest in the land. They condescend, it is true, to take your money, but at the same time seem to think it a degradation to do your work. If it is necessary to find fault with any part of their conduct, they generally return a saucy answer, or else make this rejoinder—"Bery well, as we can't agree, we best part; me no care to hire meself out again;" and immediately collecting their different articles together, (including, perhaps, some belonging to their master or mistress, of course by mistake!) away they go, and the only plan you can adopt is, to procure another domestic in their place, who, perhaps, acts even worse.

I would not wish to be thought unreasonably prepossessed in favour of my own country-people, but, conscientiously speaking, I have never met with one black domestic who acts with the same degree of propriety as most of the English servants do. If you keep them at their proper distance, they become dissatisfied, and complain of your being harsh to them; if, on the contrary, you shew them any degree of attention, and try to make their situation as comfortable as possible, they then assume too much, and entirely forget the difference of rank. Try to serve them, and it is ten chances to one you make them your enemy; do them ninety-nine favours, and refuse the hundredth, and you are reviled and blamed as if you had injured them.

An old English gentleman, who had spent the greater part of his life in Antigua, and who has several hundreds of these people under his control, used to say, that "the worse you behave to a negro, the better he behaves to you." This is a doctrine, however, which I do not admit, let the negro character be as defective as it may.

Oh! slavery, slavery! when will all the train of evils thou hast originated cease? when will thy pestilential influence be abolished in these beautiful, but (I must add it) crime-stained islands? Another and another generation will have to pass away ere prejudice is no more—ere suspicion is lulled to sleep, before the servant will learn to look up to his master as his protector, and the master view without distrust the services of his domestic, and find in him an humble friend.

CHAPTER XLII

Negroes: Employment of the women—Washing—A scene at the pond —Conversations—The sea-side—"Water frolic"—Hucksters—"Damaged flour"—Female porters—Masculine appearance of some of the females— Indelicacy—Their mode of carrying burdens.

Having given a short sketch of the manner in which the generality of the negro-men employ their time, it will be proper also to mention the occupation of the females. Many of these still follow the employment to which they have been habituated from their youth, the cultivation of the sugar-cane. But others, although used to it in their days of slavery, now they have become free, look upon it as degrading; and therefore, quitting the estates to which they formerly belonged, and all the privileges incident to their country-life, they hire a small house in some of the alleys or outskirts of the capital, and there take up their abode. Among this class of women, washing and huckstering are the principal employments; and it is from the profits arising from these means that they are enabled to bring up their daughters in comparative idleness, and send them forth on Sundays dressed in the ridiculous style I have already described.

It may not be deemed superfluous to remark how differently *washing* is conducted in Antigua to the mode pursued in England. There, among the good housewives who preside over such ablutions, it generally occasions gloom and discontent, particularly if the weather proves foul when the *water frolic* takes place; in that case (as the song says)—

"The very kittens on the hearth,
 They dare not even play;
But away they jump, with many a thump,
 Upon a washing day."

But in this country, where blue skies and sun-shiny days predominate, the case is quite the reverse.

Groups of washerwomen may be seen in the morning with large bundles of clothes upon their heads, their half-naked "pic'nees" clinging round their hips, and similarly accoutred little urchins running by their side, wending their way to some of the ponds near the outskirts of the town. When arrived at the place favourable for such sports or occupations, their bundles are first put down, their youngest children placed upon the ground with one of larger growth to watch over it, their own dress properly arranged, and then the business of the day commences.

The clothes are thrown into the pond, and allowed to remain there until completely saturated with water; they are then taken out, placed upon large stones, (which are generally to be found about such spots,) and holding a piece of wood (in shape like a cricket-bat, which they call a beetle) in their hands, they commence pounding the articles with all their might, utterly regardless of loss of buttons, causing large rents, or any other *et cetera* which may chance to happen. When they think the clothes are sufficiently *washed*, (if that term can be applied to this operation,) they are again steeped in the pond, rinsed out, and then spread along the ground, to imbibe the heat of the glaring sun.

All the time the labour of the hands is going on, the tongue is by no means idle. The news of the island is discussed; dress, dances, and religion, descanted on; and the songs upon individuals (already alluded to) composed. One party of staid matrons commence a conversation. "You no go prayers last night; bery well; massa miss yo—why yo no go? Don't you 'member what godmodder (as they call their leaders in the Moravian society) say 'bout aunty Nanny, 'cause she no go get her speak last time?[34] Well! sure the Lor' he one good Lor', (what you keep bawling so for, you cross pic'nee, eh?—me no gee you one cane to suck, you good-for-noting you!" addressed by way of parenthesis to a little crawling *black-a-moor*, who, unable to gain its mother's attention by more pleasing means, is compelled to raise its 'importunate call;') yes, me dear sister, de Lor' one good Lor', and massa parson talk all good talk." Another party of giddy, laughing girls, chatter away in a different strain. "I say, Ange', (Angelina,) you see dem *challis* se (sister) Eleanor hab selling last week? Well, I buy one, only it no make yet, 'cause I no get money 'nough to buy de black lace to trim it. I'se wants to hab it make like dat buckra lady's frock, she as come from England the oder day."—"No, me no seed em; me buy one robe dress Christmas gone. But did you hear 'bout se Margate?"—"No; war 'bout she?"—"Eh! eh! you no hear. Why, last night she war coming home past were de old play-house used to 'tan, when just as she get close de wall, dere she see one big ole jumby man—ugly so! most kill her, she so frighten. Bery well! she try to run, but he old jumby knock her down, fall to lick (*flog*) her in such a manner dat she hab feber all last night."—"Eh! eh! poor Margate! you b'lieve me, me no tink me dare go by de ole play-house at night den."

With conversations such as these they endeavour to lighten their labours; and during the time the clothes are drying, some form themselves into parties, and dance on the greensward to the music of their own voices; others nurse their little children, or boil their lunch (gipsy fashion;) while the more idle ones stretch themselves upon the grass, and sleep away the hours until the cleansed garments are perfectly dry, when they collect their different articles, and march off to their respective dwellings in the same manner as they came.[35]

As remarked at the commencement of this chapter, among those black women resident in the capital, are to be found an immense number of hucksters; indeed, in every street, at every corner, they are to be met with. These persons deal in different articles; some in cloth of various fabrics, threads, tapes, laces, &c.; some in salt-fish, corn-meal, (the flour from the Indian corn,) rice, &c.; and others in fruits, vegetables, soap and candles. Some of these hucksters occupy small shops of about fourteen feet square, (which, by the bye, in most cases they are obliged to use as their sleeping, dining, and dressing room as well,) where they vend their different wares; while others frequent the markets, or walk about the town or country with their goods. These people purchase their goods from the retailers upon a larger scale, or else buy them at an auction sale, of which there are sometimes three or four in a day, at the different merchant's stores.

There is one peculiarity attending these small dealers, which is worthy of note—this is, the great love they have for buying "damaged flour," supposing they will be sure to get a bargain. Upon this account, it is common among some merchants, when they are about to dispose of this commodity by public auction, to term it "damaged," when perhaps the only appearance of such mischance is, that the barrel is a little dirty. It has been often known for one of these sullied barrels to bring a larger amount than a better article, simply because it was put up as damaged.

Many of these women do nothing else but walk about to the different sales all day, in hopes of meeting with bargains, leaving the management of their shop (if they have one) to their children. When an article is put up, they bid in pounds and shillings, of which they have no conception; the consequence of which is, that when they retire from the sale, and get some friend to add it up in *dollars* and *bitts*, (current coins,—the *dollar* 4*s*. sterling, the *bitt* 4½*d*.,) they become alarmed at the amount of their purchases; and as there is no auction duty to be paid by them, they will not return for the articles, and consequently the merchant is obliged to bear the loss.

Some of the females work as porters, hire themselves to mix mortar for bricklayers, or even dig wells, (or springs as they are termed in this country,) and clean out ponds. Many of the negro women, particularly those who live in the country, and are employed in agriculture, are so very masculine in their voice, manners, and appearance, that it is at times a matter of doubt to say to which sex they belong. This may be attributed to the general system of treatment during slavery: they were required to work the same as the men; and when punishment was thought necessary, no regard was paid to their feelings, but their persons were equally exposed as those of the other sex. Of course, these proceedings in time rendered them callous, and in the end, divested them of all those principles of modesty which are so great an ornament to the feminine character, whether in a high or low condition of life. The manner in which they were accustomed to dress during their ordinary employments tended in great measure to have this effect. A petticoat of coarse linseywoolsey, or blue check, with a short jacket of similar materials, constituted the chief part of their covering; and even this was put on so carelessly, that frequently the upper part of their persons was left quite bare. While employed in their daily avocations, it is customary to tie up their garments almost—if not quite—as high as their knees; and even when walking about the streets of the capital, if it is rather wet weather, the same degree of indelicacy is practised. All these causes combined, tend to lessen the women in the eyes of strangers; although the Creoles appear to see no indecorum in their style of dress, or manners.

Most negroes appear to be possessed of great strength, and will carry immense loads, the women as well as the men. The head is the part appropriated by the negroes to bear their burdens. They carry tables, heavy boxes, boards, barrels, and similar articles, in this manner; and if they want to convey a cup or a bottle, it is placed in the same exalted situation. The very little children, of perhaps not more than three or four years old, will also place a calabash of water, or a bottle of rum, upon their heads, and trip along without holding it in the slightest manner.

———————

[34] A religious ordinance among the Moravians.

[35] In Barbados, the negroes make a little difference in their mode of washing. Going down to the sea-side, they make use of the sea-water, and then spreading them upon the sand, sprinkle them occasionally with the briny fluid. When (during a short visit to that island) I saw them thus employed, it recalled forcibly to my mind the description of the Princess "Nausicaa" in "Pope's Homer's Odyssey," who at the command of Pallas went to wash the robes of state in the "mazy waters."

"Then emulous the royal robes they lave,
And plunge the vestures in the cleansing wave;
(The vestures cleansed o'erspread the shelly sand,
Their snowy lustre whitens all the strand.)"

CHAPTER XLIII

Negroes: Exterior appearance—Difference of expression—White negroes (Albinos)—Description of one—Black and white negroes—Negroes' "bulls and blunders"—Exchange is no robbery, or the lost specimens—Negro politeness—Negro tongue—Inebriation—Concluding remarks

It is now necessary to make some mention of the exterior appearance of this large bulk of the population of Antigua, the blacks. As most persons are aware, the distinguishing features of the negro tribe are thick lips and flat noses, to which peculiarities may be added, their black and woolly hair; but that there are no exceptions to be met with is an incorrect statement. Even among the Africans themselves, some intelligent countenances and expressive features are to be found, while many of the Antiguan *Creole negroes* are what may be termed very good-looking. High and well-formed foreheads, black and sparkling eyes, aquiline noses, and lips with only a slight pout, are not uncommon. I would not, however, presume to assert that these pleasing outlines predominate; on the contrary, a great many of the negroes are very ill-favoured, approximating to what may be called hideous; and this is heightened when, in contrast to their ebon skins, is presented the snowy hair of old age, or when suffering from that dreadful disease, the *elephantiasis*. Many, again, are exactly like an ape, only, perhaps, they have not so much animation in their countenances; while others, from their thick, sullen-looking features, their over-hanging eyebrows, white, gleaming tusks, and faces more than half covered with hair, give no bad picture of "Master Bruin."

It has been remarked by many persons, that they could not distinguish one black person from another. A short time spent among them shews you, however, that this is not the case, there being, in reality, as much difference in personal appearance as there is between the natives of England, although, from their dusky hue, it is not so perceptible at first sight. This dissimilarity consists, not only in features, but also in complexion. Some of the negroes are black as "the ebon throne of night," or the drear raven's wing, others present a kind of "reddening gloom;" while many have that wan, *spectral* appearance, that you may fancy them suffering in the early stage of the *black jaundice*.

There have been instances in this island of Albinos being born among the negroes; one, in particular, of the appropriate name of "Wonder," belonging to an estate called "Mayers," astonished all who beheld him. He was said to be as repelling in temper as he was in person. One of these prodigies of nature was introduced to me during my stay in the West Indies, and so extraordinary was his appearance, that I cannot refrain from giving a short description of him. In person he was rather tall and slender; his complexion was of the colour of chalk and water, and no tinge of carnation was to be found either in his lips, cheeks, or gums. His hair, which, like that of all negroes, was short and woolly, was perfectly white, as also his eyebrows and eyelashes; these last were very long and thick, and completely shaded his eyes. Of this member, the iris was of a very light grey, while what is called the white of the eye, or more properly, the *albuginea*, presented a yellow tinge; and, from the manner in which he screened his eyes with his arm when looking up, he must have possessed a defective vision. Although he was not absolutely ugly, yet his appearance was such as to cause an involuntary repugnance. The person who introduced this strange creature to my notice acquainted me that he was of a very crabbed temper; but at this I was not afterwards at all surprised, for wherever he went, he was a matter of wonder and dislike, and every little negro called after him as he passed along, "You see dat white nager?—well, me no like to be one white nager, me sure!"

It is said that these "Albinos," or "Dendos," as the negroes call them, cannot see during the middle of the day, but that at night their vision is so particularly clear, that they can see to pick up the smallest object.[36]

There have also been instances of a negro being born *black and white* in Antigua; his parents were both black people, as were the progenitors of "Wonder," whom I have already mentioned. Dame Nature does play strange freaks at times; and surely when she formed these white and "black and white" negroes, she must have been in one of her most sportive humours.

Many of the negroes have very good figures; but the assertion of some authors, that there is scarcely ever a deformed person to be met with among them, is as untrue as it is ridiculous. I profess not to be a connoisseur in anatomical beauty, or to know the just criterion as to what the human shape ought to be, but with regard to this people, very many of them are anything but perfect in their organization. One very perceptible defect is, their bodies being longer in proportion than their legs; and in many instances, these last-named members have a strong inclination to *turn in*, or *turn out*,—in plain English, to be *bandy-legged*. This latter blemish may, perhaps, be attributed to the manner in which the women carry their children during infancy: leaning upon one side, they place the child upon the protruding hip, with its little legs clinging around their body, which posture, in time, causes those limbs to *bow* out. This plan of carrying children is not only commonly practised with their own offspring, but when engaged as nurses in respectable families they use their little charge to the same awkward custom, so that if you lift a Creole child, it immediately clings round you in the manner described.

The negroes, like the Irish, are famed for their "bulls and blunders," in illustration of which, many an anecdote is related.

During the period that Sir James Leith was residing in Antigua, as governor of the Leeward Islands, he was very indefatigable in his geological researches, for which Antigua affords an ample field. Upon one occasion, his excellency had been labouring very hard to collect from the bosom of "Mother Earth" specimens which only a geologist can properly appreciate; and with a well-filled bag of them, entrusted to the care of a negro servant, he left the scene of his toils to refresh his animal spirits with some of the *good things* of this life. To ensure the safety of his favourite specimens, the negro was despatched with them to "Dows Hill," (the place where the governor then resided,) with strict injunctions to make the best of his way, and carefully deposit his load in his excellency's study until they could be properly arranged.

After receiving his orders, and well poising his load upon his back, the man started upon his journey. The weather was very sultry, and the way was very long; the bag was very heavy, and poor *blacky* was very tired. Still he plodded on "his weary way," stopping only now and then to dash the flowing perspiration from his brow, and had arrived within a mile of his home, when he was suddenly joined by a friend. "Eh, buddy! (brother) why you loaded true! War you got in that great big bag?" "'Tornes, (stones,) me friend." "'Tornes! why war you go do wid dem all, eh?" "Me no no. Massa gubbunor gib me dem to *fetch* home, but me no no war he go do wid dem; me no dem well heaby though." "Well, if eber me hear de like! for one somebody to go haul all dem 'tornes sich a long way, when dere plenty ob dem all 'bout 'Dows Hill.' I tell you war me go do if deys gib me dem to carry, me go heabe dem ebery bit away, an when me get to de 'Hill,' fill me bag wid some of dem big 'tornes as stop all 'bout dere—sure one 'torne as good as anoder." "'Tank'e, me friend, me neber think ob dat me sure; but if you just help me down wid dem, me soon do war you tell me."

No sooner said than done; the splendid specimens were thrown away without compunction, and the negro, who found it much easier to march with an empty bag than with his former load, sped on his way joyfully. At the bottom of "Dows Hill" he stopped, and once more replenished his bag with the rough stones, which liberally bestrewed the pathway, choosing the largest for the purpose. These he safely conveyed to his master's study, carefully shut the door, and left them. The surprise and consternation of the governor when, upon inspecting, as he thought, his hard-earned specimens, he found only a heap of useless rubbish—the interrogations he addressed to his servant, and the ludicrous answers of the negro,—are matters for the imagination to dwell upon.

It is customary with many store-keepers in this island to wash the outside of their stores or shops, yellow, or some other colour. Should this take the fancy of a negro as he passes, he immediately exclaims— "Ah, me like dat, massa's 'tore really look gran; he whitewash he yellow, an make he stop quite good, de trute!"

With regard to the negro tongue, much cannot be said for its purity; the Creole negroes speak a dialect bad enough, but the Africans' is almost unintelligible. There is one peculiarity in their mode of speech very remarkable—the making use of only one gender. For example:—if they speak of a female, or any inanimate object, they invariably say *he*; thus, if a woman is speaking of her sister, she says, "*he*, my sissy;" or of something that particularly attracts their notice, they exclaim—"*he* one handsome house," or "*he* one gran' carriage."

They have also particular ways to designate persons of all ages among themselves; their old women they call "grandy," those of a middle age "aunté," while the younger women are nominated "see," or "sissy." In the same manner, the old men go by the title of "daddy," the middle-aged "uncle," and the young men "buddy." In conversation they seldom pronounce the "s," "th," or "y;" thus, if they want to say "story," it is "'tory," or "the," it is "de," "young," it is "noung."

They are particularly polite whenever they meet, addressing each other as "Sir," and "Ma'am." Many a dialogue have I heard pass between the gossips on their way from the Moravian Chapel, sufficient to excite the risible faculties of a stoic. "How d'ye, ma'am?" said a dirty-looking man just now, to a woman of a similar grade; "how you do?—I'se hope you well to-day." "Well, I tankee, sir—how you do?" "Oh, so so, ma'am, it one long time since me see you; war you no come up our side?" "Oh, my dear sir, me no forget you togedder, but me pic'nee been quite sick."[37] "Me sorry to hear dat, but me hopes he soon get well; me just been to see de new gubbernor land." "Yes, me here he cum, but me not able to go; war kind of a gentleman is he?" "Oh, one noble-looking buckra, an he lady on gran lady; it do you heart good to see he; me dont tink we eber hab gubbenor like he afore." "War he named?" "Gubbernor Sir Charles *Gustus Fitzoy*." "Eh, eh, one big name true." "Well, good morning, sir." "Good morning, ma'am," and so they separated.

To a stranger, the negro tongue is as difficult to *write* as it is to *speak*. In the different conversations given in that dialect, indulgence must be craved from my kind readers, both English and Creole, if they are not correctly written, observing at the same time that I write them as it seems proper to me, and in such a manner as they may be understood by those who read, not always the case when garnished by so many accentual marks. Perhaps sufficient examples of their mode of talking has been given, and that by adding more, the reader may be tired, and myself involved in a maze; I will therefore conclude this subject by remarking, that it requires more than a moderate stock of patience to deal with them, for they talk so long, so loud, and so fast, that if not blest with that virtue to an eminent degree, you will be sure to lose your temper without avail.

In my lengthened descriptions of the negro tribe, among the darker shades of their character inebriation has not been mentioned, as it is not a general vice among them. Still it cannot be altogether passed over, for alas! too many have to deplore the consequences of excessive drinking. In a country where his actual wants are sooner supplied than in a colder clime, the labourer has a larger portion to spend upon that deleterious poison, *new rum*. A few sticks, collected by himself or his wife, serves to cook his daily meal, a mat forms his couch, while a coarse garment of cloth is the dress of his children, and their little feet seldom know the confinement of a shoe. Their smart dresses (if they have any) are reserved for a Sunday, or any particular occasion; but the generality of negroes who are addicted to the vice of drunkenness, seldom pay any regard to their personal appearance.

Their excuse for indulging in this habit of drinking is, that after working all day they require something to strengthen them and allay their thirst. But the question is, will ardent spirits do this? or will they not rather, from their heating qualities, augment the craving? Now, most negroes have a sweet tooth, and a beverage composed of sugar and water would tend to alleviate their thirst, and at the same time nourish and enrich their blood.

It is very much to be wished that managers and owners of estates would try and enforce on the minds of their labourers the pernicious effects of dram-drinking; for a steady, well-ordered peasantry is a blessing to a country. True it is, the negroes have a stubborn temper; and yet there are very many to be found among them who seem willing to follow good advice; in that case, the "rum-shops" might be forsaken in time, and their frequenters become, instead of the refuse, the ornament of the class to which they belong. The time has at length arrived when this despised and benighted race are treated as rational creatures; when—

"Spite of the shade, at length confess'd a man;
Nor longer whipp'd, because he is not white."

If a society was formed in Antigua, similar to the "horticultural," or agricultural societies in England, only extending it to articles of manufacture, it would be the means, perhaps, of exciting in the minds of the lower classes a worthy spirit of emulation, and by employing them during their leisure hours, draw them from their bad associates, and conduct them, by gentle and persuasive measures, into the paths of virtue.

The humanity and generosity of the Antiguans is proved by many charitable institutions; perhaps, then, this remark may be deemed an imposition upon their goodness; but such is not the case; this society might be established at very small expense. Twice in the year, the negroes might be encouraged to bring their little productions to an appointed place; and the best made, or best cultivated articles, obtain a prize. The prizes, of course, would be but small, but surely there are some among this large body of persons who would esteem them, not for their value, but for the honour it conferred upon them. It would be well if some of the philanthropists of the present day would take it into consideration whether such a society would be advisable or not. If even but a few individuals were converted from idleness to industrious habits, the purpose of the institution would be in a great measure answered, the country benefited, and, in course of time, others might be led to follow their example.

Ambition is a principle inherent in man; in all ages, in all classes, in all shades, it more or less abounds, and when tempered with reason, becomes, perhaps, more of a virtue than a vice. While the negro was used as a beast of burden, a creature without feeling or soul, his mind became degraded, and he could not exercise his natural powers. But now he is become free, bear with his ignorance for awhile, and endeavour by every means to enlighten it. Treat him as a being endowed with the same capabilities as ourselves; lay before him a just view of life; point out to his notice the difference between a man under the control of reason and one who follows the dictates of his own impetuous will; shew him what industry and perseverance will accomplish, and, in all probability, there will be some who will lean to the side of virtue, and feel ambitious to become good citizens, and worthy members of society. Nor would this be all the good effected; being virtuous themselves, they would of course desire their children to be so; and consequently, try all possible means to procure them good instruction, and endeavour to bring them up in the paths of rectitude. This is the only way to banish the taint of slavery from the land, and exempt the rising generation from those vices which have for so many years been prevalent, and caused the man of sensibility to blush for his country.

----

[36] Wager, in his "Account of the Isthmus of Darien," published 1699, when speaking of these Albinos, says,—"They are not a distinct race by themselves; but now and then one is born of a copper-coloured father and mother." In the night they skip about "like wild bucks, and run as fast by moonlight, even in the gloom and shade of the woods, as other Indians do by day; being as nimble as they, though not so strong."

[37] In creole language, the term "sick" is applied to all ailments.

CHAPTER XLIV

Remarks upon free system—State of affairs before emancipation—
Trials and casualties—Improved price of land—Sugar estate during slavery
—Benefits of emancipation in the moral state of the colony—Benefits
arising to the planter—Pretended illness among the negroes—Propositions
in their favour—Decrease of crime—Hopes indulged—"The first of
August."

After dwelling so long upon the gloomy subject of slavery, it is pleasing
to turn to the more cheering prospects of the country under a system of
perfect freedom.

It must be allowed that, for a few years previous to emancipation, the
Antiguan planters were in a state of great perturbation. They plainly
perceived, from the state of affairs, that the thraldom of slavery must be
broken—that Britain would no longer allow her children to traffic openly in
flesh and blood; and, finally, that they must, whether with a good grace or
sullen deportment, give up their right to slaves. Still the change from slavery
to freedom was a great revolution, a mighty crisis; and urgent and inevitable
as it was, who could tell what would be its results. From this cause, property
in Antigua diminished, for some few years, greatly in value; and many
estates might have been then purchased for a comparative trifle.

But this depression did not continue long, for no sooner was the deed
done, and the chain which bound the negro to his fellow-man irrecoverably
snapped asunder, than it was found, even by the most sceptical, that free-
labour was decidedly more advantageous to the planter than the old system
of slavery. That, in fact, an estate could be worked for less by free labour
than it could when so many slaves—including old and young, weak and
strong—were obliged to be maintained by the proprietors. Indeed, the truth
of this assertion was discovered even before the negroes were free; for no
sooner did the planters feel that no effort of theirs could prevent
emancipation from taking place, than they commenced to calculate
seriously the probable result of the change, and, to their surprise, found,
upon mature deliberation, that their expenses would be diminished, and
their comforts increased, by the abolition of slavery.[38]

The lapse of eight years has proved this to be true; and there is now
scarcely one person, if any, in the island of Antigua, who would wish to
become again a slaveholder.

Since the period of emancipation, (1834,) Antigua has suffered from
many casualties. There were the severe hurricane, and the long and

harassing droughts of 1835. In 1836, and part of the following year, the drought returned with increased severity, and blasted, in great measure, the crops. In 1840, the planters had again to contend with a season of dry weather, and yet, under all these disastrous circumstances, the free system has gloriously worked its way; and by producing larger average crops, (as well as other advantages, both as regards exports and imports,) has claimed from all a tribute of praise.

Although there are some few persons who deny that free labour is less expensive than slavery, yet the general voice pronounces it to be a system beneficial to the country. It has been proved to demonstration that estates which, under the old system, were clogged with debts they never could have paid off, have, since emancipation, not only cleared themselves, but put a handsome income into the pockets of the proprietors. Land has also increased greatly in value. Sugar plantations that would scarcely find a purchaser before emancipation, will now command from 10,000*l.* sterling, while many estates that were abandoned in days of slavery; are now once more in a state of cultivation; and the sugar-cane flourishes in verdant beauty, where for so many years nothing was to be seen but rank and tangled weeds, or scanty herbage.

In days of slavery it required an immense capital to establish a sugar plantation, as well as a large annual expenditure to carry on the affairs of the estate when established. Perhaps a sugar estate had a gang of two hundred slaves upon it, yet out of this large number possibly there might not be more than sixty or seventy efficient negroes, the surplus being composed of helpless old men and women, children and infants, and emaciated and cureless invalids. Still the law obliged the owner to feed, clothe, house, and procure medical attendance for the entire number; and little as their allowance was, yet, in dry seasons in particular, when the crops of yams and other island provisions failed, the maintenance of so many persons was attended with great expense, while at the same time, perhaps, not more than one-third the number were of any use in agricultural employments.

Under the free system, this tie upon the planter is entirely annulled; for he now employs but a sufficient number of labourers to carry on the estate-work, and the negroes support themselves, as well as their old people and children, out of their weekly earnings and the privileges which they still enjoy upon the properties where they are domiciled.

But this diminishment of expense in the cultivation of the sugar-cane is not the only benefit which emancipation has brought to the colony. Setting aside religious principles—which evidently point out the *sinfulness* of slavery, as it is known among modern nations—there were many, very many circumstances, which tended to render the system obnoxious in the highest degree.

I have already spoken of the immorality practised in the West Indies. It is a topic most harrowing to the feelings, and one that a sensitive mind cannot descant upon. What was the origin of that awful state of society? *Slavery!* Illicit love was not only countenanced, but actually encouraged upon estates between the white masters and their black slaves, in order that the gang of slaves might be enlarged by such unholy means! In these brighter days of freedom there is, at least, not this inducement to licentiousness in its most hideous form, and consequently, that degraded state of morals which marked the annals of former years, has, in great measure, disappeared.

Again, slavery occasioned the *planter* immense trouble and perplexities in managing his slaves; it engendered continual heart-burnings and jealousies; it soured his temper, rendered him callous, deadened those feelings of humanity which the Spirit of Love has implanted in our breasts, and, however kind and benevolent he might be in his domestic circle, a few months spent in managing slaves, and he forgot to exercise his self-control, and gave way to bursts of passions which, in his calmer moments, he perhaps bitterly repented of.

Nor was this all: slavery engendered suspicion. There was not a single slave-holder or slave-manager who, one time or the other, was not made the prey to apprehensions, and had his brain filled with thoughts of rebellions and insurrections. Emancipation has entirely banished this hydra-like train of evils, and paved the way for more enlightened and happier times. It has also put an end, in great measure, to pretended illness among the negroes. During slavery, this was a practice universal. No sooner did Monday morning arrive than the manager's door was thronged with self-elected invalids, and more diseases were then complained of than even Dr. Buchan would have us believe "flesh and blood are heir to." Some made their appearance with their heads tied up in a bundle of banana-leaves—a negro prognosticator of a severe head-ache; others were suffering from pains in the knees and ankles, and consequently, such parts of their frame were duly enveloped in sundry particles of old cloth or dried snake-skins; while some, again, with woe-begone countenances, expressed "dat dey felt bad all ober dem." In vain the poor manager protested their pulse was good, the tongues in a healthy state—the negroes only groaned the more, gave a longer detail of their aches and pains, or else, in a very doleful voice, exclaimed—"Massa no b'leive he, (pointing to their tongues and wrists,) he no worth b'leiving, for he no 'peak true!" and so the end of the confab was, that the slaves in question were put upon the sick-list.

But now the case is generally different. The negroes work for *money*; they know if they feign illness for a week, they will be the losers at the end of the month; and as they are very quick in discovering where their own interest lies, they stick to the hoe for the sake of the dollars.

Still, however, pretended illness is not entirely extinct,—there are some of the labourers who practise it in these days of freedom, as of erst they did in slavery. In illustration of this remark, it is a customary plan upon sugar plantations, that if any of the people quit their work for a certain period, they, after that time, are required to pay rent for the cottages, with which, as stationary labourers, they are provided. This is done in order to ensure their labour, and prevent them from working upon other estates, where they may receive higher wages as strangers.[32]

In order, then, to gain this increase of wages, without having to pay rent for his house, the negro calls up some pseudo complaint, and very early in the morning, presents himself before the manager, with the usual bandages, and the notification that he is "quite sick." The manager feels grieved at this intelligence, for he had contemplated doing a particular quantity of work that week, and required all the labourers he could procure; but as the negro represents himself so very ill, and he cannot deny the statement, he is obliged to remain content. No sooner, however, has the indisposed negro gained his hut, than he throws off all symptoms of illness, and choosing his best hoe, he secretly starts away to some other estate, where he is sure to obtain the additional wages; while his proper master supposes he is reclining upon his bed, a prey to ill-health.

It must be remarked, that although the free labourer acts at times in this disingenuous manner, it is a general opinion that they work better, and in a more cheerful manner than they did in days of slavery, when a driver stood over them with his long and heavy whip, to chastise their least cessation from labour. It cannot be supposed that I am perfectly cognizant of the real truth of this statement. I must, therefore, along with my own observations, take the opinions and arguments of planters, and other persons connected with agricultural employments, as the basis of my remarks.

The facts brought forward in support of this affirmation are these:— That upon some estates the extent of acres in a state of cultivation is greater than before the abolition of slavery,—other properties make a larger annual crop with one-third the number of labourers,—and that although many efficient negroes have emigrated to other islands, estates that were dismantled have been re-cultivated. In *job-work*, as it is termed, the negroes accomplish twice as much work as when employed by the day; the simple reason of which is, that they gain a larger sum of money by such arrangements. It is a fact that has fallen under my own observation, that when a piece of land is holed[41] by *task-work*, the negroes will rise by one or two o'clock during moonlight, go to the field, and accomplish the usual day's work (300 cane-holes) by five or six in the morning; and after resting for a short time, are prepared to take another task, which they also complete, and have some hours left, in which to till their own little spot of provision-ground. When the excessive heat of the climate is taken into consideration, as well as the labour it requires to dig one *cane-hole*, the work of a negro who can open *six hundred* in one day, can be better estimated by those who are more acquainted with such matters than myself.

Another proposition in favour of the free system is said to be the greater docility of the negroes now they are emancipated. Of this circumstance I am not able to give *personal* information. To me they appear as aggravating as ever: equally suspicious, quarrelsome, and uncivil. Still there are many and great excuses to be made for them, when we consider how short has been their life of freedom!—how untutored their minds are! —how debased has been their state!—the very beast that eats the grass of the field has, in times past, been equally esteemed with the negro!

Many planters, as well as other intelligent individuals, have affirmed to the truth of the statement, "that negroes are more easily managed as free men, than they were as slaves;" and certainly such persons ought to be better judges than myself, whose intercourse with the negro population is, of course, more restricted.

Crime is also said to have decreased—that is, in offences of the higher character. We seldom or ever hear of a murder, or arson; but petty faults, such as small thefts, breaking canes, breaches of contract, and insolence to their employers, swell at times into a large amount. Still it must be remembered, such is not a proof that misdemeanours are more frequent in freedom than they used to be during slavery. The reason that these minor violations of the law appear to have increased is, that under the present system all defaulters are brought before a magistrate, and their offences thus published in the eyes of the world; whereas, in days of slavery, their owner was their judge and corrector, the whip their punishment, and they received their corporeal chastisement without any notice of the event reaching the ears of any stranger.

It is true, as I have already remarked more than once, the negroes are a class of individuals very difficult and tiresome to deal with; the greatest patience is requisite in order to bear with their strange and harassing dispositions. It is now ten years since I first came among them; and although great part of that time has been spent in England, I have lived long enough in Antigua to know what negroes are. I have studied their characters in every point, and well as I would wish to speak of them, truth obliges me to confess I have found them to be very far from perfect. Still I glory in emancipation, for I looked upon slavery as a foul and hideous monster, which ought to be exterminated from every corner of the world; and consequently, I would not have the bright star of liberty robbed of one of its rays by any remarks of mine. I yet hope to see the negroes improved in their mental, as they already are in their temporal affairs. I trust that, as years roll round, their ill qualities will be ameliorated, and their virtues increased; that they, as well as their employers, may learn and practise that golden maxim, "Bear and forbear;" and that eventually the Antiguan peasantry may be held up to the other colonies as bright examples of humble worth, adorning the sphere of life in which they move.

It is my fervent wish that the negroes may learn properly to estimate their state as a *free people*, and instead of using their liberty as a cloak for insolence and impertinence, they may fulfil the several duties which are required of them with becoming diligence, and finally meet their reward.

In summing up this chapter upon free labour, it may be deemed necessary for me to mention some few particulars of the 1st of August, 1834, that eventful day, when about thirty thousand human beings were released from the trammels of slavery, and entered upon a new state of existence as free men!

Before the abolition of slavery, it had been supposed by many of the inhabitants of Antigua, that the negroes, at such an important era of their lives—the transition from slavery to freedom, would be led into great and serious excesses, or, at least, that they would pass the first days of freedom in dance and song, in riotous feastings and drunken carousals. But when the time arrived, far different was the result. Instead of that day being the scene of wild revelry and disorderly jollity, the negroes passed it as a "Sabbath of Sabbaths," a solemn feast,

"One bright day of gladness and of rest."

The churches and chapels throughout the island were thronged to overflowing; and those persons who were unable to procure seats within the sacred walls, crowded around the open doors and windows with eager looks of joy. All the shops and stores in the island were closed—

"The   roar   of   trade   had   ceased,   and   on   the   air
Came holy songs, and solemn sounds of prayer."

From every valley and dingle and from every height came trooping joyous groups. Old men and women, whose woolly locks were silvered by the hand of time—young men and maidens—the robust and the weak—the parent and the child—all rejoicing that the day had at length come when the iron yoke of slavery was removed from their shoulders, and they, like their masters, could boast that they were free!

The 1st of August fell upon a Friday, and after enjoying themselves upon the following day with their friends, and joining in the ordinances of God upon the Sabbath, the greater part of the negroes returned to their agricultural and other employments on the Monday morning with the utmost decorum and good temper. Defective as the negro character may be, their behaviour at that eventful period of their lives must elicit praise from the lips of all, and prove a lasting theme of gratification to the friends of liberty.

[38] My readers must clearly understand, that in my remarks upon free labour, I confine myself exclusively to Antigua. In Jamaica, Trinidad, and some of the other islands, great complaints are made upon the working of the free system. Many estates are almost out of cultivation in Jamaica, and serious fears are entertained for the future prosperity of the island. To enter into any disquisition respecting where the fault lies in that colony, comes not within the focus of the present work; but no doubt, if the cause be minutely and candidly inquired into, it will be found that blame is to be attached to *both parties*.

[39] It may be necessary to explain what is meant by *strangers*, as well as the reason they receive higher wages. The average rate of wages is eightpence sterling, per day,[40] with the additional privilege of a cottage, a plot of ground in which to plant provisions, and medical attendance. Some estates which are short handed, endeavour to procure labourers from other plantations, and as they have not to provide them with anything but their actual wages, they are enabled to give these strangers (as they are termed, to distinguish them from the resident labourers) a few pence more per day.

[40] Since the late awful earthquake, 8th Feb. 1843, wages have increased greatly. The sum of 4*s.* currency, per diem, is now the usual rate; but some estates have to give from 6*s.* to 8*s.* currency, for the daily work of negroes, when grinding or cutting canes.

[41] The process of opening the ground for planting the cane. This is most laborious work; it is performed with a heavy hoe, and the holes are from three to four feet square, and about a foot deep.

CHAPTER XLV

A chapter on colour—Gradual removes from the negroes—Middle classes—Personal appearance—Devotions at their mirrors—Style of dress —Chapel belles—Passion for dress—Home and home scenes—The young men—Extreme officiousness—Higher classes of colour—Coloured Hebes —The chapel tea-party—Gastronomy and speeches—Wesleyan bazaar, and lunch-table—Gastronomic relics.

In commencing this "chapter on colour," it may, perhaps, be deemed *unnecessary* for me to mention, that there are as many gradations in *tint* as there are in *rank;* but as some of my readers may not be perfectly aware of the fact, I prefer to be branded with the title of a "multiplier of words," rather than omit any subject on which I may be able to afford information.

The several removes from a black are as follows:—The *mongrel*, the offspring of a black and mulatto; the *mulatto*, the offspring of a black and a white; the *mustee*, the offspring of a mulatto and a white; the *fustee*, the offspring of a mustee and a white; and the *dustee*, the offspring of a fustee and a white.[42] This last gradation is the connecting link between the degraded children of Ham, and the descendants of his more honoured brethren. It is to be noted, however, that the *mulatto* is not *always* fairer than the *mongrel*, or the *mustee* than the mulatto; and children of the same parents often exhibit as much, if not more, difference of complexion, as those of Europeans.[43]

Perhaps it may be considered almost an impertinence in me to remark —the fact is so well known both in England and the West Indies—that, among this numerous body of her majesty's subjects, there are some of the highest respectability. Every West Indian island has its *élite*, and Antigua is not behind the rest. Many, very many, could be mentioned, who are superior in every way—well-read, strong-minded, with excellent natural talents, and unexceptionable, both in public and private life. It would afford me pleasure to name them; but I refrain from doing so, knowing that their applause will be sooner gained by remaining silent, and therefore will skim over the more general character of the class, noting, in the first place, some peculiar traits in their personal appearance.

The chief peculiarities in the coloured race are, the extreme pliancy of limbs, attenuation of person, large black eyes, and a profusion of black curling hair. The men are generally *under* than above the middle size, but in most instances, possessed of good figures.

The females are also small and slender, and are noted for an ambling gait, combined in many of them with an extreme affectation of manners. Many of them, unknowingly, are warm admirers of Lord Chesterfield's "Advice," and practise the "airs and graces" before a looking-glass with an intenseness and indefatigability which, no doubt, that *great philosopher* would fully appreciate.

We hear of the beautiful Narcissus being so enamoured of his own lovely features, when reflected in the clear waters, that he pined into a jonquil. Now, I cannot take upon myself to state this is exactly the case with the West Indian brunettes; but they do certainly "lingering look," until a pretty considerable stock of patience would be exhausted.

Their toilets are laborious in the extreme; and they might exclaim, with Lady Mary W. Montague's "Flavia,"—

"———————— I oft have sate,
While hours unheeded pass'd, in deep debate
How curls should fall, or where a braid to place;
If blue or scarlet best became my face!"

Sundays, marriages, and funerals, are the occasions appointed for making the greatest display. At other periods, a long dressing-gown, or "wrapper," as it is termed in Antigua, with a many-coloured cotton kerchief around their shoulders, and their heads perhaps enveloped in a similar article, and *slip-shod* shoes, constitute their attire. But when "high-days and holidays" come, and an *étalage* is contemplated, one or two of their friends are generally called in to officiate as tire-women, and it must be allowed, their place is then no *sinecure*.

The style of dress adopted by ladies of this rank, when abroad, is very superb! Silks and satins of the most approved colours, challis and mousseline-de-laines of the gayest patterns, mantelets, and "Victoria cloaks," bonnets covered with flowers, silk stockings, parasols of the most fashionable dimensions, gloves of the softest dyes, shoes and boots of every shade, reticules, with tassels and all complete, and pocket handkerchiefs, ornamented with lace in the manner dictated by the changeful goddess, added to a rather exuberant display of *bijouterie*, whose gold is deeply alloyed, and whose gems owe their brightest rays to the aid of different coloured *foils*, serve to increase the charms of the olive-tinged creole beauties.

Those of this class who frequent the chapel, and term themselves Methodists, make some slight difference in their apparel. Their bonnets, for example, are divested of flowers on the *outside*, for which they make amends by various twinings and *counter*-twinings of glossy ribbon and cotton lace, and filling their caps—I beg pardon, I mean their *brides*—but I am such an indifferent votary of fashion, that I am ever forgetting her technical terms —their *brides*, then, with such a profusion of flowers, which be they of Amaranthine birth I know not, but I am very sure, they are like nothing earthly—that their eyes, nose, and mouth, just peep forth like sentinels from some guarded fortress. Others, more scrupulous I suppose, discard the use of flowers altogether, and in their room call to their aid snowy *blondes*, and bows and puffs of choicest ribands. Jewellery is also interdicted, although a few of the smarter of the "chapel belles" contrive to smuggle a ring or two, a mock-cameo brooch, or a treble-gilt chain, into their outward adornments. Fashion is, however, worshipped by all. Their bonnets must be of the proper size, their collars and capes of the proper shape, their dresses of the proper length and breadth, and their waists reduced to the proper circumference.

But the *sleeves* of their dresses are the parts appropriated to the display of their most exquisite skill. *One* poor human brain could never invent the puffings, plaitings, and gatherings; quiltings, flutings, and bandings, which are lavished upon that peculiar portion of their dress; to devise them must be an arduous task, to construct them an herculean labour. The arrangement of their hair is also a work of no trifling nature, and takes up no small portion of their time; and the dealers in oils and pomades derive no small profit from such articles, which are indispensable in making their masses of black locks repose in their proper position.

But, jesting apart, it is really the very pinnacle of absurdity, to see the rage to which dress is carried, by this class of persons in particular, when their style of living and rank in society are taken into consideration. Their mothers are of that class who have been already described when speaking of the negroes, but who, it must be mentioned, disdain that term. Others again are mongrels or mulattos; themselves the offspring of those illicit alliances for which the West Indies, in their days of darkness, have been so disgracefully noted. These mothers have had, in almost every instance, the entire management of their children. Perfectly uneducated themselves, they of course see no charms in knowledge, and except the simple act of being able to spell through an easy lesson, or scrawl their own names, these unfortunate girls are brought up with no higher ambition than the wearing smart clothes, utterly unbefitting their station, and spending their lives in brushing and dressing their hair, or rubbing their teeth with a roll of tobacco. While their mothers, who keep a small shop, sell in the market, or huckster about the town to gain a subsistence, think they have performed the part of a good parent, by procuring for their daughters clothing which every well-thinking person must mourn to see them arrayed in.

Their houses are, in many instances, the domiciles I have also already described in the negro chapters, where, amid all these smart habiliments, the young persons whom you may see walking out with the air and dress of a *duchess*, herd together, eat the coarsest fare, perhaps never know the luxury of a table-cloth; and where the whole family, including male and female of every age, take their nightly repose together. Some of these young females are more industrious, and take in needlework of different kinds; but the amount of their earnings is lavished upon that all-absorbing object—dress. This, however, is the only species of work they will condescend to perform, for as to going out to service, they scorn the very idea.

The young men are equally scrupulous in adorning their persons; although, in many instances, very negligent in improving their minds. Their dress, which has been already described when speaking of the *black beaux*, they procure by following the several trades of tailors, shoemakers, joiners,[44] &c., and sometimes, I am sorry to say, by less honest means. They are far behind the females in appearance; for the latter, let them be ever so uneducated, have a certain gracefulness of manners, which, as long as they keep their mouths shut, tends to gloss over their ignorance. I have had opportunities of noticing this in public places of resort; the missionary bazaars, for example. The females sit or stand quietly in groups, and offend not the eye or ear by their coarseness of mien; but, on the contrary, the men have that dissolute, vulgar, cavalier manner, so characteristic of low, over-dressed vanity, that, were it in England, we should be led to keep a steady eye upon our pockets and watches, and feel ourselves safe only at a distance. Even in the West Indies, where the "swell mob" does not exist, a kind of unpleasantness of feeling steals over one upon their near approach, heightened, or rather produced, by their boldness and vulgar, officious conduct. They appear to know no difference of rank, but, in their obtruded remarks, forget their plebeian origin. This is more apparent in their behaviour to the higher classes of their own colour, whom they approach with the utmost familiarity, and unless they are speedily and properly discountenanced, prove as troublesome as the impertinent little *gad-flies* do to a quiet herd of cattle, when standing musing in some marshy pool.[45]

The higher class of coloured persons, which embraces a large portion of the community, I have already slightly glanced at; but still my work would indeed be incomplete did I not more fully endeavour to portray their worth and superiority. These are men, who, if not educated in England, have received the best instruction the West Indies could afford, aided by their own strenuous endeavours for information. Hospitable in the highest degree, with a hand ever open to grasp in friendship that of the strangers whom fate or the winds may lead to their pretty little island; living in an easy elegance of style—the possessors of warm and generous thoughts—

the doers of high and noble actions—patriots in the full sense of the term, their services ever at the command of their country; of agreeable conversation and polished manners; these are the characteristics of many of our Antiguan coloured gentlemen. Their wives and daughters are, in several instances, as unexceptionable as themselves, and perform their social duties in the same pleasing manner.

Within the last few years, the young people have been more generally educated in England, and many of them exhibit superior talents, and have attained to no mean proficiency in the fine arts. Their manners, too, are, with but few exceptions, very graceful; their voices soft and mellifluous; and although, perhaps, rather more silent than in the present age is expected of women, what they do say is generally to the purpose.

Among these young daughters of a glowing clime, many very beautiful girls are to be met with. With a sufficiency of *embonpoint* to prevent the appearance of any "right angles" in their frame, they possess a sylph-like movement and an elastic step; while the large, black liquid eyes, the glossy jet hair, the long eye-lashes, and the soft olive tinge of their complexions, relieved by rosy lips and dazzling white teeth, would form no bad model for one of Mahomet's *houris*.

Our sweet little queen has, unwittingly, done much to improve their beauty, in wearing her own fair hair in the simple style she does. As true and loyal subjects, the Creole girls can do nought but follow the example of their royal mistress; and the massy bunches of curls, which tended to give their features a degree of thickness really not their own, and caused them to look more sallow by the contrast, have given place to the more elegant, Madonna-like bands and braids.

The place of all others where the greatest display of coloured beaux and belles are to be found is at the tea-parties given at the Methodist chapel for charitable purposes.

It being a beautiful moonlight evening upon the last occasion of the kind, we determined to avail ourselves of it, and attend the party whose gastronomic performance was to commence at seven o'clock. Upon gaining the outer wall of the chapel, we found the gate guarded by a few of the "new police," and the porter appointed to receive the tickets of admission, for which the sum of 2*s*. 6*d*. sterling was demanded.

Passing across the court-yard, we stopped for a few moments at an open window, to view the interior. The entertainment was held in the school-room, a large apartment, forming the ground-floor of the chapel; the walls of which were hung round with various pictorial embellishments, seen to advantage by the aid of the numerous lamps. We entered at that auspicious moment when nearly the whole of the company were assembled, and before the actual business of the evening commenced. The effect was really very picturesque, and the scene would have been worthy the painter's pencil. The whole of the interior, with the exception of a space all round the apartment, reserved for a promenade, was laid out with tables, placed breadthwise, surrounded by well-dressed groups, and covered with all those delicate "cates and confections," generally introduced at that social meal, which Cowper has celebrated.

The heat of the climate rendering it necessary to have all the windows thrown open, renders the use of large glass shades also necessary to prevent the tapers from being extinguished by the fresh land-breeze. On every table a pair of silver candlesticks supported the delicate sperm or wax candles, the clear light of which, heightened by their glittering screens, threw an air of cheerfulness on all. Many elegant little vases, filled with choice and fragrant flowers, were placed at stated distances, interspersed with baskets and plates of the most luscious fruits, while, at each end of the table, with their tea equipages of silver and china placed before them, was seated a lady-member of the chapel, whose zeal prompted her to prepare all this pretty display, for the benefit of the society. Every pillar of the apartment supported its appropriated lamps, which, reflected in the bright eyes of the assembled girls, shewed their brown faces to more advantage.

In about the centre of the apartment, elevated a foot or two from the floor, was placed the seraphine, at which a young lady (sister to the wife of one of the missionaries) presided, with quiet grace and great skill; and around this instrument were gathered the missionaries themselves. The business of the evening commenced by singing a "grace;" upon the conclusion of which, tea-spoons rattled, tea-cups danced from hand to hand, and every one appeared resolved to prove, *par experience*, the goodness of the plenteous fare placed before them. As for myself, I had full work for my eyes, and postponed the exercise of my masticatory powers until another opportunity.

Now, be it known to my English readers, that *tea* is a beverage West Indians seldom, if ever, indulge in; except those of the higher classes. When, then, such a mixed party of coloured persons meet together for the express purpose of partaking of that cup "which cheers, but not inebriates," it is done by the lower classes merely for the sake of fashion, or to shew off their gala dress. Accordingly, some most ludicrous caricatures might have been taken, had Cruikshank or Phiz been of the party instead of myself. Some of this class sipped their tea with the same apparent relish they would have partaken of so much decoction of senna, or any other similar luxury the pretty new "druggist's shop," lately established in St. John's, under the auspices of a son of "mighty Scotia," so neatly dispenses. Others, with many a rueful look, talked of the *delights* of tea-parties, and of their own fondness for that fragrant herb, while they beat a tattoo upon their tea-cups; and some, again, with noble determination of purpose, stirred their smoking cup until a little cool, and then gulped down the whole quantum, much in the same way, and with the same happy countenances, as a *débutant* generally swallows his first glass of water from some of our English chalybeate springs.

The "young men" of the class already noticed, appeared to have been engaged the preceding forenoon in studying attitudes, for, collected in groups, they stood leaning against the pillars, distorting their forms and faces, and striving, I suppose, to emulate the statues of the "Apollo Belvidere," or the "Farnesian Hercules."

Everything in this world has its end, and consequently the time at length arrived when the repast—to which all appeared to do justice, and consumed such huge pyramids of cake as was marvellous in my eyes—was over, and at a signal from one of the preachers, they all knelt down to prayer; but while thus engaged, I could hear the repressed jingle of many a silver spoon, which some more careful dame was placing in security in her box or bag.

After the prayer, a few hymns were played and sung; during which period, I took the opportunity of walking with my companion around the space already mentioned, in order to obtain a full view of the assembled guests; and then followed some speeches by the missionaries and one or two of the leading members, which afforded much interest to the assembled group.

One old gentleman—a very excellent man, by the way, but rather too much given to prosing when in the pulpit—spoke in favour of tea-meetings and of the chapel debt, (to pay off which, these entertainments were given, as one means of raising money.) Another preacher gave us a long rambling anecdote of a bowie-knife; paid high compliments to the ladies, which were received by a grin of applause; said how much better it was to have these agreeable parties, and thus raise money, instead of the old way of trudging about from house to house, begging the inmates to put down their names for certain sums, and attributing the happy change to the fertile genius of the "tender sex;" and concluded by remarking, that in the course of a week or two there would be a bazaar held at the court-house, for the purpose of raising more cash to liquidate the chapel debt, at which he understood there was to be a *solid lunch-table* spread, besides one for confectionary; and although he liked tea very well, he liked lunch a great deal better.

After Mr. ———— had concluded, a mild, quiet-looking man rose, who spoke of social intercourse, referred to Job's sons and daughters; talked of heaven and heavenly enjoyments; and then, after a few more speeches, more compliments to the ladies, a few more hymns, and a concluding prayer, came the cloaking, shawling, and bonneting, and we returned home, altogether pleased with our visit, and leaving the lady-givers of the repast packing away their silver urns and tea-pots, and all their other "goods and chattels," with a clatter and clamour that would have awakened the "seven sleepers."

Having been so well pleased with our visit to the tea-party, we resolved to attend at the Wesleyan Bazaar held at the court-house; and accordingly, on the day appointed, we drove to that handsome building, whose walls have seen many a smiling face, and echoed the sighs of many a heart—so mutable is everything in this world, sorrow ever treading upon the steps of joy!

The day was very warm; and upon entering the crowded apartment, the smell of the various viands from the predicted *lunch-table* completely overcame me for a few seconds; but recovering myself, after a short sojourn in one of the wings of the building, I ventured to return and look about me. The upper rooms of the court-house, where the council and assembly hold their meetings, had been appropriated to the occasion; the council-chamber (after having one of the temporary partitions taken down, thus including the lobby) was cleared of its chairs and tables; and in their place, fitted up with stalls, placed around the sides of the apartment, at which some of the chapel-ladies presided.

Here several little fancy articles were exhibited for sale, at the usual high prices; the best of which were, a pretty little baby-house, illustrative of the style of architecture most used in Antigua, and which was made from the long arrow (or sheath) of the sugar-cane, and a "pedlar woman" of old England in her red cloak, black bonnet, and basket on her arm, containing her numerous diversified wares, and hung round with other miniature symbols of her trade—the make and gift (with many other elegant trifles) of the accomplished daughters of a lady of Upper Holloway, England.

The other apartment, where the house of assembly hold their conclaves, was appropriated for the eating part of the amusement; and a very good amusement some of the company seemed to think it, if I may judge from appearances. On one long table was displayed a cold collation, consisting of savoury dishes, suited to the tastes of all, and where, for the charge of 1*s.* sterling, any one might fare most sumptuously. Those who preferred it, partook of sandwiches, for which the moderate charge of 2¼*d.* sterling was demanded; and upon my entrance, my eyes were first attracted by seeing a huge widow-Barnaby-looking woman, devouring them with a voracity I certainly did not expect to witness in that place. The other table displayed confections of various beautiful forms and kinds, interspersed with fruits and flowers; and where the younger people also seemed to find full employment.

Here again I could not help observing the low appearance of many of the "young men," who, with hats placed on one side of their heads, and immense quantities of black hair smoothed to a half-straight fashion by the assistance of a plentiful supply of lard pomatum, and their thumbs stuck most (*un*)gracefully in their waistcoat pockets, were pacing the room and shewing off their smart apparel. I afterwards understood that many of these over-dressed specimens of mortality contrived to enter the room without paying the "quarter dollar" (1*s*. sterling) entrance money, by fascinating, I suppose, the door-keeper, who was too *simple-hearted* to denounce these peacock-like persons of conduct a sober-robed owl would scorn to be guilty of.

At length the appetites of all seemed to be appeased,—their motives for coming (to see and be seen) fully answered,—their appropriated sum of money expended,—and themselves loaded with pincushions and *scent-bags*, babies' caps, and reticules, they began to disperse, and we ourselves took our departure, leaving some of the matrons, who had *an eye to business*, very eagerly making bargains for sundry portions of beef and ham, tongues, poultry, and cold mutton, jellies and cheese-cakes, and other gastronomic relics.

---

[42] This is the creole way of terming these different castes: the Spanish call them *mulattos, tercerones, quarterons*, and *quinterones*. There are also some intermediate names for the issue of unions between the negroes and coloured people, as sambos, &c.; but the general term for persons of colour is, quadroons.

[43] In illustration of this it may be remarked, that there are families where some of the brothers or sisters are fair enough to be taken for English people; while the rest are scarcely distinguishable from negroes in colour.

[44] In these remarks, the author begs to say, she means no disparagement to the other professors of these several trades. She is well aware that Antigua boasts a most respectable class of tradesmen—white, black, and coloured—who are an honour to the colony in which they reside.

[45] A great portion of this class of persons are the offspring of those illicit alliances already alluded to in the times of slavery, and who did not receive their freedom until after the general emancipation in 1834, or within a short time previous to that event, when they became so depreciated in value, that their owners were satisfied to dispose of them at a trifling remuneration.

CHAPTER XLVI

Prejudice—Its former and present character—An act of resentment—The "Prejudice Bell"—Exclusion of persons of colour from offices of trust and polished society—The dawn of better days—The assertions of some authors contradicted—Domestic character of the coloured gentry—Hospitality—A day at a coloured gentleman's country-house—Dwellings—Marriages—Great suppression of illicit connexions within these last few years—Funerals—A scene of riot in former days—Provincialisms.

Before continuing my sketches of colour, it is necessary to say something about *prejudice*. I mentioned in a former chapter, that possibly it would be better to bury such a subject in the gulf of oblivion; but upon mature consideration, I think it advisable to portray a few of its many instances as well in times past, as now.

A candid mind cannot but allow the illiberality, not to call it by a harsher name, of despising or underrating persons, because it has pleased their Creator to give them less fair skins. Yet that these feelings have existed from time immemorial to the present day is a well-known fact; and the West Indies in particular has been the place where Prejudice has erected her stronghold.

Although, as before remarked, the negroes were only considered as beasts of burden, their polished and urbane white masters had no objection to making them the partners of their illicit intercourse; and then, casting aside all natural affections, doomed their unoffending children, the issue of such unions, to a state of degradation.

In former years, the cruelty of such an act was not, perhaps, so keenly felt by them. Without any knowledge of religion or share of education, they grew up devoid of the finer feelings. The girls, as they approached womanhood, became themselves the mistresses of white men, or, in the West Indian term, *housekeepers*, while the males were content to drag on their existence much in the same way as a tolerated spaniel, which at one moment is noticed by a gracious nod, and allowed to lick the feet of its master, while at the next it is kicked out of the apartment, or spurned from the pathway.

As time wore on, and knowledge slowly progressed, the fathers of these poor children were led to send them to some place of instruction, where, besides acquiring the mere rudiments of reading and writing, they became grounded in plain, but solid learning. Having thus passed through the early stages of life, the males followed mercantile or agricultural pursuits; and as, perhaps, wealth poured in upon them, and they felt in their own bosoms their superiority to many of the white inhabitants, their eyes became more and more opened, and they more and more felt their degraded state.

They were debarred from holding any office of trust—were not allowed to act as jurors—and were prevented from serving in the militia, until the year 1793, when, as a great concession, or else because the "great folks" thought it for the public good, they were allowed to serve as pioneers, or drag the heavy artillery. The very churchyard was denied them, and their mortal remains were deposited by the roadside, where only the suicide or the murderer found a grave; while, should a white man be seen to take one of them, even the most respectable among the class, by the hand, in the way of social intimacy, that white man would be scouted from all ranks of society for his indecorous behaviour.

In 1798, Mr. Gilbert, (a relation to the Mr. Gilbert, the founder of Methodism in Antigua,) for many years the superintendent of his majesty's dockyard at English Harbour, was united in the bands of wedlock to a highly respectable and accomplished coloured lady of Antigua. The *iniquity!* of this action, as they deemed it, was resented by his brother whites; himself and his lady were openly insulted; and some wag of the island, who, with the brains of a calf, fancied himself an Ulysses in wisdom, gave to the world an example of his would-be wit, by painting Mr. Gilbert's office-door half *black* and half *white*.[46]

Not only were the coloured people refused interment in the churchyard, but so fearful were the whites of profanation, that the very *bell* which tolled out *their demise* was prohibited from being used to perform that service for those degraded ones through whose veins flowed the least drop of Afric's tarnished blood. Accordingly, a smaller bell (which still hangs in the belfry) was obtained from an estate in the island, called "Golden Grove," and which was regularly kept for the sole use of persons of colour, until within these last few years, when their rights as fellow-creatures have been allowed, and those mean and pitiful distinctions of caste, in great measure, done away with.

The first coloured person who was buried in the churchyard at St. John's was a merchant's clerk, (whose own blood was tainted, it is said, but who passed as a white man,) the favourite of his master. The merchant ordered the funeral to proceed to the churchyard, and upon the clergyman making his appearance, and no doubt expressing his surprise at such an unprecedented circumstance, he (the merchant) insisted upon his performing the burial service, and dared him to prevent the interment taking place. The rector thought it prudent to comply, and accordingly the coloured man reposed by the side of some white person, who (following the idea of Pollock in his "Course of Time") will, indeed, feel surprised at the last day, when each one takes again his own body, to find how long his ashes have been polluted by mingling in one common dust with him who perhaps was the offspring of one of his own despised negroes.[47]

How the coloured people bore all these accumulated indignities, which were heaped upon them for so many years, would astonish any sensitive mind; nor if they had joined the negroes in one common cause against their tyrants would it have produced much surprise. But they did bear it, and with magnanimity, until time and circumstance worked the cure, and delivered them from that thraldom of the mind more galling than any servitude of the body.

It was not only the soreness of spirit which this state of affairs inflicted upon the coloured man, but as Prejudice was the offspring of Slavery, it was consequently the ground-work of that horrible system of licentiousness which rendered Antigua among the other West India Islands famous, or rather *infamous*, for so many years. The coloured women participated in the *prejudice* of their masters, and as they became the mothers of female children, they reared them up in the same spirit, and inculcated into their minds that it was more honourable and praiseworthy to inhabit the harem of a white man, than to be the lawful wife of a man of colour. This conduct was, of course, the grave of all domestic peace, the destroyer of connubial love; and by its dire, its *demoniacal* influences, caused the fairest island in the world to become, in a moral point of view, a dreary marsh, exhaling the poisonous miasma.

Brighter days have, however, at length dawned; the unhallowed custom of concubinage has greatly decreased; and, indeed, except among some of the old white planters or merchants, who have retained the sins of their youth, and some of the low coloured people, such alliances are generally reprobated.

The assertion, however, that prejudice is entirely done away with, is incorrect. It still exists, and that, perhaps, very strongly; but policy forbids, in great measure, its outward show. It is true, that white and coloured gentlemen walk, and talk, and dine together—drink sangaree at one another's houses, sit in the same juror's box, and are invited, *sans distinction*, at "Government House;" yet, at the same time, there is a lurking dislike to them on account of colour, which ever steps in as a barrier to social intercourse. It is said, that the white ladies are the strongest upholders of prejudice; but that their refusal to mix with this class of persons is not occasioned from any shade of colour, but on account of their general illegitimacy. This, however, is not the sole cause; for there are illegitimate white people, whom they are in the constant habit of meeting without any aversion; while, at the same time, many of the people of colour, particularly the younger ones, are the offspring of parents who have been legally united within the sacred walls of the temple of God, and whose intellectual attainments fit them for any society.

It has also been said, that the coloured classes are not of a sufficient respectability to move among the white inhabitants; and some few years ago, the question was asked, (in excuse for excluding them from society,) by one who then filled the highest station in Antigua—"Would you wish to ask your tailor or your shoemaker to dine with you?" To this query a most unequivocal negative might have been given. Differences of rank ought to be observed; and no one can be blamed for preserving a certain degree of *etiquette* in the arrangement of their parties. But, at the same time—"Are all coloured people tailors and shoemakers?" "No!" as before remarked, among them are some of the most respectable merchants and planters; and the whites themselves, with but few exceptions, follow no higher occupations.

Let the lower class of coloured people know and keep their proper distance, the same as the lower classes do in the mother country; but allow the upper ones to hold that place in society which their worth, respectability, wealth, and general deportment, entitles them to.

I have already spoken of the extreme familiarity of some of the low persons of colour, who rest all their pretensions to gentility upon their smart clothes, or their ability to keep a horse or a horse and gig. It could not be expected or wished that such persons should be received into good society, any more than the low and ignorant of my own countrymen. There is also another class of coloured people which, although, perhaps, equally talented and prosperous, from the nature of the business they follow, are excluded from the tables of the great. Such distinctions as these are but equitable, and consequently, cannot be called prejudice; but to debar the whole caste from polished society on account of *colour*, is an illiberality unworthy of the "age we live in."

From a glance at prejudice, and its attendant evils, I will proceed in my remarks upon the domestic character of the coloured Creoles. I have already spoken of their hospitality, which is a virtue apparently indigenous in the island; for white, brown, and black, rich and poor, seem, as far as lies in their power, equally open to its influence. The country, as any part of the island beyond the precincts of the capital is termed, is divided into small towns, (described in the previous pages;) a few settlements, which have sprung up since emancipation, and sugar-estates, or grazing-farms, which, with their "great houses," managers' and overseers' dwellings, and negro huts, form themselves complete villages. There are no hotels or places of public entertainment, where the *sun*-worn traveller can obtain "rest and refuge;" but if only acquainted by name, you can take the liberty of driving to any of these country residences, where you are sure of meeting with a polite and cordial reception.

Most of these dwellings are very pleasantly situated, generally upon a gentle slope, and every breeze that blows finds a ready entrance at the open windows. Some of them are built in the cottage style, with only one floor, elevated a few feet from the ground; just affording sufficient room for a snug and cool cellar, where the good inmates store their generous wines. These houses contain a spacious hall, (the principal room in a West Indian house, occupying about two-thirds of the whole dwelling, and where meals are taken,) a parlour, or drawing-room, generally opening with folding-doors into the first-named apartment, a small morning room, four or five bedrooms, and the remainder of the building is divided into butler's pantry, larders, and a kind of lobby, where the numerous domestics assemble, and when not actually engaged in waiting at table, or ministering to their own ungovernable appetites, stretch themselves along the floor in all the luxuriance of idleness. The kitchens are detached from the house, for the purpose of evading the heat and smoke from the wood fires; and contiguous to them are a long line of "negro rooms," (as they term the apartments in this country intended for the use of the domestics,) stables, and coach-houses, interspersed with "stock" houses for poultry, and pens for the accommodation of those unseemly animals vulgarly called hogs.

These country residences are seldom devoid of company, who, in parties of three or four, leave the confinement of the town for the advantage of the purer air. The days are spent much after the same fashion. Between the hours of five and six in the morning, a tap comes at your chamber-door, and a black-visaged smiling damsel enters with shoeless feet, and grinning lips shewing their two rows of ivory, and with the accustomed "mornin', missis," presents you with a cup of delicious coffee. The morning's costume arranged with due precision, you quit your chamber, and passing through the "hall," where two or three black servant boys are spreading the snowy damask, and otherwise preparing for the plentiful breakfast, you gain the drawing-room. Stepping through its open windows or doors, you find yourself in a covered gallery, amid, perhaps, a group of children and their nurses, busily employed in various little infantile amusements. Upon the appearance of "the lady" these, however, are immediately postponed, as each miniature man or woman comes forward with native courtesy and outstretched hand, and offers the usual compliments.

A grateful breeze greets your cheek with its bland whisperings; and the early sunbeams, devoid of their intense meridian heat, glisten on the dew-besprinkled leaves, or dance in the ripples of the neighbouring ponds. If the property should be a sugar estate, and it is the season of harvest when you visit it, many a jocund laugh comes from the mill-door, where, under direction of the manager or overseer, the sails are unfurled and given to the wind; and with shout and creak, and cracking of whip, the sober oxen are dragging home cartloads of golden sugar-canes. Thus the time wears on;— at one moment watching the busy group at the mill-door, at another holding converse with the lovely skies, or following with dazzled glance, the rapid flittings of the honey-seeking fly-bird;[48] and anon poring over the pages of some spirit-stirring volume, or in occasional snatches of conversation with the hospitable hostess.

At length the master of the domain, in his snow-white dress, and broad-brimmed hat, returns from his morning ride around the property, and the other guests assemble; and as the bell rings for nine o'clock,[49] a black boy, with napkin on his arm, announces "*breck-fus* (breakfast) ready, ma'am," and a general movement takes place. The lady of the house, in her simple morning dress, presides at the head of her well-stocked table with a quiet gracefulness of manners, and amid a little racy talk and pleasant jest the meal proceeds. Tea and coffee, the light roll-like bread, roasted yams or potatoes, cutlets, ham, tongue, eggs, *caveached* fish,[50] and potted meats, are among the lists of excellences found at a West Indian breakfast, while fresh butter, (which is reckoned a rarity, and is very troublesome to procure, being churned in a bottle, by continually shaking it, and which is served up without the addition of any salt,) and tempting fruits, fresh gathered from the tree, with the purple bloom upon them, form the lighter delicacies of the repast.

The meal over, and finger-glasses handed round, the company quit the table, and assemble in the drawing-room in order to pass the morning. The gentlemen leave, on various cares intent—some ride to town, to pursue their customary avocations, while the master inspects the labours of his people, settles some magistracy business, or visits some other estates under his management. The ladies in the meantime settle themselves to various little womanly employments. There is the piano, the paint-box, and the embroidery-frame; a selection of periodicals, new works, (most of the genteel people are subscribers to the "Library Society,") or a *porte-feuille* of prints to look over; lively conversations of "home and home scenes," (all West Indians call England home,) promenades in the galleries or verandahs, or romps with the children to while away the hours.

About two o'clock the lunch-table is spread, when some of the gentlemen find time to be present, and more good things are partaken of. Pepper punch is brewed for "the lords of the creation;" Hock and Seltzer water introduced, and the delicious lemonade, made from the limes that moment gathered; and sparkling water from the peculiar porous jars, which keep it as cool as if drawn from the bottom of some gelid grot.

The flies are very troublesome in Antigua, particularly at those moments when meals are going forward, flying into the plates and dishes, and almost upon the very portions of food you are conveying to your mouth; indeed, in one instance, I observed one of these intruding little insects actually fly into a gentleman's mouth upon his opening it to utter some witty saying. To guard against these disagreeable associates in your repast, it is customary to have a black boy stand behind your chair, with a large green bough in his hand, with which he brushes backwards and forwards, in order to drive the intruders away. If the bough made use of be gathered from any aromatic shrub, it is particularly agreeable, as it throws a pleasing fragrance around, at the same time it raises a gentle breeze.

After lunch, your former amusements are resumed, until the sun loses a little of its intensity, when bonnets and shawls are called into requisition, and you stroll to the "boiling-house" to see the preparation of sugar-boiling going on, and taste the "sling," (the name given to the sugar when in its liquid state,) canter over the short turf on the back of some "Bucephalus," or wander through scenes of sylvan beauty, until the time arrives when it is necessary to repair to the house to dress for dinner.

Seven o'clock is the usual time appointed for "this momentous meal," a time better fitted for this warm climate than an earlier hour. The dinner generally consists of fish and soup, with the accompanying Champagne, followed by flesh and fowl, and concluded by pastry, game, (when in season,) butter, cheese, and shell-fish. Madeira and Sauterne are the wines generally used at dinner; and port, claret, cherry-brandy, and other liqueurs, with luscious Malmsey, are introduced with the dessert, which of course embraces the choicest of the West Indian fruits. Most of the higher families possess a good stock of silver and glass, and the table linen would please the most fastidious.

The gentlemen do not sit long at their wine, but join the ladies in the drawing-room, where tea and coffee soon make their appearance, and the evening is spent in music and conversation until the ornamental clock points to a late hour, when, family prayers over, you retire to your chamber, and under cover of a single sheet, repose in quietness, unless disturbed by an officious mosquito, which, *sans ceremonie*, has entered by a peep-hole in the "net" which surrounds the bed.

The houses of the coloured gentry are neatly and tastefully furnished. The hall contains its complement of dining-tables, side-boards, with their glittering burdens, butler's trays and stands, chairs, and sofas; wall-shades, hand-shades, suspension-lamps, and china tables—sometimes a book-case and writing-table, and a few prints in gilt frames. The drawing-room has its couches, lounging-chairs, and ottomans; its pianofortes, chiffoniers, and "what-nots;" loo and sofa tables; and all its little fancy embellishments of ornamental china, albums, and or-molu clocks. The floors are generally covered with oil-cloths of various patterns, which are found to answer better in this warm climate than carpeting; but the days when *mahogany floors* were rubbed with *orange juice* are long since passed, if they ever existed. I have never seen floors of more costly materials than "pitch pine," which certainly takes a good polish if rubbed, but which in that case are very disagreeable to walk over.

The marriages of the coloured people are more private than they used to be formerly—that is, among the genteel classes; the common people still drive about in borrowed gigs and phaetons, after the fashion already spoken of in the negro chapters. Some years ago, it was customary to marry by special licence, the ceremony being performed in the evening at their own dwellings. This practice has become extinct, and they are now married in their parish church. The favourite wedding-dress is blonde and white satin.

A great reformation has also taken place in their funerals. In former days, a wake used to be held by all classes on the night the demise took place; and on the following day, (the day of the funeral,) immense quanties of "dyer bread" and "biscuit cakes" (species of pastry) were made, enveloped in white paper, sealed with black wax, and handed round to the assembled guests, who often amounted to two or three hundred. Mulled wines, Port and Madeira sangaree, "mixed porter," (specified quantums of porter, water, sugar, and spice,) and different kinds of spirituous liquors, were also provided, sufficient to satisfy the thirst of Baron Munchausen's whale. If accounts be true, many of these funeral guests paid such particular attention to these several preparations from the vine and the hop, that they became greatly elated thereby, and not unfrequently left the *house of mourning* in a state of inebriety.

Every article of furniture in the house was covered with white, and many other fatiguing ceremonies observed; but these have long ago fallen into disuse, only the chamber of death shewing its white drapery. The corpse, if a male, is attired in his usual dress, with the exception of coat and shoes; over which is placed what is termed a *scarf*, made of the finest white muslin or lawn, crimped round the edges, and fastened round the waist by a broad band. The ends of this scarf are brought in folds to the feet, and terminated with bows and rosettes of the same material. A cambric muslin shroud, also crimped in a deep border, is first placed in the coffin; which, before the last sad office of screwing down the lid takes place, is carefully covered over the corpse, and shuts out from the glance of friends, the features which they have so often gazed on with pleasure. If the deceased is a female, an elegant white dress is chosen, with a white satin band around the waist, white silk gloves and stockings, and a blonde cap ornamented with white satin.

If the deceased were unmarried, the coffin is covered with fine white broad cloth, and elaborately ornamented with silver lace, nails, plates, and "little angels," (as the negroes term them;) if married, it is covered with black cloth and black ornaments. Crape hat-bands and scarfs are now given to the bearers, and hat-bands to the intimate acquaintance only, for if the deceased is much respected, three or four hundred persons of all colours attend the funeral. In the arrangement of the procession, (which is always a walking one,) an eye is kept to prejudice. Formerly all coloured persons had coloured bearers, then came a change; and two white and four coloured men officiated in those characters; then it came to be three white and three coloured, and in a late instance, four white and two coloured persons formed the complement.[51]

The common coloured people still keep "a wake" upon the death of their friends; and on such occasions, while one part of the company are engaged in singing psalms, the others are filling the women's hats with water, putting pepper into wine, pulling off their shoes, and playing other vulgar practical jokes, most irreverent and disgusting at such a season.

The Antiguans have a peculiar mode of calling articles by particular names:—thus, potatoes are invariably called *Irish potatoes*, come they from what part of the world they may; the common Prussian-blue pea, and wheat-flour, are always termed *English* peas, and *English* flour, although such articles may come from France or America; ducks are English ducks; *negus* is denominated *sangaree*, and spirits and water, *swizzle*.

This practice is illustrated by the following anecdote, related of a West Indian, who upon arriving for the first time at a London hotel, rang the bell for the waiter. Upon that necessary appendage to such an establishment making his appearance, the West Indian saluted him in the following Creole manner: "Boy! d'ye hear? give me a glass of *sangaree;* and let me have for dinner English ducks and Irish potatoes."

The waiter, not used to this specification of articles, was astounded; he passed his fingers musingly through his lanky locks, looked up to the ceiling, and down to his Warrenized shoes, minutely inspected the movement of a fly upon the gilded mirror, in hopes, no doubt, of deriving information from it, smoothed the *un*rumpled table-cover, and then being still utterly unable to comprehend the order, exclaimed, in a very lamentable tone, "I ham werry sorry, sir, but we have not got no ducks or potatoes but the *common ones*, and has for the *other thing* you *hordered*, we have none in the house just now."

There are several other peculiar modes of dialect observable among the Creoles. For instance: If an order is given to open or shut a window, it is, "Heave up that glass sash," or, "Haul down that glass sash;" when speaking of east and west, they invariably say *windward* and *leeward;* to throw a stone, is to *fire* a stone; if a person is fortunate enough to procure a good situation, it is immediately said, "He has got a *capital berth*," and their men-servants, of every age, are always termed *boys*.[52]

Soon after my arrival in this island, I happened to be present, one evening, when a gentleman was deploring an accident which had lately occurred. With my mind running upon "wounds and bruises," I inquired into the circumstances. "Why, that good-for-nothing *boy* of mine," was the rejoinder, "went to the pond this morning, and on bis way back, he *knocked down my horse*." I was certainly surprised at such an herculean feat, and began to think of Maximin, the Roman emperor, who, with one blow of his fist, could knock out a horse's tooth, or break its leg with a kick; but my wonder was considerably increased upon the entrance of the *boy* in question, for instead of his exhibiting any appearance of great strength, I found him to be, in reality, a decrepit old man. How this pilgrim of sixty summers could knock down an animal of such vast strength as a horse, I could not imagine —the mystery was more and more intricate—but at length, an elucidation was afforded, and I found out that instead of *the boy* knocking down the animal, the animal had knocked down him; or, in other words, the horse had fallen down with the poor old man upon his back.

My sketches of colour are completed. True it is, there are many other little peculiarities which might be noticed; but for the present I will bid the coloured classes "farewell," and turning over the page, mention a few of the "traits and trials" of the white inhabitants.

---

[46] This was not the only indignity offered. Mr. Gilbert was at that period the notary public, and when the news of his intended marriage got abroad, "the acting governor of Antigua wrote to the acting general governor of the Leeward Islands, resident at St. Christopher's, representing that he (Mr. G.) had so basely degraded himself as to be unworthy of that office." The governor-general thought so too; so the public whipper was sent to demand his notarial commission, and some unknown patriot removed the painted board, placed over his office, bearing the words, "John Gilbert, Notary Public," and threw it into the sea. Mr. Gilbert also held a commission in the militia; but so horrified were the officers of the corps to which he belonged, that one of them, in the name of the rest, waited upon Mr. Gilbert with the pleasing intelligence, "that they were determined to have no intercourse with him, and would apply for a court-martial to try

him, *for acting in a manner inconsistent with his rank and station, and the character of an officer, if he proceeded with this marriage.*" For peace' sake, Mr. Gilbert resigned his commission. When, according to "the universal practice in these islands," he applied for his marriage licence, he was refused; the "bans were therefore published in the church." It is almost needless to remark, that had he made the lady the object of an illicit intercourse, his conduct would have been thought nothing but proper by the white inhabitants of Antigua in those days!

[47] This circumstance occurred at a period when the clergymen officiating in Antigua were not of that exemplary character which distinguishes the generality of the present divines.

[48] The humming bird, or colibri.

[49] A bell is rang, a conch shell blown, or an old copper struck with a piece of stick, to notify the hour when the negroes leave their work, for the purpose of getting their morning meal; and this is the usual hour for partaking of that repast among all classes.

[50] Fish stewed with vinegar, limes, mace, pepper, onions, &c., and eaten cold.

[51] How often trifling matters like these speak a mighty change in the "spirit of the times!"

[52] Although these *provincialisms* happen to occur in this chapter, it is necessary to remark, that they are made use of by Creoles of every colour.

CHAPTER XLVII

Grades among the *pure in blood*—Aristocrats—The tribe *fungi*—An overseer's duty—Managers and attorneys—Pickings and gleanings—Managers' wives and managing ladies—Aristocratic shops—"My daughters"—Education—"Field days" of the militia—The Antiguan aide-de-camp.

As in commencing my chapter on colour, I deemed it necessary to mention the different grades and gradations among that olive-tinted race; so in writing upon the white population of Antigua, it will be first proper to remark, that there are two *distinct classes* to be found among them: the one born in the island, (but of course of European extraction,) and consequently termed Creoles;[53] the other, persons of both sexes, who have emigrated from England in search of wealth, or whose domestic ties, or government appointments, have caused them to leave the land of their birth, and made them, for a time at least, residents in this bonny little island.[54]

In these two classes, then, are to be found all the descendants of the fair-haired Saxons, from the president of the island, down to the low, ignorant, but proud, pauper—proud of his untarnished blood! who, in Antiguan vulgarism, is known by the appellation of "bottom-foot buckra." Of this last-mentioned class much may be said. Many and various are their "traits" of character, and arduous their "trials" to enable them to "keep up appearances." But perhaps it may appear more orthodox to scan over the peculiarities and "manners and customs" of the "tip-tops" first.

The head of Antiguan society is of course her majesty's representative —"His Excellency the Governor." Then comes the "President of the Island," who, in absence of the commander-in-chief, exercises his duties, and takes his place in society. After the president, the members of the council and house of assembly rank next among the grandees, all of whom, no doubt, are—

"Most potent, grave, and reverend signiors."

Then comes the "bench and the bar,"—the occupiers of pulpits, and the followers of Galen,—government officers, and the officers of her majesty's customs,—a few gallant sons of Mars from some of England's "wooden walls," who in cruising about these seas, pay Antigua an occasional visit,—officers from the stationed regiments,—and a long line of merchants, attorneys, managers, and nondescripts—and there the line is drawn. "These several gentry," with their wives and daughters, aunts, sisters, and cousins, constitute the first class among the white population, or more properly speaking, form the aristocracy of Antigua.

But it must be observed, these aristocrats, although forming one body, mixing in the same society, and equally looking upon themselves as *exclusives*, may yet be divided into two distinct classes—the one springing from a good old stock, the other comprehending the *self-elected* ones. I shall confine myself more particularly in this chapter to the latter class, as being better exemplifiers of the "ups and downs of life."

Now although the tribe *fungi*, of which the mushroom is a member, luxuriates better in a damp climate, than in one so excessively hot; yet some species of them may be met with in all parts of the world. I have often seen their long slender stalks, and pallid-looking caps extending the limits of the *vegetable world* in Antigua; and therefore it does not surprise me to find so many of the mushroom family among the animal creation in that part of the globe, obtruding their tall heads, even in the aristocratic circles of the community. Like their brethren among the vegetables, some of them grow upon the ground, and "derive their nourishment from the soil," while others "spring up on various substances, presented by nature or art."

The first of these two varieties of mushrooms are to be met with among the descendants of those poor white persons, who in former years came to Antigua to act, in the literal sense of the word, as "servants of servants," but whose offspring, by dint of petty traffickings and small gatherings, amassed a sufficient sum of money to make them forget their origin, and contemning their natural parents, look for some "Jupiter Ammon" to stand progenitor for them in their stead. The latter class are the wild branches of some sapless tree, who, with scarce a change of raiment in their wallets, or the clink of a coin in their purse, were shipped off to the West Indies to be killed or cured—reap dollars like thistles, or starve in the attempt.

By the "good luck," as it is termed, which sometimes attends such needy adventurers upon their arrival in this country, they obtained, perhaps, employment as overseers upon the different estates, (I am now speaking of the manner in which such affairs were conducted some years before emancipation, when the proprietors were obliged, by law, to maintain so many white servants to so many slaves,) where they were quickly installed into their duty. This consisted in calling over the names of the negroes before daylight of a morning, seeing them properly whipped, when such chastisement was deemed necessary, or perhaps whipping them, as the case might be; inspecting the labours of the gang of negroes in the field, who were cutting canes or preparing the land for planting; flying from thence to the mill-door, where some awkward "boatswain" had let the mill-tackling get wrong, (for which crime he was coolly ordered a dozen or two,) or, perchance, if it were a "cattle-mill" instead of a "windmill," a gang of mules had turned restive, or one unfortunate over-driven animal had dropped down dead, or else three or four of the wooden cogs of the mill were broken, and the cattle were obliged to be taken out until it should be mended. Then he had to visit the "rum-still," and overlook the process of distillation, taking down, upon a dirty piece of paper, the number of gallons of "high-wines," "rum," and "low-wines." From the "still" he marched to the "boiling-house," to inspect the making of sugar; and from thence to the "curing-house," to see the sugar "potted," (that is, packed in hogsheads, tierces, or barrels.) Then there were staves to be given out to the coopers, and boards to the carpenter, besides dispensing medicines to the sick slaves, and cane-tops to the hungry mules. And then, when all these multitudinous occupations were performed, and the different store-houses well secured, he proceeded to the "great house," and, after scrubbing his face with brown soap and a jack towel, smoothing, if possible, his straggling, sun-burnt locks, and exchanging his dirty white jacket for one of broad-cloth, or a coat whose cuffs and collar bore ample marks of time, he made his appearance in the dining-room or hall, where a high stool or an education chair was placed for him near his master, at whose old jokes and worn-out tales he felt obliged to laugh, while he indulged in such luxuries as fowls' necks and odd ends of pudding, washed down by a single glass of wine.

His labours were now over for the night, unless it were the sugar harvest, and then he was expected to return to the boiling-house, where, amid clouds of densest steam, he remained until twelve or one in the morning, and then, as the last copper was cooled down, he marched off the tired negroes, and, having well locked the door, quitted the furnace-like heat of the building to wend his weary way home in the cold night air.

During former days of slavery, it has often been the practice to carry on the boiling of sugar throughout the whole night. Upon such occasions, the poor overseer had to keep his place in the boiling-house, to see that the slaves attended to their duty. There is an anecdote told of a West Indian overseer which proves him to have been rather clever in the art of dissimulation. He was a man of reserved manners and of extreme taciturnity, seldom speaking to the negroes, unless, indeed, giving them a stroke or two from a rattan which, from custom, he carried in his hand, can be termed *speaking;* but he was a favourite with his employer, who thought him *watchful* as well as careful—two very necessary virtues in days of slavery. From some cause or the other, he had lost the sight of one of his eyes, but which disaster, from a latent spark of pride, he was very desirous of concealing. While in the "boiling-house" during the day, quietly seated in his cherry-tree chair, and narrowly watching the movements of the negroes, it was his custom to place his hand over the affected organ. But as evening came on, and "tired nature" craved repose, he altered his plan of operation, and covering his other eye, he allowed his rayless orb to glare "horribly stern" upon the toiling slaves, who, unconscious of his visual defect, and noting his movements, by which one of his eyes was ever apparently fixed upon them, exclaimed—"Eh! eh! war dis?—buckra oberseer cleber true; he make one yeye (eye) sleep while toder keep watch!"

To return to our overseer's duty. Perhaps some of my readers may be inclined to think this kind of life described not the most enviable, and their "good luck" in meeting with such a situation very illusory. Like, however, the solitary waste in the Eastern story of "Abdallah," this life of drudgery leads to riches. A few years over, and if the overseer is "smart" in his business, he gets promoted to "manager," marries, perhaps, his former master's daughter, or some other fair one, starts his horse and gig, purchases a dozen or two of wine, and a decent suit of clothes; and what with his salary, and the pickings and gleanings procured from off the property, he begins to make a show, and ventures to give a dinner-party to the "great people."

Another year or so, and if the island is blessed with fine and copious rains, and the estate makes a good crop in consequence, the proprietor in England experiences great delight, and by the return packet, despatches a commission, promoting our *ci-devant* overseer to the situation of attorney as well as manager. Now, in truth, he begins to raise his head, like other mushrooms after a shower of rain, and thinks himself a man of family. His gig is replaced by a rattling, shaking, tumble-down carriage, drawn by a pair of spavined horses, and further graced by a shoeless coachman, his head surmounted by a pitiful beaver, encircled by a gold or silver band, his only other article of livery consisting of a scarlet waistcoat, made perhaps from some cast-off militia uniform. A little meagre black boy, whose habiliments are upon a similar scale to the coachman's, serves the office of footman, and attends upon "the ladies" in their morning drive, with a grace and grimace most admirably seconded by the monkeys in the zoological gardens of London. Nor is the starting of this equipage all that marks the change; Mr. Attorney becomes more egotistical every day—his cellar receives a stock of champagne, (*or perry*,) and he cries, "Taste my wine—it is excellent, I do assure you. I cannot drink bad wine; I have never been used to it!" His larder becomes replenished with richer fare. "Try this turtle-soup," says he; "you'll find it superb—my cook is celebrated for his skill. I can tolerate nothing that is indifferent at *my table*." He procures a commission in the militia, and sets up for the house of assembly; and being elected, takes his place among that august body with a vast deal of dignity. He makes no long speeches, 'tis true; but, instead, shakes his head with an overpowering gravity, and insinuates, "I think the more," taking good care, however, to chime in with the strongest party.

His family becomes of some importance; his sons are intended for the bar, or the church; and one is destined to step into his own shoes. He next looks out for some poor damsel, who, to save herself from actual starvation, agrees to wear out her strength, and prostrate her talents in endeavouring to inculcate into the minds of his daughters the elementary branches of education for a sum your washerwoman would scorn to take.

Thus, as we have seen, the overseer rises to manager, the manager to attorney, and, like the worthless grub, when it puts on the butterfly's painted wings, and, soaring on the bland and beautiful zephyr, scorns his former race, who yet remain grovelling in the dust, and fancies itself of a higher creation; so the attorney, as he gains the pinnacle of his ambition, forgets his former lowly state and penniless pockets, and, with haughty brow and over weening pride, proclaims himself an aristocrat. How very fast mushrooms do spring up!

But it may be asked, "What salary does an attorney receive to enable him to keep up all this state of grandeur? surely it must be something handsome?" In answer, it must be remarked, that such affairs are not conducted in the West Indies as they are in England. This is the country for a poor man to make a display in—here he may run his carriage without fearing a visit from a tax-gatherer; or dress up his servant in livery without having to pay 1*l.* 4*s.* per annum. His wine costs him about 2*s.* sterling per bottle; claret, 1*s.*; and "real Cognac" can be obtained for 2*s.* 6*d.* Before emancipation, the attorney and manager employed as many of the slaves as suited them, in the capacity of domestic servants, which slaves were of course fed from the estate provision; then the attorney has one or two horses allowed him, and if he purchases any more from his private funds, the estate finds them in corn and grass; he keeps a flock of sheep, for which the property also stands caterer; and now and then his employer may forward him a hogshead of porter, or a pipe of Madeira, besides other little presents, consisting of barrels of beef, or pork, or any other little matters. Thus, in the end, his pomp and grandeur is kept up at a very moderate charge to his own pockets.

It cannot be supposed that I intend to assert, that the aristocracy of Antigua is wholly composed of the *fungi* tribe, or that all her planters are of the upstartish class it has pleased me to describe. Far from it; an attentive perusal of these pages will prove, on the contrary, that there are to be found among them families, whose genealogical tree bears many a goodly shoot— through whose veins runs a stream of England's richest blood: the names of Warner, Williams, Byam, Martin, Ottleys, with many others, have long stood pre-eminent in the annals of Antigua; while their descendants have kept up their high station in the society of the island.

But to return to the mushroom gentry. While they are travelling the high-road to preferment and honour, their wives are proceeding with railway speed in the paths of affectation and conceit. From the more useful occupations of washing their own clothes, and mending their own stockings, they now play the part of "my lady," and pass their time in lolling upon a sofa, with an open book before them, ready to take up should "company" arrive; or with wondering ears, listen to their daughters bungling through one of Mozart's waltzes, or stammering over a French fable.

Yet it is but proper to observe, all the "ladies" of this class of aristocrats do not spend their time in this indolent manner. No—far from it. Many of them have an eye to business amid all their grandeur, and keep, in a little tenement adapted to the purpose, a good stock of salt pork and salt fish; mackerels, herrings, and "alewives;"[55] corn-flour, tobacco, and candles; besides various articles of finery and coarse cloths, which they dispense to the negroes upon the neighbouring estates, at the very moderate profit of about 50 per cent.! Nor is this the sum-total of their industry; their yard is well supplied with poultry, their gardens with vegetables, if they lack flowers; and many a goodly-sized swine enriches their pigsties. When these last-mentioned quadrupeds have exchanged their Saxon for their Norman names, as "Wamba" observes, the lady of the house, on "notable thoughts intent," packs up their delicate "sides and quarters," and conveys them, or has them conveyed, to a snug corner of the carriage about to convey her honourable husband to the capital, to meet in "conclave grave" his noble compeers. After setting down their master at the door of the court-house, "Mr. John," the coachman, or "Mr. Thomas," the footman, draws these choice viands from their retreat; and while the owner of the defunct pigs is busy in making laws, or settling the affairs of nations, his servants are disposing of them to the best bidder, or laying in a store of bread in their stead. In the same manner, corn-fed mutton, poultry, eggs, and fresh butter, find their way to St. John's market; and, by the magician-like wand of commerce, return to our manager's managing lady, in the form of wine, tea, or loaf-sugar.

Of course, when these "ladies of distinction" draw on their mitts, and make their appearance in the drawing-room, the *shop* is banished from thoughts and conversation; and if not literature, at least topics of scandal, rank, and lineage, are discussed in its place. Some great-great-grandfather, who, from some freak of royalty has been dubbed knight, or else some imaginary kinsman, is called up from their long-forgotten tomb, to stand as a kind of foundation to their present greatness.

Their daughters are carefully instructed in all the various modes of setting forth their own charms, and of publishing their own exalted rank, by expressing their contempt for all beneath them. The scornful toss of the head, the disdainful curve of the upper-lip, the affected heave of the shoulders, the insolent stare, and the air of proud condescension, is studied with far more intenseness than their grammars or geographies. Meet them where you will, in the place of worship or the "public show," their manners are equally haughty; and their boasted pretension to superiority is even expressed in the very bending of their knees, when in acts of supposed adoration.

The more juvenile part of the community are, of course, debarred by their youth from keeping up with proper dignity their rank in life; but in the very nursery, the lessons of pride and affectation are engrafted, soon to become strong and flourishing shoots.

The days of extreme ignorance are certainly passed; the days when the young white Creole was left entirely to the care of their black, or low-coloured nurses, who imagined they could not better discharge their duty than by giving them their own way. The days when girls of fourteen could find no other amusement than, seated upon the floor, amid their negro attendants, to pass their time in eating "sling," or sucking sugar-canes, while their listless mothers lay stretched upon their couch, leaving their children to learn their alphabet as best they could. In later years, as before remarked, a poor English girl is generally procured to instruct them in the early branches of knowledge, curl their hair, and teach them their "steps," until the period arrives when their parents deem it necessary to send them to England, and place them at some suburban seminary. Here they are taught to sketch a landscape, complete a butterfly in Poonah painting, play some of the fashionable airs, with variations, upon a piano, speak Anglicised French, dance a quadrille, and perhaps embroider a footstool. Their education is then supposed to be completed, and they are re-shipped to the West Indies, to astonish "papa and mamma," play their part upon the theatre of life, and swell the ranks of the female *coterie*.

In the days when the militia was in being in Antigua, the ladies of these self-elected aristocrats, were very fond of alluding to the martial rank of their relatives, particularly in their visits to England—talking of "my husband, the colonel," "Capt. X———, my papa," or "Lieut. Z———, my brother." The gentlemen, many of them, were also very proud of wearing their uniform upon "field-day," which occurred once a month, and no doubt felt themselves, as they buckled on their glittering swords, like

"Hudibras, grow valorous." The governor, as commander of the force, was allowed by the militia laws an honorary staff, which consisted of six officers, who bore the local rank of lieutenant-colonels.

An anecdote is related of a gentleman of Antigua, who formed one of this *cortège*, and who was no little pleased with his high rank, and garnished shoulders. Business or pleasure called him to England, and he carried "home" with him his growing daughters to gather instruction, and his smart aide-de-camp's dress to reap applause. Arrived in London, and the fatigues of the voyage over, our aide-de-camp arrayed himself in his gay uniform, and hiring a carriage, drove with his daughters to a fashionable seminary. His card was sent in "Lieutenant-colonel ————" and the lady of the establishment met him with all possible grace, and bowed and courtesied to his inquiries with elegant obsequiousness. No references were of course asked for—no entrance money demanded: his gay apparel was a sufficient passport, and the gentle "*maitresse d'ecolé*" only thought herself too happy in acquiring the patronage of an officer of such high rank.

Time sped on, and the recess was at hand—the young ladies remained with their instructress during its period—the scholastic duties were again resumed, and another six months passed away. The various items swelled to a vast amount, yet no remittance came—no aide-de-camp made his appearance. A faintish tremour played around the lady's heart, and, unwillingly, she began to think of moneyless "soldiers of fortune." Letters were despatched to put the tardy sire in remembrance of his daughters' improvements in their various studies, and urge for a remuneration. But alas! like "sleep," at the call of our fourth "Henry," it came not; and in the end, the lady was only too happy to get rid of her fair charges without receiving any payment, resolving, however, in her mind, never to trust again a West Indian *aide-de-camp*.

———

[53] It is an erroneous opinion held by some English people, that only coloured persons are called *Creoles;* the word being, in its proper sense, applied to all who are born in the West Indies.

[54] These two classes are of coarse subdivided into many others, according to their different stages in society.

[55] A description of salted fish, brought from America.

CHAPTER XLVIII

The pure in blood—Aristocrats of the higher order—Law, physic, and divinity—Merchants and planters—Proprietors' dwellings—A day at a country-seat—Gastronomy—Beef—"Mary Swift"—Mutton—Pork—Turtle and City aldermen—Christmas.

Having, in the preceding chapter, glanced at the "rise and progress" of the *mushroom* part of the aristocracy, it may be deemed requisite for me to enlarge upon the merits of those members of that body who, to present high bearing, add the claim of good descent. And yet I know not what to say more than I have done already in many parts of these pages, that they are fully entitled to the respect they so universally meet with. For among them are to be found men of superior knowledge, and distinguished by the possession of all the cardinal virtues; men in whom dignity of station is blended with kindliness of heart, and who, amid the blessings wherewith Providence has blessed them, have an open purse, and an outstretched hand, ever ready to administer to the wants of their less fortunate brethren; men of agreeable manners and pleasing conversation, and whose intercourse with the polite circle in other parts of the world has corrected any little errors they might have imbibed from their West Indian mode of life, and divested them of that narrow-minded spirit so much to be deplored.

In this class of individuals are to be found the Creole proprietor, as well as those who may have purchased estates within these last few years, and, in consequence, emigrated from England, clergymen, barristers, and physicians, merchants and planters, the offspring of the soil itself, or wanderers from the several countries of England, Scotland, Ireland, and Wales.

I have already spoken of the worth of many of the clergymen; men who practise what they preach, and who, in their private as well as public life, shew forth, by the fruit they bear, that they are branches of the *true vine*. The barristers are generally considered men of distinguished abilities, and some of them plead with powerful eloquence. They also act as solicitors and attorneys; but they honour the profession too much to speculate in cargoes of horses or corn-meal, as some of their brothers of the profession are said to do in an island not seventy miles from Antigua. In that colony there is at the present day a firm, consisting of three parties, who, to their numerous duties of pleading before the bar, add the more primeval occupation of agriculturists, the partners taking it by turns to play the planter for the space of three years,[56] and so leaving Coke, Blackstone, and similar other worthies, study instead the art of *planting canes* and *boiling sugar.* How far their professional knowledge retains its vigour in the interim their several clients can best tell; I suppose they refrain from tasting the waters of Lethe, but pay daily orisons at the shrine of Mnemosyne. It must not be supposed that all the barristers of the island in question engage in such diversified occupations; many of them pay as much respect to their profession as their brethren of Antigua do, and among them are to be found some very clever men. One in particular is possessed of very superior qualifications, and his eloquent pleading would gain attention and merit applause even within the ancient walls of Westminster. His name is also known in the literary world, and his "Commentaries" upon the laws of his native island have no doubt often materially benefited his brother barristers. It is, of course, a work that would not call for general attention, from its local nature; but if once taken up, the author employs so many pleasing bands with which to bind his bundle of *law leaves* together, that the reader is irresistibly led to peruse it to the end.

To return to Antigua. Perhaps the most eminent member of the Antiguan bar is a Mr. James Scotland, who, although he does not often indulge in that flowery style of oratory which some of his brethren of the long robe do, speaks with powerful emphasis, and is grounded in all the mazy doctrines of the law. Mr. S. is a scion of a goodly stock. His ancestors emigrated from the mother country, and became settlers in Antigua, in which island they filled official situations at an early period, and where they have ever maintained a high character for philanthropy and liberal principles, even in days of prejudicial darkness. Such a line of conduct has often drawn down persecution upon the members of this family; but at length they have met with the reward of their unflinching perseverance in seeing that large portion of the Antiguan community whose interests they have ever supported, enjoying the privileges of British subjects, without regard to complexional prejudice.

The merchants are in most instances unexceptionable characters; the planters rank high in agricultural knowledge and respectability; and the physicians are, I believe, generally noted for their eminent skill. It must be remarked that in this last-named profession there are no gradations, all the medical men ranking as M.D., whether they have attained that degree or not; and so far is this custom carried by the illiterate, that the very black or coloured boys, who are generally employed to handle the pestle, also go by the title of "doctor;" nor is it an uncommon circumstance for these illegitimate sons of Galen to be called in to visit patients and perform those particular branches of surgery, phlebotomy and extracting of teeth. The first physician in Antigua is a Dr. F., a man of versatile and brilliant talents—an able logician, well versed in polite literature, of energetic manner, and, what is above all, possessed of deep, heart-felt philanthropy, based upon that golden maxim, "Do unto others as you would have others do unto you."

Some of the proprietors' dwellings, situated upon their several estates, in the most cultivated parts of the island, are mansions which would not disgrace the parks of our English country gentlemen. They, in most instances, are built upon gently swelling eminences, spots of extreme beauty; and the contrast they display between their dazzling white walls, and the deep verdure of their surrounding groves, over-canopied by a sky of intense blue, strikes pleasingly upon the eye; while the interior is fitted up in a style worthy the taste of the occupiers.

The approach to many of these edifices is by stately avenues of cedars, whose bright laurel-like leaves set off to advantage the bunches of delicate trumpet-shaped flowers. Others, again, have the carriage-road bordered by noble rows of cocoa-nuts or palmettos, whose long graceful branches bend to the breeze, which makes pleasing melody as it sighs among them. Their country-seats embrace prospects of inexpressible loveliness. Nothing of what is generally termed the sublime, it is true—no frowning precipices or gigantic mountains, whose hoary heads are ever hid in the clouds—no impetuous cataracts rushing down the face of wild and blackened rocks, and hiding at length their angry waters in some dreadful abyss; the scene is of a more quiet nature, one where there is such a rich harmony of colouring, such a blending of earth, and sea, and sky, (for from almost all parts of the island the ocean can be seen,) that as the eye gazes thereon, a pleasing calm comes over the beholder, and every discordant passion sinks to rest.[57]

In these mansions, a system of open but elegant hospitality is kept up; and like gentlemen's country-seats in England, they are seldom devoid of puissant knights and lovely damsels. The day passes as most days do in the country. Ample respect is paid to the well-stocked breakfast table, where every West Indian luxury abounds; and then the gentlemen separate to pursue their respective avocations; ride round their estates, and mark the progress of their canes, or as it is said, to hear them grow; visit the capital, to perform their legislative duties, pay their respects to his excellency the governor, or scan over accounts with their agents. The ladies, in the meantime, amuse themselves with various feminine and elegant employments; sometimes accompanying their soft voices upon the piano, or on well-strung harps, playing over those melting ditties which once brought tears into the eyes of the "gentle shepherd," or the matchless ploughman of Ayrshire. Others frequent the library, where the works of our best writers may be met with; but the spirit-stirring volumes of a Gore, a James, or incomparable "Boz," are much more eagerly sought after, than a Boyle, a Locke, or a Newton; but few of our West Indian ladies study philosophy or metaphysics; a novel, a poem, a book of plays, or modern travels, are the highest steps they take in literature.

At length comes the hour of luncheon, when other delicacies are produced, and duly indulged in; and then the duties of the toilet have to be attended to—a stray ringlet or a captivating dimple taken to task—a smile, a look, or an attitude studied, until the time arrives when a drive in the carriage, or a stroll through some pleasant vale, is practicable. After enjoying these exercises for some time, the dressing-room is once more sought, and beauty receives every assistance that art can give her, in direct opposition to the advice of the author of the "Seasons."

About seven, the whole party assemble around the dinner-table, where luxurious fare and choice wines receive additional *gusto* from a profusion of handsome plate, rich glass, snowy table-linen, and a well-lighted apartment. I cannot in this place, pass over the head of all West Indian confectionary, a *floating island*, without further mention. Could I give an authentic recipe for the making of it, my patriotic spirit would lead me immediately to do so; but as that is not in my power, I can only say it is compounded of cream, sugar, guava jelly, and citron, and is of all sweets the very sweetest. Despite what Baron Munchausen says to the contrary, I could, were all floating islands like it, willingly live upon them; and consequently, his strenuous exertions in driving stakes through them, to render them stationary, as of erst he says he did St. Christopher's, would meet with no thanks from me.

Dr. Johnson has remarked that the hour of dinner is the most important of the twenty-four; be it so; like all other important, as well as unimportant matters, time at length brings it to a close. The drawing-room is once more sought, and in lively conversation, or listening to soft strains of music, which our lamented *Mrs. Hemans* has so beautifully eulogized, the evening passes away, or is closed in with a sprightly quadrille.

All West Indians of the higher rank keep a good table; indeed, the custom has become proverbial. Not only does the island contribute its fish, flesh, and fowl, but France and England pay a tribute in the shape of potted meats and soup. The native beef, it must be allowed, is horrible—lean, tough, and sinewy, it requires all your masticatory powers to demolish it, and proves not a bad illustration of the conundrum, "*If* tough beef-steaks could speak, what English poet would they name?" "Chaw-sir," (Chaucer.) Some West Indians, however, have asserted that they do not like English beef, it is so "fat and tender!" so much for custom. But the indifferent quality of the Creole beef is easily accounted for, when the state of the animal before it is killed is considered. The cattle bred upon the island, although very small, are used instead of horses in agricultural labour, and are of consequence of great value to the planter. They therefore seldom think of killing them while it is possible for them to be put to the plough, or worked in the cart; but when the planter finds that they are utterly unfit for work, and that death will soon put an end to their toil, or when a cow has become so old and emaciated as to be unable to rear her calves, they make a virtue of necessity, and give them up to the care of one of the old men or women, who feed them about the estate for a few weeks, and occasionally give them a little corn-meal to fatten them, and then sell them to the butcher.

I have seen some of these *antediluvian* creatures, if I may be allowed to use that term, coming into the capital, particularly about Christmas, lame and blind, faltering at every step they made, that it has been a matter of surprise to me how they were able to reach the shambles; but, poor creatures! there they arrive, sooner or later, are quickly despatched, and, about seven o'clock the next morning, you may hear the bellman hallooing out—"Oyes! oyes! a fine fat ox, bery fat, indeed, to be had at the shambles of Mary Swift," of famed renown! who, in person, amply makes up in longitude what she loses in latitude. I cannot help remarking, in this place, how much more humane the mode of killing these animals, practised in Antigua, appears than that customary in England. Here are no horrible slaughter-houses, still reeking with the blood of those slain before, to harass the poor animal's sense of smelling, and call for the assistance of those cruel ropes to pull it in; neither is the dire mallet used, which often requires so many strokes before life is extinct. A little grass is scattered down beneath the shade of some spreading tree, to which the creature is tied, and as it bends its head, the butcher, with a sharp knife, separates the spinal marrow between the horns, and death is instant.

The mutton introduced at the table of the gentry is super-excellent— small, tender, and not too fat; something like the Welsh mutton so justly esteemed by the opulent in England. It is generally fed upon the Indian-corn, and gentlemen kill for their own use. That procured at the shambles is generally very indifferent, and not unfrequently goat mutton. Pork is another viand admitted at times to enlarge the table-store. It is considered by some to be the first meat in the West Indies; this, however, I cannot accede to; the warmth of the climate is against it, and makes it appear unseasonable. Goldsmith, in his "Manners and Customs," mentions that pigs in the West Indies were always fed upon sugar-canes. I have made inquiries upon this *important* subject, and from the answers received, and my own observations, am inclined to think that the family of grunters are forced to be content with less luscious fare. Upon estates, when grinding, they may, perhaps, get a share of what is termed the *mill-bed*, but that is all the production of the cane they are allowed to participate in, unless they march into a cane-field of their own accord, and stand a chance of getting shot or stuck for their pains, for a watchman is ever looking out for such intruders, to whom he plays the executioner's part, and, after decollating, takes, by right of law, the head for his own share.

Poultry is also a standing dish at a West Indian dinner. Before emancipation, all kinds of feathered stock were very plentiful, and very cheap; fowls could be purchased for from 6*d.* to 8*s.* each, and turkeys, geese, guinea-birds, and ducks, in the same proportion; but now it is different, the negroes requiring higher prices for them. Most country gentlemen have, however, a poultry-yard attached to their residence, and thus escape the necessity of having to send, perhaps, half over the island before their want can be supplied.

Rabbits and pigeons are occasionally added to the luxuries of the Creole banquet; and venison finds its way from the neighbouring island of Barbuda. Several very excellent kinds of fish, the produce both of sea and fresh water, and shell-fish, allure the eye of the epicure; and last, *not least,* the delicious turtle, which at certain seasons is vended weekly at 9*d.* sterling per pound! with all its rich green fat, its white and yellow eggs! What would a city alderman say to this? would not his imagination revel in all the delights of *calipash* and *calipee,* and *real* turtle soup? not made of beef and calf's head, with a few pieces of turtle floating in it, to *stand its god-father,* as a late gastronomic writer so aptly describes such soup as may be obtained at the "London Tavern," or Cornhill, although that is reckoned very excellent in its way. We are very soon to have the steam ships running, or rather galloping, between England and these islands; and I really think it would well repay that very honourable body the "lord mayor, the sheriffs, and aldermen of London," to take a trip, if it was only to partake of turtle in perfection, and quaff a glass of Madeira, mellowed beneath this burning sun.

Although hospitality is ever practised in Antigua, Christmas is the season of the year when conviviality is at its height. Then relatives meet together from all parts of the island,—then friendly compacts are renewed, and family differences happily adjusted, and sweet Concord, with beaming smile, wreaths once more her golden chain. Although no glittering green mistletoe, that "holy bough," hangs pendant from the ceiling, and calls the attention of flashing eyes to its mystic berries, the fragrant pimento adorns the halls of the rich, as well as the cottages of the poor, while the laugh and song and

"Mirth-moving jest,"

throw around their pleasing witcheries. The tables groan beneath their burdens; and among their goodly fare may be found, as the old Christmas carol expresses it—

"Plum-pudding, goose, capon, minced pies, and roast beef."

---

[56] The estate belongs to "the firm."

[57] The principal of these country residences are—"Claremont," the seat of the Hon. R. E. Williams; "Cedar Hill," the seat of the Hon. Wm. Byam, both of them truly paternal looking edifices; "Gilbert," the seat of the Rev. Nat. Gilbert; "Mount Joshua," the seat of the Hon. Bertie E. Jarvis; Green Castle, the seat of Sir H. Martin, &c.

CHAPTER XLIX

The pure in blood—Places of amusement—The theatre—"Romeo Coates"—Jugglers and rope-dancers—Maroon parties—Shooting season—The Creole beauties—Dress—"The lords of the creation"—Fops and foppery—Business hours—Scene at the Antigua post-office—Auction sales —Militia doings—The gallant dragoon—Guard-nights.

There are but few places of public amusement in Antigua; no malls, or parks, or Kensington gardens,—no morning concerts, Colosseums, or exhibition-rooms,—no "Almacks" of an evening,[58] or box at the opera, where the Creole beauty may shew forth her charms with *eclât*. The Antiguan *belle* has to trust to fortune to bring her admirers;

"Unknowingly she strikes, and kills by chance,"

as Dryden expresses it.

A few years ago, however, there was a theatre in Antigua,[52] which now and then was frequented by a straggling company of players, who, in their trips about the West Indies, called in at Antigua to delight and surprise the inhabitants with their dramatic lore. Then "Macbeth" grasped his gory dagger,—"Hamlet" stalked about in sable suit,—"Othello" raved, or "Jaffier" stormed,—then poor "Juliet" wept, or "Desdemona" prayed, and many other heroes and heroines of the stage "mouth'd" and "saw'd the air," with all the grace that strolling players are noted for. Their ranks augmented by some gentlemen amateur performers of Antigua, who, not content with entering the lists as knights of the "buskin and sock," like Hercules, put on the *petticoats*, to shew, I suppose, their diversity of talents. Much cannot be said for the performance upon these occasions. One gentleman, in his metamorphosis, forgot to divest himself of his "Wellington boots," and there was such a clattering and stamping about with him, when playing the part of the waiting woman, that I verily believed the boards were in danger.

The well-known and eccentric "Romeo Coates," as he is generally called in London, is a native of Antigua; and many and oft have been the nights, when he has made his bow before an Antiguan audience, and trusting in his histrionic powers, claimed the chaplet which Fame has woven for stage-struck heroes. The playhouse has, however, been levelled with the ground; and its site is now occupied by a very respectable private dwelling-house, in place of the shabby temple, formerly appropriated to the tragic and comic muse.

Although the theatre is "no more," Antigua is not always devoid of public exhibitions. A juggler, or a rope-dancer, now and then makes his appearance, and having procured an empty store or loft, throws his body into ten thousand different contortions, for the amusement of those who feel inclined to throw in their dollars. At other times, a dwarf, or an "infant phenomenon," do their best to call a smile into the face of their audience; or a ship-load of *yankees*, with their stud of horses, and an "incomparable female rider," as their play-bills have it, erect their marquee upon the barrack-ground, and for the small remuneration of a dollar, spring over the moon almost, or act the part of a spitted ox, dressed by the heat of fire-works.

During the absence of these "professional characters," the Antiguans have other methods for getting rid of the time that hangs too heavy upon their hands. Now and then a *maroon party*, or West Indian *fête champetre*, is given; when groups of beautiful girls and gallant youths, stayed matrons, and gentlemen of riper years, assemble together, with full purpose to enjoy the passing hours. Some sweet spot, generally near the sea-side, is chosen for the day's resort; or else some

"—— green and silent spot amid the hills,
A small and silent dell."

And beneath the shade of some far-spreading trees, whose boughs form natural arcades, their rural banquet is spread. Various pastoral sports are here enjoyed; and although no "Weippert's band" is in attendance, the sound of the lively violin, or soft-breathing flute, often floats across the blue waters, and mingles with the murmur of the playful wavelets.

At different periods of the year, fancy sales are held in the court-house, when all classes congregate together, from the governor's lady, to the lady of the agricultural labourer. These, with balls at government house, now and then, and occasional quadrille parties at private houses, Bible and missionary meetings, and rides and drives in the afternoons, or walks by moonlight, constitute the chief *amusements* of the Creole beauties.

The gentlemen vary these pastimes with occasional regattas and races, a day's rabbit-shooting upon Long Island, or, in the season, they deal destruction with their murderous guns upon the poor winged tribe, who pay us annual visits. The shooting season commences about September, when plovers, teals, and wild ducks migrate from America to these islands, although the quail remains with us throughout the year. There are game-laws now in force in Antigua, and consequently, every sportsman has to take out a licence, before he is at liberty to endanger the lives of the birds, or may be, the safety of the queen's subjects. Some few years ago, this was not the case; and whoever felt inclined, went out shooting. Cobblers, tailors, butcher-boys, and carpenters, were immediately metamorphosed into gentlemen, and gun-in-hand, shot-belt and powder-flask slung round them, left the trammels of the shop and the work-bench, to wage war against the feathered race.

Many of the white Creole girls are very beautiful. Their complexions may vie with the purest Parian marble; while the softest, most delicate rose-tint mantles in their cheeks, and every blue vein can be traced, as it courses through their polished foreheads. The long glossy ringlet, the drooping eyelash, and the penciled brow, relieve, while they set off, their natural white; and the little coral lip, and pearly teeth, make up a *tout ensemble*, more lovely than can be told. Beauty has ofttimes been compared to flowers, and when looking at some of these lovely Creoles, they bring to mind that sweet and elegant rose, known in England as "the maiden's blush." In person they are generally *petite*, and their hands and feet are faultless as regards shape or size. Canova might have chosen them as a model for his Venus. What a pity it is, that extreme affectation should, in so many instances, spoil their manners, and deteriorate from their natural charms. Dress is carried to a great extent. Every pew in the church looks as gay as a box at the opera. Such feathers and flowers, mantelets and cloaks; such *capotes* of *tulle*, and cardinal pelerines; such corsages *à la vierge*, and skirts *à la Corinne*—crispins of lace, and I know not what besides, are exhibited by the Antiguan belles, as would surprise any one who is not well versed in all the changes of the arbitrary rule of fashion.

From a glance at the ladies it is but right I should turn to the "lords of the creation," and remark a few of their peculiarities. In a small community like Antigua, it is not to be supposed there are to be met such extreme contrast in dress and appearance as in the crowded streets of London—and yet some of the gentlemen emulate the "fops" of Regent-street, while others, again, are so *outré* in appearance, that we involuntarily exclaim, "From what habitable part of the globe could this creature have sprung?" As is generally the case, the younger gentlemen are those who enlist under the banners of "foppery;" and then there is such a display of exquisitely-fitting coats, brilliant satin waistcoats, and voluminous stocks, or reversed collars and cuffs, and throats *à la Byron;* such pointed boots and pumps, clerical-looking hats, and elegant canes! with wasp-like waists, flowing locks, and languishing manners, that had Adonis lived in these days and seen the Antiguan beaux, he would, most undoubtedly, have despised his own inartificial charms, and have cried with King Richard—

"I'll be at charges for a *looking-glass*
And entertain a score or two of tailors
To study fashions to adorn my body."

The gentlemen of more advanced years very generally patronize the blue-coat-and- white-waistcoat school, and some of them follow the almost obsolete custom of powdering the hair; but white is the prevailing morning-dress among all classes and all ages, a dress of all others best suited to this warm climate.

As bright Hyperion takes from the Creole maidens the *glowing* tints for which England's daughters are so famed, so he thinks it but fair to play many pranks with the complexions of the gentlemen who own his much-loved and frequented island as their home. Some he renders so pale and wan, that they appear like gliding spectres; others are as fiery red as the old English country market-women's cloaks with which they enwrap themselves when Winter holds his despotic reign; while some, again, present the deeper tinge of a full-blown peony; when to these latter shades are added the silvery honours of old age, the *tout ensemble* is most striking.

The hours of business in Antigua are from about six in the morning to four in the afternoon; after that period, the lawyer leaves his musty books and all his *pros* and *cons;* the merchant quits his counting-house, his day-book, and his ledger; the dealer in fashions and furbelows shuts his varied store; even the professors of the lancet abandon, for a time, the *cure* of the *incurables;* and away they all hurry, on "pleasure bent," to enjoy the exercise of riding, driving, or walking, until the day draws to a close, and their watches point the hour of dinner.

Many circumstances, however, occur during these "business hours" which calls for the presence of the trader as well as the professional man. The packet from England is signalized, and away they scamper to the post-office, almost before the mails are landed, to the utter consternation of the poor post-master, and, with anxious eyes and clamorous tongues, crowd the office-door. At length, two or three burly sailors, followed by the commander of the packet, a lieutenant in the navy, are seen approaching the spot, bearing upon their broad-built shoulders the long-looked-for mail-bags, well secured in their leathern envelops. The pushing and jostling increases, as gig after gig dashes up and sets down its several passengers—horsemen curvet about, at which lank and miserable-looking dogs bark, servant-boys grin and chatter—and a group of little children, just dismissed from one of the free schools, stand gazing thereon, and wondering "war make dem buckra care so much 'bout letter?"

Oh, what a *hurly burly* it is! what a noise and discord! what a pushing, and scrambling, and puffing, and panting! At length, the door is opened, and the postmaster announces, in not very dulcet tones, "the letters will not be out for two hours," and closes the portal again. A look of dismay and vexation overspreads the countenance of all. The first turns to his neighbour, and he, in *his turn*, looks to the one behind him; one mutters, "How provoking!" and another says, "I hate to be served so!" while one of the applicants, a melancholy-looking man, observes, in an important voice, "The letters *must be sorted*, you know." As no good can be effected by waiting, they finally disperse, and endeavour to while away the time until, the two hours having elapsed, they again besiege the office. A well-applied rap summons the postmaster. "Are the letters out?"—"No, they will not be out for another hour!" Time, however, brings many things to pass, and the letters are at length sorted. Happy now does that individual feel himself whose name begins with an "A"—for they always conduct this business alphabetically. A silence ensues, the letters are distributed, and, too anxious to know their contents, their several receivers open them upon the spot.

Various is the intelligence received, as seal after seal is broken—manifold the subjects discussed. Some talk of failures of mercantile houses, others of legacies received or in prospect; some descant upon politics, and others upon the price of sugars; while another group peruse the London newspapers, inspect carefully the list of births, deaths, marriages, and *bankruptcies*, look to see what the Queen and the court are doing, and then go forth to publish the "varied accidents by flood and field."

Another figure emerges from the office-door. A fine portly-looking man, whose complexion rivals in colour the *château margaux* he so liberally indulges in: a pair of gold-rimmed spectacles surmounts his well-formed nose, a substantial-looking umbrella is stuck beneath his arm, while in one hand is borne an open letter, and in the other, a voluminous silk handkerchief, and a gold snuff-box almost large enough to play the part of a portmanteau. "Not bad, though," he mutters to himself, as he carefully looks out for the lapses in the stone platform which runs along the front of the post-office—"not bad, though; my last ten hogsheads brought 78*s*. per cwt.; and my agent tells me the sugar was not so good as the former shipment, or he should have got higher prices. I must look to what my manager is doing; he must exert himself more, or he and I must part. Ay—rain again!" and he inspects the movements of the clouds, and glances for a moment at the vane upon the church-steeple visible above the surrounding houses. "Well, let me get home first, and it may rain as long as it likes—all the better for my canes." So saying, he gains his "top-gig," and carefully stepping in, and placing his umbrella between his knees, he tells "John" to gather up the reins, and make haste home. This is a resident proprietor of a sugar-estate, a man with whom the world has long dealt well.

Another event that makes an inroad into business-hours, is the occurrence of an auction-sale. When a gentleman or his family intends paying a visit to England, one of their first preparations is to "call an auction," and sell off all their household furniture, carriages, and horses. Upon these occasions, they print no compendious catalogues, as is the custom in England; but an advertisement is inserted in the island weekly papers, calling the attention of individuals to the fact, that

"The subscriber being about to proceed to England by the first opportunity, will dispose of all his fashionable household furniture, lately imported, consisting of,
HANDSOME FRENCH POLISHED MAHOGANY SIDEBOARD,
Dining, Loo, Card, and other tables, Glass, &c.
Also, a few choice articles of plate and plated goods; also, an English-built Phaeton and Pair of Horses and
A FLOCK OF SHEEP.

Y. Z."

Now, this last announcement is but very seldom true. But as Mr. Robins, of well-known auctioneering celebrity, calls to his aid all the high sounding words and flaunting descriptions he can get, to ensure company at his rooms, so the Antiguan auctioneer, or *vendue-master*, as one of the craft calls himself, throws out all the sprats he can in hopes of catching whales. The country managers and overseers are often good purchasers; and to ensure their company, the bait of a *flock of sheep* is held out, which has more effect in bringing them to the scene of action than anything else. "I have no sheep," observed a gentleman one day to an auctioneer he had employed. "Why do you put such notice into the papers?"—"Oh! I know you have not," quoth the knight of the hammer; "but it makes the advertisement look so much better, and draws the attention of the planters—they all like to come when sheep are to be sold."

Upon the day of this important undertaking, a red flag is hoisted before the house, and the bellman perambulates the streets, announcing that "the sale is just begun." Carpets are not taken up, and beds taken down, mirrors torn from their resting-places, and pots and pans brought into the drawing-room, as is often the case in England; but everything remains in its usual situation, only, perhaps, with a rather stricter eye to order than is practised in common; and the auctioneer proceeds from one apartment to the other, until the whole of the articles are disposed of.

The company assemble about twelve o'clock, and the first lots, consisting of glass-ware, china ornaments, or similar little *knick-nacks*, are knocked down *very cheap*. Sangaree is then handed about; and as its potent influence becomes apparent, the heavier articles are brought forward, and often obtain high prices.

As another means of ensuring good company and biddings, a kind of lunch is provided; and then there is such a cutting-up of hams, tongues, and salt-beef: such a calling for sangaree, punch, "swizzle," and porter; such a laughing, choking, talking, and eating, that a poor quiet body is glad to get into a corner, and offer up a prayer for silence.

It is not always, be it remarked, that "the subscriber is going to England," although such intimation heads the advertisement that occasions these "auction sales," for very frequently they are nothing more than an Antiguan scheme for "*raising the wind.*"

Previous to the abolition of the militia, field-days and reviews often occurred, to abstract attention from business. Upon such occasions, the gentlemen took great pride in exhibiting their epaulettes and garnished coats.

In proof of this assertion, I need but relate the following anecdote. A resident of Antigua, who, in days of militia glory, served in the dragoons, went to a neighbouring island, of which he was a native, to pay a visit to his friends. In order to astonish the inhabitants, and create a "sensation," Mr. —— determined to land in full uniform. The dress of the dragoons was very smart, and the swords and steel scabbards they carried, very long and heavy. Fancy, then, our brave *militaire*, who, by the bye, is a very short and corpulent personage, with a redundancy of colour, landing upon a sandy beach, beneath a burning sun, in all the glory of blue cloth and yellow worsted, with his Goliah-like weapon, scarcely twelve inches shorter than himself, dangling, or rather dragging, gracefully by his side. Although of little stature, he is big of heart; and proudly erecting his head, and settling his shoulders, he marched along, amid a herd of astonished boatmen and sea-side loiterers, with all the dignity of a commander-in-chief. The news spread like wild fire—astonishment was at its height—for rich and poor, black, white, and coloured, all thought their *ci-devant* neighbour was Fortune's child, and had been promoted governor of his native island. Before, however, any procession could be formed, or salute fired to welcome his arrival, his real rank was discovered; and as the truth became known, the assembled multitude one after another departed, and left our gallant dragoon "alone in his glory."

In speaking of the militia, I am reminded that I have not yet mentioned the Christmas guards. Before the emancipation of the negroes in 1834, martial law was put in force upon the 24th of December, and continued during the three following days, which, by law, constituted the Christmas holidays; and a militia guard stationed at the guard-house in St. John's, in order to protect the arsenal from any attack which might be made upon it by the slaves, who were more at their leisure during that period than at any other part of the year.

At such times, the whole body of the militia appeared in their tinselled jackets, and the churches and chapels presented such an array of glittering steel, and burnished epaulettes, blue and gold, and red and silver, that the pews looked like beds of ranunculi. When the guard for the night was comfortably fixed in the guard-house, a complete scene of dissipation ensued. Wine, cards, and dice, were liberally indulged in; and not unfrequently, mirth and festivity paved the way for sorrow, care, and quarrels. Upon one of these guard-nights, a wealthy German, since deceased, met with such a run of ill luck at the gaming-table, that the next morning he was obliged to hire porters, and despatch the dollars he had lost to the house of his adversary in *wheel-barrows!* That was, however, in a time when dollars were more plentiful in Antigua than they are at the present day, and when doubloons were in such abundance, that, it is said, the possessors of these costly coins found it necessary to deposit them in barrels! But, alas for the bonny little isle! that golden age has long ago passed by, and in its place we have one of copper and paper money.

Before concluding this part of my work, I contemplated to enlarge upon the "traits and trials" of that portion of the Antiguan community, who, in absence of other qualifications, rest all their claims to superiority upon the reputation of their being *white people.* As these sketches, however, have been already lengthened more than at first intended, but a very brief mention of this class of individuals can be given.

I would not for one moment have it supposed that I am so heartless as to upbraid them with their poverty—far be it from me to hint at such a thing—no; it is their pride, their overweening pride, I notice, and their hard struggles to ape *the ton,* while at the same time they condescend to receive the parish allowance, which ought really to be applied to the benefit of those who possess humbler minds. The "son of Sirach" in his wisdom, saith—"Three sorts of men my soul hateth, and I am greatly offended at their lives;" and first among the trio he mentions, "a poor man that is proud." Now, without making use of such a strong expression as *hatred,* who can help noticing the fulsome attempts of these persons to appear greater than they are? while their wives and daughters, instead of dressing as becomes their station, and thus rendering themselves respected, figure away in rainbow-coloured gowns, and bonnets that would better suit a strolling player, and then falsely think they merit reward! Some few years ago, about the smartest ladies in the Episcopal congregation were receiving parochial aid; but upon its being officially notified that the names of all paupers would be published, many of these dashing damsels became alarmed, and resolved rather to depend upon their own unaided exertions than let the world know how they procured their ribbons and laces.

But there is another class of white persons, who, although not dependent upon parochial relief, dress and act equally beyond their sphere in life. In illustration of this—A lady brings to Antigua an English servant-girl, and before her mistress can collect her scattered thoughts, after all the rolling and bounding, pitching and jumping of the vessel in which she took passage from Old England, the *femme de chambre* is turned into the fine lady; and ere, perhaps, six moons have waned, is united in the holy bands of wedlock with a *ci-devant* Irish soldier, who plays the part of a policeman; a lately-imported English ploughman; or, in lack of these, some red-faced overseer, who may stand in want of that somewhat necessary appendage—a wife. Servitude at an end, our fair lady makes a display of her dignity, and all the cast-off graces of her former mistress—wears very fashionable blonde caps, and long-skirted gowns—patronizes hysterics and *eau de Cologne*—and laves her previously hard-worked fingers with Rowland's Kalydor. Equipped in all her finery, she next makes her appearance at church, and when the service is over, bows and courtesies with self-approved grace to any other *white lady;* and then takes promenades with her fiery-faced husband, while visions of future grandeur and *invites* to Government House float through her brain.

If "her lord" should be an overseer, the estate upon which he is employed generally furnishes him with servants; but if instead, he is an ex-son of Mars, or some similar grade, our *lady* employs a black servant-girl of about eight years of age, to conduct her domestic affairs; while her husband obtains another specimen of juvenility, (but of course of an opposite sex,) to play the part of groom to the Canadian pony he has lately purchased for about four pounds sterling.

Although not *quite* so thick

"As autumnal leaves that strow the brooks
In Vallambrosa,"

still ladies and gentlemen of the grade above described are no *raræ aves* in Antigua; in all parts of the island they more or less abound, while in affectation and outward adornment they are not to be equalled among the *pure in blood.*

---

[58] In former years there was a subscription assembly held at "Smith's Tavern," then a noted house of entertainment, where cards and dancing were resorted to until twelve o'clock, when supper was introduced, and the festive party broke up about two in the morning.

[59] The first Antiguan theatre was established by a party of amateurs, and opened on 17th Jan. 1788, with Otway's play of "Venice Preserved." The orchestra was composed of the band of the 69th regiment, (then stationed upon the island,) conducted by Mr. Green, the late organist of St John's. The prices of admission were, two dollars to the boxes, and one and a half dollar to the pit; the funds being appropriated to the erection of a Free Mason's Lodge (never finished), the remains of which are to be seen at this day, at the east of the town.

CHAPTER L

Zoology—Rabbits—Rats—Horned cattle—Horses—Mules—Asses—Sheep—Goats—Domestic animals—Whales—Thrasher—Grampus—Porpoise—Shark—Anecdote of the Young Creole—Death of the sailor-boy—Remora—Pilot fish—Dolphins—Jew fish—Stingray—Corramou—Beautiful colours displayed in fish—Parrot fish.

In an island like Antigua, destitute of every wild animal of larger growth than a rabbit or a rat, it may be deemed risible to talk about its *zoology;* but as that word embraces a description of all living creatures, I intend to include under it the several doctrines of ichthyology, entomology, and ornithology.

Having mentioned rabbit and rats, I will reverse the general order pursued in writing upon subjects of natural history, and commence with a slight mention of those animals. The wild rabbit more particularly abounds in Long Island, a pretty and delightful spot, already mentioned as belonging to the Hon. Bertie E. Jarvis. Although rabbits sometimes form a dish at genteel tables, they are not generally esteemed in Antigua as an article of food. Many of the Creole negroes express the greatest antipathy to them, on account of their similitude to a cat; and to offer to them such a repast would, no doubt, be deemed an insult. I remember upon one occasion, hearing a woman inquire of a black carpenter, who was employed about our premises, if he would purchase from her a rabbit which she had in a basket. "Rabbit?" interrogated the artisan, his face wearing a most sardonic grin, "I should *jist* like to no war you take me for, ma'am? You tink me go buy *rabbit?* No, ma'am, me no cum to dat yet; for me always did say, an me always will say, dat dem who eat rabbit, eat *pussy,*[60] and dem eat pussy, eat rabbit. Get out wid you and your rabbit!"

The rats are a numerous race in Antigua, and feed most lusciously upon the sugar-cane, to the grief and loss of the planter. The present race are said to have been introduced into the West Indies by Sir Charles Price, in hopes of exterminating the Creole rat. The emigrants' tribe fulfilled their duty with great fidelity in this respect, and waged a vigorous war with their brothers of the *furry coat;* but while thus employed, they multiplied so fast themselves, that they overran the whole island, and proved a more troublesome and dangerous foe to the planters, than their predecessors. These quadrupeds are so fat and sleek, from feeding upon the juice of the sugar-cane, that some of the country negroes find them an object of value, and with addition of pepper and similar spiceries, prepare from them a delicate *fricassé,* not to be surpassed by a dish of French frogs!

The horned cattle of Antigua, as well as beasts of burden, and domestic animals, are all of Lilliputian dimensions. Agricultural labour is generally carried on by help of oxen, and upon this account, each plantation is provided with a large herd of these animals, whose patient drudgery often calls for an expression of sympathy. The horses bred upon the island are, in most instances, but a very sorry race; still there are some handsome Creole ponies to be met with, whose slender limbs and bright wild eye give them the appearance of "sons of the desert." The donkeys and mules are of diminutive sizes, but retain their asinary qualities in as great a degree as their patient brethren in the other parts of the world.

Sheep, like "Miss Cowslip," are as tall and slender as a poplar. Their wool falls off as they gain maturity, and is succeeded by short stiff hairs, like a goat. Many of them are so spotted and marked, that they might be taken for spaniel dogs, were it not for their length of legs, and *sheepish* visage. The sheep, however, at Long Island, are very deservedly admired. Their backs are of a deep warm brown colour, and the underneath part of the body, with the breast, feet, legs, and head, of a glossy coal black. Their eyes are also black, and very piercing, very much like the eyes of the stag; and as they raise their long necks, throw back their well-formed heads, and gaze earnestly at the stranger who intrudes upon their haunts, they display a higher degree of animation in their features than any of their species I ever saw.

Goats are also a numerous race in Antigua, almost every negro possessing one or more of these sure-footed creatures: their milk, as well as that of the sheep, is generally used for domestic purposes. Cats and dogs also degenerate greatly in size, and present as attenuated an appearance as if they had been keeping strict fasts and vigils for a month; the young puppies are sold for two shillings currency, and the cats are sometimes bartered between the negroes for a chicken: this last-named animal often forms an article of food to negro watchmen, who rear them especially for that purpose.

The lordly whale at times frequents the West Indian seas. These huge marine animals generally quit their hyperborean homes in the summer months, to take a trip along the eastern shores of North America, and passing through the West Indian Archipelago, return to their icy regions, where they enjoy, with redoubled pleasure, their unwieldy gambols amid the stupendous icebergs. In their passage between the several islands they often meet with various trials; at times they quit their right course, and flounder about in shallow water, until at length they are perhaps cast ashore, where they suffer an untimely and lingering death. One met this fate at Antigua a few years ago. It was driven upon an unfrequented part of the coast, where it must have remained for a long time, until at length the effluvia became so offensive that it attracted the attention of some negroes, who, going in search of the cause which so tainted the air, discovered the defunct whale. It was a very large one, measuring from sixty to seventy feet in length, and of about thirty feet in circumference; many of its bones were preserved by the curious as commemorative of the event.

But the greatest enemy the whale meets with in the tropic seas is the thrasher, (a species of squalus;) a fish so called from the manner in which it attacks its prey. As soon as the thrasher perceives the whale, he swims rapidly up to it, in a kind of orbit, until at length, when it approaches near enough, it compresses its tail, and by a great effort, throws itself out of the water and falls heavily upon the body of its unoffending victim. This exploit the thrasher performs again and again, until at length the whale (which very seldom escapes by speed) spouts up volumes of blood and water, and with one dreadful convulsion sighs out its last breath, and its immense carcase floats upon the ocean until some playful wave flings it upon the shore of some neighbouring island. In one of my trips from Antigua to Barbados I witnessed one of these conflicts, and although at a considerable distance from the place of battle, the blows sounded audibly in our ears.[61]

Among the other *Cetaceæ* which sometimes frequent the waters of the blue Caribbean, are the grampus and porpoise.[62] I have heard some master of the small trading vessels express great apprehension of grampus, who, they say, will at times approach so near a craft as to endanger its safety; but during my sojourn in these islands, however, I never heard of such a casualty taking place. A few years ago, an immense shoal of grampus were driven ashore at Antigua during a season of stormy weather, and by the oil they yielded, became a valuable prize.

But the greatest dread of the mariners in these seas is the shark—that rapacious and terrific monster whose very name conjures up a train of horrors. The usual length of the white shark is from 25 to 30 feet; the body oblong, and tapering to the tail, which is of a semiannular form, and of great strength; the head is rather flat upon the top; and the jaws, of horrific dimensions, are armed with numerous rows of flat, jagged, triangular teeth, (which it has the power of erecting at pleasure,) down to the very gullet.[63]

The eyes of the shark are large and prominent; and they appear to watch their hoped-for prey with the malign glance of an ogre; while their vision is so acute, that they can distinguish objects at an immense distance, and will brave any danger to procure booty with which to fill their ravenous maw. A circumstance occurred some years ago which evidently proves that the optics of a shark are anything but defective.

A young Creole one day escaped from the vigilance of her nurse, and, attracted by the numerous wild flowerets and gaudy butterflies she met with, rambled on, reckless of danger, until at length she approached the seaside. Here she watched for awhile the waves as they dashed their snowy foam over the pointed rocks which lined that part of the beach, until, impelled by the beauty of the scene, and the heat of the weather, she threw off her simple tropic dress and wended her way into the smiling waters. Although not more than six years old, from being accustomed to bathing, she had learnt to swim with agility; and gaily did she sport with the bounding billows, until her attention was arrested by a violent rushing of the waters, when, upon looking behind her, she saw, fast approaching, what instinct immediately told her must be a shark. It was but the thought of a moment to make for the land, upon whose confines she fortunately was; and urged on by fear, she gained the pointed rocks, followed by the rapacious monster. Springing from one to the other of these natural coast-guards, she at length reached the land in safety; while the greedy shark, fearful of losing its prey, and regardless of hazard, dashed after, until it became entangled in the intricacies of the beach, where it floundered about, unable to extricate itself, until a party of negroes (who had been working near the spot, and whose attention had been attracted by the cries of the child) came to the scene of action, and with ready good will despatched the encaged monster.

The shark is viviparous, and sometimes five hundred young ones, of about a foot in length, have found in the stomach of the mother. The mouth is placed so far beneath the snout, that the shark is obliged to turn upon its back to seize its prey. The fins are large and strong, which enables it to dart quickly through the water, while the huge dorsal one may often be seen above the surface of the sea for a long time together, marking the spot where the dreadful creature lurks beneath. The bays and harbours of Antigua abound with this voracious marine animal, and woe betide the unfortunate swimmer who approaches its lair.

On board the ship which first conveyed me to Antigua, was a remarkably fine and intelligent lad, "the only son of his mother, and she was a widow." He had been placed under the care of the captain of the ship, in order to gain some knowledge of the sea before sailing with his uncle, the master of a South Sea whaler. Robert had never quitted his fond parent before, and anxiously did he look forward to the end of his voyage, hoping that a letter from his mother would be awaiting his arrival at Antigua.[64] At length we gained our wished-for haven, and the passengers quitted the ship to seek their several places of destination. The packet had arrived, but there was no letter for poor Robert, who, with a disappointed heart, was obliged to wait the arrival of another mail. In the meantime, according to the rules of the merchant's service, he was employed along with the other lads in many little duties aboard the ship, until one fatal Saturday, as he was drawing a bucket of sea-water from over the ship's side, he overbalanced himself, and fell into the depths beneath. The steward, who was passing, raised an alarm; a boat was lowered, but without success, for he never rose to the surface. At length drags were procured, and (after an ineffectual search of some hours) his body was discovered, but the merciless sharks had made it their prey; the head, legs, and arms were gone, and his mutilated trunk alone reposes in the churchyard at St. John's. It was an untimely and dreadful death, so far from the land that gave him birth; and the circumstance was rendered more affecting, by the arrival of the packet the next day, bringing a letter for him from his mother, expressing her hope of her darling boy's quick return.

It is a general custom in St. John's when a horse dies to have it towed over the bar,[65] in order that it may be cast away in deep water. These defunct animals are very often made a bait for shark-fishing; but at times the sharks are so large and so greedy, that these would-be fishers are obliged to let go their bait in order to prevent their boat being overturned, and they themselves become the prey of the monsters. Young sharks are often exposed in the Antiguan markets for sale; and their flesh, stewed down with rice or "sweet potatoes," forms, among the negroes, a savoury supper.[66]

The common attendants upon the shark are the *remora*, or sucking-fish, and the pilot-fish, the former deriving its name from the firm manner in which it can adhere to any foreign substance. This adhesion is performed by means of a piece of hard thick skin, of an oval form, about five inches long and two broad, and which is attached to the head of the fish. This curious appendage is indented like the roof of a cat's mouth, and can be drawn up or expanded at pleasure. By these means the remora fixes itself so firmly to the back of the shark that no effort of that animal can dislodge it. Some naturalists are of opinion that the sucking-fish is the friend of the shark in directing its course and warning it of approaching danger, in the same way as the hermit-crab acts towards the pinna-marina. Others think this is a fable, and that, instead of befriending, it in time becomes the destroyer of the shark by draining its body of all moisture. I have heard seamen assert, who are often better observers of nature than is generally supposed, that if by accident a sucking-fish becomes separated from the shark, it is unable to provide for itself, and has not even the sense to swim from approaching danger. A remora was caught by the crew of a small vessel on board of which I was passenger. It was placed upon the deck for a few moments in order that I might be better able to inspect it, but when about to be removed, it was found to have adhered so firmly to the planks, that no effort, save the cruel one of cutting off the part, could disengage it. It belongs to the ray kind, and measures generally from two to five feet in length; but one was captured off Guadaloupe, which had attained the unusual length of thirteen feet from head to tail. Many strange tales have been related of the remora being able to stop a ship when in full sail, as well as performing other prodigies of valour; but in this age of wisdom all such statements are deservedly regarded as fables.

The pilot-fish, the other attendant upon the shark, is a very beautiful fish, of a tapering form; it is represented as encompassed "with chains of pearls, corals, emeralds, and other precious stones;" and really, from the brilliancy of its scales, such an idea might be entertained. It was formerly supposed to precede the shark in order to point out its way, and for this cause it obtained its name of "pilot-fish." This supposition is, however, exploded by later observations, which point out that it attends the shark at a respectable distance, in hopes of participating in its prey.

The dolphin, or *delphinus,* is the next most remarkable and beautiful fish which frequents the Caribbean. Painters and sculptors have represented it of a semiannular shape; but the true figure of the fish is straight and tapering, with the back very slightly curved. The snout is long and narrow, and armed with numerous sharp-pointed teeth; the French give it the name of *Porc de mer;* it has also been called the "prismatic fish," from the assertion, that when in the agonies of death it presents the seven primary colours. Much has been said about the dying beauties of the dolphin; but how far more beautiful it looks sporting in its parent element with all the brightness of the emerald, and enjoying the life that has been given it! The flesh is firm, and of a very good flavour, although it is a rapacious fish, waging incessant war upon the poor little flying-fish, and devouring them with the greatest avidity.

The largest among the fish esteemed in Antigua as articles of food is the "Jew-fish," which commonly weighs from three hundred to four hundred pounds. The flesh is reckoned one of the greatest luxuries the West Indian seas afford. It is, however, but seldom caught—probably one reason for its being in such repute—its visits, like angels', being "few and far between." A superstitious notion is attached to this fish—that its appearance bespeaks the death of some magnate of the Island; and accordingly, when tidings are brought that such fish is captured, all the old women lay their heads together to plan out who is to die. The king-fish, grouper, barracoota, cavallie, are equally esteemed for their gastronomic qualities; there are seasons, however, when the flesh of the barracoota is poisonous—a circumstance attributed by some persons to their feeding on copper banks.[67] The other poisonous fish found near Antigua are principally the "horse-eyed cavallie," the yellow-billed sprat, and the conger eel: the flesh of the yellow-billed sprat has often proved fatal to those who have eaten it, and it has been known for death to take place six hours after tasting it. The poison is said by some to be contained in the head.

The stingray is another native of these seas, the meat of which is much esteemed by the Creoles. This fish is armed with a long, slender tail, in the middle of which is a sharp barb; with this instrument the stingray beats the water, or anything that approaches it, rapidly, when attacked. The negro fishermen allege, that the stroke from the stingray's tail products leprosy, for which cause they are very careful in approaching it; and a circumstance has been related of a person having been thrown into a frenzy for forty-eight hours after being struck by this formidable weapon.

The *corramou* is the salmon of the Antiguan fisheries, as far as regards superiority of flavour. It is caught in the fresh-water stream which runs throughout the Island, but is rather scarce; it is the most delicate of the West Indian fish, and ought to be cooked as soon as taken from its parent stream. Snappers, hinds, silks, mullets, doctors, angels, old wives, nurses, Spanish mackerel, &c., are among the other kinds of fish exposed for sale in the Antiguan markets, some of which are noted for their excellent taste, the others for their brilliancy of hue; indeed, the most diversified colours, as yellow, purple, pink, orange, green, and blue, chequered with gold and silver, and the whole happily blended together, are to be observed in almost every species. The parrot fish is the most beautiful of its tribe. Its scales are of the deepest emerald, and its eyes, composed of different coloured circles, are as clear as crystal. It feeds upon shell-fish, which it crushes between its bony jaws, nature having armed it with such instruments in place of teeth. The negroes always call it "blue parrat;" its flesh is much esteemed by them, but the flavour is so rank, that it is never admitted at any respectable table. It sometimes attains the weight of from sixteen to twenty pounds. There are a great number of other edible fish which might be deservedly mentioned, but the pages of this work have so multiplied, that I must pass them over without further mention.

---

[60] The negroes term all cats, but more particularly kittens, "pussy."

[61] The whale belongs to the class *mammalia;* order, *cete.* The food of the whale is lump fish, and small marine insects. Whalebone is procured from the lamina in the upper jaw, (commonly called whiskers,) which supplies the want of teeth. It is split and prepared for use in England.

[62] The grampus generally measures from 15 to 25 feet, and is of great circumference. It is a very voracious fish, feeding upon its neighbour the porpoise, when able. It also attacks the whale, and sometimes makes that

huge animal cry out with pain. Pliny, the great Roman naturalist, who perished in that awful eruption of Mount Vesuvius, in A.D. 79, which also destroyed the cities of Herculaneum and Pompeii, when speaking of the grampus, says, "it is an immense heap of flesh, armed with dreadful teeth."

The porpoise measures from six to nine feet in length, and may be found in all parts of the ocean, and even in the mouths of large rivers. It keeps in large shoals, and if one of the company receives a wound from the harpoon, the rest fall upon him and devour him. Formerly, it was esteemed a fish of such rarity, as to be introduced as royal fare; but in this degenerate age, its savoury qualities are generally over-looked, unless by sailors, who sometimes make a portion of it into a sea-pie.

[63] Some naturalists are of opinion that a fresh row of teeth is added every year. I have counted five rows in a shark's mouth.

[64] We went by way of America, and consequently our time from England was long.

[65] A shoal running across the harbour of St John's from north to south.

[66] Shark, in ichthyology, a species of squalus.

[67] Labat thinks the reason some of the West Indian fish are poisonous is on account of their feeding upon the "galley-fish," a genus of the Zoophyte tribe.

CHAPTER LI

Zoology: Orb-fish—Echinus, known to the ancients—Hippocampus
—Trumpet-fish—Toad-fish—Sea-blubber, and galley-fish—Sea-polypus—
Cat-fish—Crabs, oysters, &c.—Turtle—Land-crab—Soldier-crab—Lizards
—Guana—Wood-slave—Scorpions—Centipede—Snakes—Tarantula—
Cockroach—Caterpillars and butterflies—Ants—Bats—Aquatic birds—
Land birds—Humming bird—Anecdote.

Among the *curiosities* found about the shores of Antigua, are, first, the
orb-fish, sea-porcupine, or *orbus-major*, as it is severally called. This fish
varies from seven inches, to two feet in length; it has no scales, but is armed
with sharp spines, measuring from one to three inches in length, which it
can erect at pleasure—the longest of these spines are placed behind the
eyes, the shortest beneath the body. The mouth is shaped like a frog; the
eyes are round and prominent, and behind them rises two strong, circular-
shaped fins, which it uses with great agility when swimming. The anal and
posterior fins are large and curved; and the tail strong and well adapted for
making way through the waters. In the middle of the stomach is a bladder
filled with air, by the aid of which it can inflate itself at pleasure, until it
presents the figure of a complete sphere. The meat of the orbus is said to
be excellent, with exception of the head, which is always thrown away; it is
dressed in the same manner as turtle. When alive, it is a dangerous and
formidable enemy in its native element, as it is not blessed with a very
amiable temper. And when stuffed, it is an object of great curiosity, and
well worthy of a place in a museum. The *echinus*, or sea-urchin, is another
species of the class and order *vermes, mollusca*. It does not attain the size of
the orbus major, being seldom found more than five inches in length, but it
is covered with sharp prickles, and can equally inflate itself when angry. The
flesh is eaten with oil, vinegar, and pepper; and in flavour resembles the
lobster. This fish was known to the ancients, who esteemed it a royal fare,
when dressed with mead, parsley, turmeric, and mint.

The trumpet-fish, or *fistularia*, is a genus of the order of *abdominales*. It
measures about 18 inches in length. The snout is cylindrical, like a trumpet,
from whence its name; the jaws are at some distance from the eyes, which
are very bright, and the body tapering to the tail. Its principal food is small
fish and marine worms.

The hippocampus, or sea-horse, is another surprising little animal,
never exceeding in length nine inches, and about the thickness of the little
finger. The formation of the head is very much like that of a horse—from
whence its familiar name—the snout is a kind of tube, with a hole at the

end, which it can open or shut at pleasure. The eyes are bright and jut from the head; behind them are two fins, of the shape and appearance of a horse's ears, and above them two orifices for respiration, through which it can spout up the water in a similar manner to the whale. Down the back runs a line of short, stiff hairs, like the mane of a horse, which falls off when the animal is dead; and the whole body is composed of rings with intermediate prickles. It belongs to the *cartilaginei* order. The ancients considered it extremely venomous, even to the slightest touch, but like many other assertions, it is ill-founded, for I have handled many of them and received no hurt. Some of the hippocampus are of a dull chesnut colour, others of a dark grey; when swimming, they compress their tails, and raise themselves with an undulating motion, which gives them the appearance of a miniature horse cantering.

The toad-fish is another curious little denizen of the deep, of the same dusky hue as the toad—from whence its name. When gently rubbed with the finger, it inflates itself into the form of a ball; and if pressed while in this state, bursts with a sharp report. It is eaten by many of the negroes, who are not famed for the delicacy of their palates, although the flesh is very rank.

The sea-blubber and galley-fish are other varieties of the *mollusca* class. They float like a jelly upon the surface of the sea, near its margin; and are dangerous to fishermen, and those persons who are in the habit of going into shallow water without shoes, wounding the feet sorely. If trodden upon, they explode with a loud noise, like an inflated bladder. These sea-nettles, (so called from the stinging pain they occasion if touched,) like the rest of their tribe, feed upon minute shell-fish and sea-insects. They are viviparous.

The sea-polypus also inhabit these seas. These wondrous phenomena of nature belong to the genus *hydra*, class *vermes*, order *zoophyte;* the distinguishing character of which is, that if any part of the body be severed, it instantly becomes a perfect animal. For example, if a polypus be cut transversely into two or three pieces, each portion becomes a regular animal, and a new polypus will also be produced from the skin of the old one. If any of the young polypi be mutilated while growing upon the body of the parent, the parts cut off will immediately grow again; and even if the polypus be dispossessed of its extremities, it will produce young ones before it has attained head or tail. The sea-anemone is very beautiful when alive. It is of a most lovely purple, and throws out its numerous feelers like radii from the centre; these feelers it can contract or expand at pleasure. They feed, like the rest of their species, upon small marine worms, insects, and shell-fish, which they have the power of rendering motionless, (after being entrapped in their long fibrous arms,) by means of a gluey liquid which oozes out of their bodies.

The *chætodon,* or cat-fish, is another inhabitant of the Caribbean. It is one of the most voracious of its tribe, preying indiscriminately upon all who approach it, and who it is enabled, by stratagem or open warfare, to overcome. The body is oblong, the head small, and the teeth slender, but extremely sharp, and bending inwards. The fins of the back are scaly, and the gill-membrane six-rayed.

Among the shell-fish are lobsters, (some of which attain to an immense size,) several kinds of crabs,[68] oysters, (which generally adhere to the mangrove trees,) conchs, whelks, cockles, star-fish, sea-eggs, and smaller multivalves and bivalves. This part of the ocean is also very prolific in marine plants, (some of which, as "sea-feathers," "sea-fans," &c., are very beautiful,) and corals of several shapes and kinds; the latter substance is principally used for burning lime. The brain-stone is also frequently found, as well as many other curiosities, which are purchased from the negro divers and sent to England, as presents, but which I must pass over with this brief notice.

The *testudo Mydas,* or sea-turtle, frequent the bays of Antigua. The female is so very prolific, that she sometimes lays 1000 eggs, which are hatched by the sun, in about 25 days. The merits of this amphibious animal are too well known to descant upon. The shell[69] is very hard and strong, and it will carry as much as 700 or 800 lbs. upon its back. One was captured in these seas, a few years ago which measured six feet across the back, and the shell formed a good boat for a boy to sail about the harbour in. In Cuba, they attain a great size, and have been known to walk off with five or six men standing upon them. A full-grown turtle has often attained the weight of 500 lbs. There are none of this race of giants at Antigua; those caught upon her shores are of smaller dimensions, although of rich flavour.

The *cancer ruricola,* or land-crab, is another inhabitant of Antigua well worthy of note. They live in clefts of rocks, hollow trees, or deep holes which they dig for themselves in the earth, and are much esteemed by Creoles for the sweetness of their meat. Once in the year they march down from their mountain dwellings to the sea-shore in immense numbers, for the purpose of casting their spawn. Before starting upon these expeditions, the whole body meet in "conclave grave," when leaders are chosen, the route agreed upon, and the whole company divided into three battalions. The strongest males most gallantly take the lead in order to face any foe, as well as to act as pioneers; they are followed a short time afterwards by a battalion of females, and the rear is brought up by a medley group of stragglers of all ages and sex. They travel by night, and, as far as possible, keep as straight a line to the sea-side as if they were going by rail-road, only that they neither cut through hills, nor fill up dingles, but march over every impediment with the greatest nonchalance. While upon their travels, they commonly march with their long nippers held aloft, and which now and then they clatter together, as if in defiance of any one they may meet; and if assaulted, they will grasp their assailants so firmly by them, that very frequently they leave such members behind them. They have something of the *ogre* about their disposition, for if one of their companions meet with an accident which prevents it travelling as fast as the rest, the others immediately fall upon and devour it, without any compunctive feelings.

As soon as they reach the sea-side, the females prepare to cast their spawn upon the surface of the sea, leaving it to chance to bring it to perfection. The females are very prolific; but it is supposed two-thirds of their eggs fall a prey to the numerous shoal of fish, which are apparently hovering about, waiting for their expected treat. After remaining for some time by the sea-side, they prepare to return to their mountain homes; but many of them are fatigued by their long journey, and dig holes about the adjacent parts of the country, where they remain until they again become strong and fat. It is during these annual peregrinations that the negroes employ themselves in crab-catching; which exploit they perform at night by aid of a torch, when the crabs come out of their holes to feed. Land-crabs cast their shells annually, and at such periods remain closely concealed in their holes, almost without motion and without food, for about the space of six or eight days, during which time the new shell hardens. They vary in size and colour, some being of a deep coal black, others of a light yellow, and some streaked in red and yellow. Their favourite resorts are the burial-grounds, upon which account many persons have a great antipathy to them as an article of food.

The soldier-crab is a curious little animal, totally unprovided by nature with any shell, so that in order to protect its delicate body from the attack of its enemies, it is obliged to look out for the vacated covering of some shell-fish in which to take up its abode. As the "soldier" increases in bulk, it changes its habitation, and sometimes, for want of a better dwelling, is fain to content itself with the cast-off claw of a lobster or a defunct crab. Although of small size, they are extremely quarrelsome, and their combats for a favourite shell are very terrific, and often end fatally to one of the party; upon which event, the conqueror immediately takes possession of the fought-for dwelling, and to put an end to the affair, makes his dinner off the body of his enemy.

Lizards abound in Antigua; from every fence, from every tree—from the copsewood thicket and the wavy cane-field—you may see their bright little eyes peeping at you. There are about eighty species of this tribe found in different parts of the world, included under the name *lacertæ;* those commonly found in Antigua are the *agilis,* or common tree lizard, the ground lizard, and the guana, or iguana. The common lizard is of a bright green colour, with the head and feet of an ashy hue; there are some, however, of a dirty olive brown, with the feet and tail approaching to black. Like the chameleon, they have the power of changing their colour; and when angry, they swell out the skin of the thorax into a kind of pouch, inflating and contracting it with a clock-like motion. Their tails, of the extreme length of their bodies, are verticillated, and armed with sharp scales; their snouts are long and pointed, and their jaws furnished with numerous small and sharp teeth. They feed upon insects and young buds, and are particularly quarrelsome among themselves, often losing the greater part of their tails in their combats. The lizard is very susceptible of melody, and will remain couched upon a tree for a long time together, listening to the soft strains of a flute or piano, or the sound of the human voice. They are also capable of being tamed, and will frequent the spot where they have once been fed with bread crumbs. The lizard is oviparous, and deposits its eggs (which are white, of the shape of a hen's egg, and about the size of a small kidney bean) in holes in the ground near the roots of trees, or even in the ashes by the fire-hearth.

The ground-lizard is considerably larger than the tree-lizard. It is of a greenish brown hue, with a blood-red stripe running longitudinally down each side. The head, ending in a pointed snout, is also of the same colour, which gives the animal altogether a disgusting appearance. The mouth is armed with an infinite number of sharp, slender teeth, the bite from which is supposed to be very venomous on account of their often leaving such weapons in the wound they have inflicted. The negroes have a superstitious notion, that as soon as this reptile has bitten any one it immediately makes the best of its way to the sea-side, and as the only means of preventing any ill-consequences to itself, bathes in the water, and the wounded person receives the punishment in the shape of leprosy. If, on the contrary, the individual bitten can reach the sea and perform the ablution necessary, before the lizard has time to gain that spot, the reptile pays the penalty, falling a prey to the effects of its own venom. The tail of the ground-lizard is of extreme length, and trails along the ground, giving the creature, when walking, a kind of snake-like motion; when, however, it is attacked by a dog, or frightened by the sound of approaching footsteps, it throws this unwieldy member over its back, and starts away with the greatest activity. The ground-lizard lives in deep holes, which it burrows in the ground, (from whence its name;) its food is the young herbage, fruit, vegetables, or anything of the kind that falls in its way; it holds its prey firmly with its fore-feet, while it tears it to pieces with its teeth, and then swallows it with much apparent *gusto*, putting out its long slender red tongue, in the manner of a dog. I have often fed a ground-lizard with the fruit of the soursop, for the purpose of watching its movements; and if a piece of its favourite fare was delayed for a little longer than it deemed necessary, it would turn up its bright round eyes upon me, as if asking why I balked its appetite. Ground-lizards are also extremely choleric, and will fight with their own species for an hour together. The mode of warfare is to spring forwards, grapple each other with their fore-paws, throw their long tails around each other's body, and in this situation roll over and over in the dust, until one of them acknowledges itself conquered by striving to retire.

The iguana, or guana, sometimes attains the length of from four or five feet, measuring from the point of the snout to the extremity of the tail; its usual size, however, is from three to four feet. It is of a deep emerald green, with the upper part of the head, the feet, tail, and legs, of a dull ash colour. Along the summit of the back and tail runs a deeply serrated membrane, almost like the fin of some fish; the head is surmounted by a kind of crown, or crest, from which circumstance it has obtained the name of "king of the lizards;" and underneath its jaws hangs a kind of comb, which it can inflate when angry or excited. Like all the *lacerta* tribe, its mouth is well furnished with teeth, with which, when exasperated, it inflicts deep wounds; but, in general, it is a quiet and inoffensive animal, feeding in its wild state upon leaves of trees, vegetables, insects, or, when it can procure them, young birds. It climbs with agility, and will spring from one branch of a tree to the other, like a squirrel. The flesh is said to be excellent, rivalling in delicacy that of a chicken. It is eaten in the French islands as a great luxury; but from its outward appearance, few strangers would be led to partake of it, unless deceived by its form of cookery.[20]

The wood-slave is about the same size as the common tree-lizard, but with a shorter tail. The bite is said to be extremely venomous, as also the wound inflicted by its sharp claw, which ends in a kind of nipper, and with which it adheres to the part with such tenacity, that no power but that of a knife will extricate it. In colour it approaches a toad; its haunts are amid old timber or old dwellings, from whence it attains its name of wood-slave.

Scorpions are another formidable foe. They are well equipped for battle, having eight legs, besides two shorter ones fixed on the fore-part of the head, and answering for hands, with which they hold their prey; eight eyes, three upon each side of the head, and two on the back; two feelers, and a long tail, terminated by a curved sting, underneath which are two instruments resembling a comb. The poison is contained in a small reservoir, and is evacuated through two oblong orifices at the top of the sting, at the moment of the wound being given. The effects are extremely painful, producing a burning heat, which, if not alleviated, produces fever. If encaged, and it can discover no means of escape, the scorpion stings itself to death, rather than remain in captivity. The body of the parent scorpion becomes the nest of the young ones, which remain sticking and feeding upon their mother until she dies, and all nurture is absorbed, when they fall off and shift for themselves; fifty of these terrific little creatures have been counted at one time adhering to the body of their dead parent.[71]

The *scolopendra,* or centipede, is another member of the *aptera* order, whose bite is equally dreaded with that of the scorpion. They sometimes attain the length of six inches, and are as thick as the finger of a man; the common size is, however, from two to three inches. They lurk in the dark holes and corners of houses, in the lumber-yards, in the stores, (or warehouses,) in stone-walls, rotten wood, or indeed, any place where they think themselves secure from molestation; and from whence they issue forth and attack whoever falls in their way. They feed upon insects; and their wars with the cockroaches are most terrible. Sometimes, however, they fall a victim to their stingless enemy, who in that case makes a hearty meal upon their remains. The scolopendra is furnished with numerous feet, from whence it derives its name of centipede—there being as many of these members (on each side) as there are joints in their body. The antennæ are covered with short hairs; they wound with two curved feelers in the head, armed with two short teeth. The bite is very painful, and produces (like the scorpion's) severe fever, if some antidote is not immediately applied. In illustration of this, a sailor on board a West Indiaman was so severely wounded in the hand by a centipede, that his life was thought to be in danger; he was, however, eventually cured, by having roasted onions applied to the part affected. The workmen employed in pulling down old buildings, or in removing stacks of lumber, are also very often dreadfully bitten by these terrible creatures.

The Antiguan snakes are perfectly harmless; some of them are beautifully streaked and speckled. Spiders are also very numerous in this part of the world, and call for the constant use of the housemaid's broom. The *tarantula,* or "horse-spider," is the most celebrated in Antigua. It is about the size of a pigeon's egg; the body and legs are stout, and thickly covered with stout black hairs, and the feet armed with triple claws, with which they hold their prey, while they tear it to pieces with their forceps. Their bite is very sharp, and is also often attended with fever; but the strange stories which have been related of the bite of the tarantula throwing its victims into a state of lethargy, from which the power of music can alone restore them, has long ago been proved a fable.

The cockroach, or *blatta,* is a most disgusting insect, although perfectly harmless, being utterly devoid of any weapon of warfare. It belongs to the order hemiptera, and is furnished with four plain wings, which, when walking, it conceals beneath its outward covering. The common cockroach is of a bright brown colour, with long antennæ, and wings exceeding the body in length. They are most destructive creatures, preying indiscriminately upon the contents of the larder, the linen-chest, or the book-case, or upon any insect they can overcome by treachery or open combat, or vary their repasts at times with a taste of the little negroes' fingers, when they go to-bed with such members in a greasy state. Cockroaches cast their skins once or twice in the year; during those periods they present a most revolting appearance, being of a milky white instead of their usual brown hue. In the day, they lurk in holes and corners, but no sooner does night approach, or the clouds threaten rain, than they issue forth by legions, crawl over the floor or furniture, dash in your face, or commence their work of devastation upon your property, leaving their nauseous odours behind them upon whatever they may touch. The *drummer*-cockroach is of a dingy ash colour; it receives its name from the drumming noise it makes by striking, it is said, its horny head against any wooden substance it may come near. It is even more disgusting than the common cockroach, both as regards form and odour; the antennæ and wings are shorter, and the body of greater breadth, and differently marked; the feet are furnished with an adhesive liquid, which stain anything they pass over. The eggs of the cockroach are about one-third the size of their bodies; they are rather flat and long, and are covered with a hard shell of a brown colour. The parent insect attaches them to walls, curtains, the interior of boxes or drawers, or, indeed, any place which they deem convenient for the purpose, by means of a kind of animal gum with which they are provided. The cockroach has many enemies to contend against, among whom the domestic fowl is, perhaps, the most formidable, picking them up, impaling them alive upon their beaks, or swallowing them with a relish which none but a fowl could conceive. The avidity with which fowls seek such food gives rise to the negro proverb, "Dat time cockroach hab dance, he no ax fowl for to come." They certainly are the pest of the West Indies; nothing escapes their depredations; and as the North American Indians have remarked of the deer, "The more you kill, the more they come." The redeeming qualities of cockroaches are said to be, that they improve the flavour of wine, and make excellent fish-sauce!

There are immense hordes of caterpillars (*erucæ*) in Antigua; some among them are of great magnitude and beauty, although sad plunderers of the garden. After grovelling for some time upon the ground, and then undergoing the transformation of a nympha, they at length burst from their shelly covering, and, in the plenitude of life and joy, bound forward in the bright sunshine as so many gorgeous butterflies. Some of them are beautiful in the extreme, their velvety coats displaying every tint of the rainbow; but, alas! like all other beauties, their triumphs are soon over; the sun rises and sets but seldom for them, and after laying their 300 or 400 eggs, their business in the world is achieved—their little lives are over, and they again become a "thing of nought."

Ants also abound, and infest every comer and cupboard in your dwelling. They have been held up as patterns of industry, and surely they possess that virtue in an eminent degree, for in vain does the thrifty housewife use her best endeavours to secure the contents of her larder from their depredations. They never tire, but surmount every difficulty, and, like the "Goths" and "Huns" of old, pour their countless legions over the whole face of the country. You may, with the greatest caution, suspend your choicest preserves from the ceiling, thinking that a place of security, but in a short time it is sure to be discovered by some roving ant, who, without loss of time, communicates the results of his foraging to his neighbours. The whole tribe are soon in motion, the discoverer acts as pioneer, and with great judgment conducts them over every impediment along the ceiling, down the string, until at length they gain the sweetmeat, where, *sans ceremonie,* they luxuriate at will. At other times, in order to guard the delicacies from the attacks of the ants, the vessel which contains it is placed in water, and there all is deemed quite secure. But not so; the ants are indefatigable; for no sooner does their sense of smelling tell them some choice dainty is inclosed therein, than they form a kind of bridge across the water, by one ant embracing another by the antennæ, and in this way they transport and enjoy the luxury at pleasure. There are ants of various sizes, and colours; the large black ant, the small black, the red ant, the wild ant, &c., but of all these varieties the sugar-ant is the most disagreeable. It is supposed the sugar-ant was first brought into the West Indies in a slaver, from the coast of Guinea, and after destroying vegetation to a great extent in Dominica, found its way to Antigua, where it committed great havoc upon the sugar canes. They are of small size, and of a light-brown colour, tinged with black, and when crushed, emit a mucilaginous substance of a fœtid smell.

As for flies, it would take an entomologist months to describe them, so numerous are their varieties; and of insects of a viler name, not to be mentioned to ears polite, the negroes would no doubt tell you they are far from being an extinct race. Bats are among the other denizens of Antigua, whose company is not very desirable. Some of them attain the size of pigeons; but although the dreaded "vampire" may be found among the number, we never hear of any creature falling a prey to its thirst for blood.

The principal aquatic birds are, boobies, or gannets, man-of-war birds, coots, gorlings, (a kind of heron,) gulls. The other birds are, chicken-hawks, (or killa-a-killa, as the negroes call them,) buzzards, turtle-doves, ground-doves, wild pigeons, quails, a brown bird, with a most melodious note,— "the nightingale of a tropic noon," as Coleridge poetically calls it; sparrows, finches, yellowbreasts, blackbirds, (but not like those sweet songsters of old England's woods,) several other birds, with whose names I am unacquainted, and lastly, the pigmy humming-bird. Speaking of these beautiful little creatures, a modern author remarks: "The consummate green of the emerald, the rich purple of the amethyst, and the vivid flame of the ruby, all happily blended and enveloped beneath a transparent veil of wavy gold, are distinguished in every species, but differently arranged and proportioned in each." Pretty as this description is, it is not quite applicable to the humming-birds of Antigua; for although the "emerald" may be found, as well as the purple and gold, in some degree, "the vivid flame of the ruby" will be sought for in vain. Still it is a lovely little creature, with its long slender bill, its graceful little head, its sparkling black eye, and its fairy-like flittings among the fragrant blossoms of its sunny home. It has been asserted that the humming-bird is one of the shyest among the feathered tribe; but to express my own opinion, I think it has as good a stock of assurance as is possible to conceive for such a minute creature; while its passions are very strong, and it will attack any bird who comes within its range.

An anecdote was related to me during my stay in this island, which proves how strong maternal love reigns in the breast of a humming-bird. In order to increase a cabinet of birds, a negro was dispatched in quest of these little creatures, with orders to capture all he could; and in the course of his perambulations, he alighted upon one which had built her tiny nest of cotton in a secluded dell, and which, at that moment, was engaged in the office of incubation. Void of pity, the negro seized upon his prize, (which, with an expectant mother's love, would not quit her eggs,) broke off the stem of the tree to which the nest was attached, and carried it the distance of ten or twelve miles to his master's house, where it remained for four days; and although under no confinement, the humming-bird would not forsake her nest, but was conveyed in that situation on board ship, where she must have died of starvation; for who was to administer to her the ambrosial dews which formed her food?

There are many other creatures whose lives and habits might be given; but as I have already extended this part of my subject to greater lengths than I had intended, I must conclude, or my task would reach to many more pages.

---

[68] The *cancer graspus* is the handsomest of its species, being of a pale yellow, beautifully streaked and spotted with red, and deeply serrated claws of a pure white. When in its native element it spouts out the water from two orifices near its eyes, forming a beautiful and never-ceasing arch.

[69] It was the shell of a turtle which served that great monarch, Henry IV. of France, for a cradle.

[70] The guana has the power of fascinating small birds &c. in the same manner as the anaconda, or rattle-snake, does. When bent upon such deeds, it stretches itself baskingly in the sun, and darts out its long red tongue; the birds, attracted by the sight, hover round, apparently irresistibly approaching the creature's mouth, until at length, when drawn within a convenient distance, the guana makes a sudden start, and with one effort swallows the poor bird.

[71] Oldmixon, in his history, says, the scorpions in Barbados are as big as rats. If so, the present race of scorpions must have degenerated greatly in size, or else the rats are of a Lilliputian family.

CHAPTER LII

BOTANY.

In commencing this chapter upon botany, I deem it proper to mention first the forest trees, confining myself to those vegetating in Antigua. As, however, it will be necessary to insert the botanical names, as well as their classifications, and wishful of throwing as much interest into the subject as possible, I have, along with my own observations upon these beauties of the creation, consulted other and more efficient botanists. It must be remarked, that nearly all the West Indian trees continue to bud and blossom throughout the year; so that there is no naked sprays and branches to be seen, as in old England's woods in winter, but instead, every grove presents an unchanging canopy of the deepest green.

One of the commonest flowers in Antigua is the FOUR O'CLOCK, *mirabilis jalapa,* or *marvel of Peru,* so called from the circumstance of its opening its pretty petals at that hour of the day. The leaves are of dark green, and shaped like a heart; the flowers are of a tubulous form, and of the several colours of red, white, or purple—the latter are the most common. The seeds are black and hard, and of a conical structure; the leaves are of much repute among the old nurses of Antigua, for their efficacy in relieving tumours, &c., but if it be only fancy, or if they really possess some medicinal qualities, I leave the gentlemen of the lancet to determine.

The PALMETTO, *areca oleracea,* cabbage palm, or mountain cabbage, is the most beautiful tree in Antigua, and richly deserves the epithet of king of the West Indian forests. The trunk rises straight and smooth, and is of a most graceful form, being about four to seven feet in circumference at the base, and gradually tapering upwards to the height of from one hundred feet; it is of a silverish grey colour, and indented with rings, marking the place of former foot-stalks. The upper part of the trunk presents a finely turned polished column, of a beautiful green colour, which diverges gradually from its pedestal until it attains the centre, when it diminishes in the same manner to the top, from whence springs an acuminated spatha terminating in a point. The branches spring from the top of the trunk in an elegant plume-like manner; as they decay and fall off, they are succeeded by others bursting from the centre of those that remain. The young leaves are esteemed delicious when boiled, as well as the cabbage, which is found in the interior of the green part of the trunk. The flowers are hermaphrodite; the male calyx sends forth three petals and nine stamens; the female flower is like the male, and turns to an oval fruit, enclosing an oval seed, which will bear a fine polish, and was formerly used for buttons. A grove of these trees presents a beautiful appearance, forming indeed a colonnade of finely turned columns, from the top of which springs a verdant canopy.

COCOA-NUT TREE, *cocos nucifera,* belongs to the order monœcia hexandria. Male calyx is trifid, the corolla three-petalled, with five stamens; the female calyx is quinquefid, the corolla divided into three segments, and furnished with three stamens. The cocoa-nut tree is supposed to have been brought from the Maldives to the West Indies. It loves a sandy soil, and sometimes attains the height of eighty feet. The trunk is a straight column, slightly annulated, and tapering from the base to the summit, where it expands into branches of about fifteen feet long, and in a circular form, among which break forth the sheaths, which are open from top to bottom and full of flowers, or clusters of embryos. The branches are apparently fastened at the top with stringy threads, interwoven like a piece of coarse sackcloth; the pinnæ are of a deep glossy green, and, near the trunk, are often a foot long. The nut is much esteemed for the sweetness of its kernel, as well as for the milk and oil it produces. When the kernel first begins to grow, it is in the form of jelly, which lines the interior of the shell; as it increases in age, this jelly thickens, and becomes a solid mass of about a quarter of an inch thick, and of the whiteness of unsullied snow. The jelly nuts contain the largest supply of milk, or water, as it is generally termed in Antigua, often as much as a pint, or a pint and a half; it is most esteemed in this state, the ripe nut being seldom eaten in its crude form, but generally compounded into different kinds of sweetmeats, or shipped to England. Thomson, speaking of the cocoa-nut, observes—

"Amid those orchards of the sun,
Give me to drain the cocoa's milky bowl,
And from the palm to draw its freshening fruit."

These nuts are enclosed in a thick husk, composed of strong fibres, thickly matted together, which, when young, is of a bright green, but which attains a dull brown as it arrives at maturity; from these husks an excellent dye can be obtained, while the dried ones are now manufactured into mattresses, floor-cloths, and all kinds of brooms and mats. The trunk of the cocoa-nut tree is capable of being made into cordage, and, if tapped, a clear liquid issues, to which the name of arrack is given, which, when fermented, becomes an intoxicating drink. The shell of the nut is sometimes beautifully carved and polished, and, when mounted in silver, is used as cups or sugar-basins. From the kernel a clear white oil is extracted, which burns with great brilliancy, and emits a pleasant odour.

WHITEWOOD-TREE, *bucida buceras,* is a beautiful forest-tree, and one that lives to a great age; there are some still remaining in the island which are said to be coeval with the first settlers. It rises to the height of forty or fifty-feet, and is thickly covered with a light-green foliage, here and there sprinkled with a leaf of the brightest red. It is said that ships built from its timber never breeds worms.

CEDARS belong to the *juniperus* tribe. There are two species in Antigua, the white and the red. The white is a very beautiful tree, clothed with a dark-green glossy foliage, from whence spring flowers of a trumpet-like shape, and of the most delicate pink or pearly white. It forms a very beautiful avenue to a gentleman's seat, as well as a road-side border; but the timber is not of so much value as the red cedar, which is another most lovely forest-tree, rising sometimes to from sixty to seventy feet, and of proportionate circumference. The foliage is very thick, the leaves in form like the English ash; the flowers (which have not the beauty of its sister tree) are succeeded by oval berries of a purplish colour. The wood of the cedar is too well known to need much description. It is of a reddish colour and of a fragrant smell, and is almost incorruptible, as no worms will breed in it. It has been related that cedar-wood was found in the temple of Apollo at Utica, full 2000 years old.

SILK-COTTON TREE, *bombax seva,* or *Ceiba,* of the polyandria order, class monodelphia, is one of the most beautiful forest-trees of the western world, and a great ornament in tropic scenery. The trunk rises smooth and straight as a column, to the height of sixty or seventy feet, and of immense circumference. It is said to have originally been brought from Africa to the West Indies, where it now flourishes in splendid magnificence. The leaves are broad, and of a glossy green, the flowers of a delicate primrose, and campanulated; the corolla is quinquefid, from whence rises the pointal, which afterwards turns to a pod of about four or five inches in length, containing the seeds, and a profusion of bright beautiful silk. From its extreme shortness, it has been for a long time held as unfit for any use; but within these last few years, it is discovered it can be manufactured into hats. The East Indians use it for stuffings to their ottomans, cushions, and sofas, on which they recline during the heat of the day; but the West Indians, less effeminate and luxurious, allow it to float about in its native copses unheeded, except by the pretty little humming-bird, which sometimes builds her fairy nest from its silky fabric.

The MANCHINEAL, or *hippomane,* rises from twelve to thirty feet, branching into several stems, but the main trunk sometimes attains three feet in circumference. It is a very beautiful tree, the bark smooth and of a brownish hue; and the leaves, of about two or three inches in length, are of the same glossy bright green as the laurel; they are thick and unctuous, and, when pressed, yield an oily milk. This tree has male catkins, which are produced at some distance from the embryos. The female pointal turns to a globular fleshy fruit, containing a rough woody nut, inclosing fewer or more flat seeds. This fruit is the celebrated manchineal apple, which, with the most beautiful exterior, possesses the most poisonous qualities. So dire is this plant, that the very sun, darting its rays upon it, calls forth all its dangerous odours, and renders it unsafe to the touch; while if any one takes shelter beneath its spreading boughs during a storm, the rain-drops as they trickle off the leaves blister any part of the skin they fall upon. Its timber is, however, made use of by cabinet-makers, although, when felling it, the wood-men, it is said, are obliged to cover their faces with thick cloth. The Caribs used to dip their arrows in this juice, which rendered the wound fatal. Poison extracted from this tree will preserve its venom for 100 years. The apples, if eaten, are said to be certain death to everything but goats.

LOBLOLLY-TREE, *varronia-alba*, (*pisonia subcordata?*) is another denizen of Antigua, which shews its verdant green canopy throughout the year. The leaves are broad, glossy, and ovate; the trunk rises from the bottom in numerous woody stems, which, though they present a beautiful road-side scenery, are of very little use, except for fire-wood.

SANDBOX-TREE, *hura crepitans*, rises to the height of from twenty to thirty feet. The trunk is straight and thick, and is armed with short prickles; the branches start from the top, and abound with an acrid juice. The leaves are broad and long, and of a dullish green. The male flowers are formed like a tapering column, and close over each other like the scales of fish; the female flowers consist of a trumpet-like style, with a quinquefid stigma. The germen becomes a round woody capsule, compressed at the ends like an orange, divided into twelve cells, each containing a flat oblong seed. When these capsules are ripe, they burst with a loud noise, scattering their seeds and severed cells to a great distance, and occasioning the negro, who may be passing at the time, to exclaim, "Eh! eh! de jumbies (ghosts) dun dere dinner hark dere plates; how dey *mash 'em!*" Before these pods burst, they are sometimes plucked by the Antiguans, and after being scraped and garnished with gold paper, are made into sandboxes, (from whence this tree derives its common name,) and sent to England as presents for the curious. This tree belongs to the natural order *tricoccæ*, and to the monœcia class of plants.

LOGWOOD, *hæmatoxylon Campechianum*, grows in Antigua, but no use is made of it in the way of commerce. It rises from the height of eighteen to thirty feet. The trunk is generally uneven in its growth, with somewhat of a knotty surface; the branches are thorny, and thickly covered with lanceolated leaves, and the flowers, five-petalled, are of a delicate pale purple and yellow. The pointal afterwards becomes a flat oblong pod, containing a few kidney-shaped seeds. Altogether it forms a very beautiful object in woodland scenery. It belongs to the decandria class of plants.

CALABASH-TREE, *crescentia cujete*, rises to about the height of the English apple. The trunk is straight and columnar, branching off at the head into numerous long slender branches, clothed with dark green foliage. The flower is insignificant; the pointal afterwards becomes an oblong or globular fruit, of a fine green colour, and covered with a rind, which, as it approaches to maturity, attains the hardness and stability of maple wood. The interior of the fruit is filled with a white pulpy substance containing the seeds. This the negroes scrape carefully out, and after divesting the nut of its outer green covering, dry it in the sun, and then use them as culinary articles, instead of the more brittle cups and basins of English ware. Some of these calabashes, as they are generally termed, will hold from one to two gallons, while others will not contain more than a gill.

The PIMENTO, or *Jamaica-pepper*, is a species of myrtus. It is one of the most beautiful trees in the western hemisphere, the trunk rising smooth and shining, and of a silver-grey colour, to the height of from fifteen to twenty feet, when it branches off into a rich canopy of dark-green foliage, like the leaves of the bay-tree. These leaves are very odoriferous; from them may be expressed oil like that of cloves, and when distilled with rum or high wines, they rank first among the West Indian simple waters, known as *bay-rum*. The flowers are white with green stamens, and emit a pleasing fragrance; while the berries, round, black, and small, partake of the flavour of all the different spices, from whence their name, *allspice*. It is said of this tree, as of the nutmeg in the Moluccas, that the chief means of propagation is by the birds, who, swallowing the seeds, void them again whole, when they immediately take root and flourish.

BARBADOS-LILAC, *melia azedarach*, is a very beautiful tree, rising from twelve to twenty feet. The bark is smooth and of an ash colour; it is bitter and astringent, and when compounded with aromatics, has been used (in the form of powders or decoctions) in fevers and chronic rheumatism. Toddy is said to be extracted from the young trees. The leaves are of a light green, and the sweet pale umbelliferous flowers hang in graceful tassels from every branch.

TURPENTINE TREE, *burseræ gummifera*, belongs to the order diœcia, class polygamia; the calyx is triphyllous, the corolla three-leaved, and the seed-vessel tri-valved. It grows very fast, and sometimes attains a great height. The trunk is of a bright brown, sometimes mottled with red, and presents a glossy appearance; the leaves are broad, and of a deep green. It is so tenacious of life, that it will bud and blossom after being cut up and planted as posts.

NICKEL, or nickar tree, *guilandina,* is a curious genus of the monogynia order, decandria class of plants. There are two species, the *bonduc,* or yellow nickar, and the *bonducella,* or grey nickar. They are both of them climbing plants, sometimes attaining the height of fifteen or eighteen feet. The flowers are quinquefid, the petals of a yellow colour, and growing from the wings of the stalks. The germen becomes an oblong pod, thickly covered with slender spines, two-valved, and containing two hard seeds of the size and shape of a marble; those of the bonduc are yellow; the bonducella, of a beautiful grey colour, from whence their respective names.

LOCUST-TREE, *hymenæa courbaril;* order monogynia, class decandria. This tree sometimes rises to the height of sixty or seventy feet, in a straight column-like trunk, of two or three feet in circumference, covered with an ash-coloured bark. The leaves are of a dark-green, and the flowers, divided into five segments, and of a pale purple, streaked with yellow, come out in loose spikes at the end of the branches. The germen becomes a thick fleshy pod, of four or five inches long, covered with a hard brown shell, and containing a farinaceous substance, in taste something like gingerbread, but of a most intolerable odour, but which is eaten heartily by the negroes. In it is seated two or three hard brown seeds, of about the size of marbles, but of an oblong shape. The timber is used for making bedsteads, &c., while from the roots a dark transparent gum may be procured, which, when dissolved with spirits of wine, forms an excellent varnish.

The CASHEW-NUT TREE, or *anacardium,* belongs to the order diœcia, class polygamia. The cup of the flower is oblong and quinquefid. The flower is deciduous, and is formed of a single leaf, divided into five concave segments, with five lanceolated petals; at the bottom of the calyx is the ovarie, which turns to a fruit the size and shape of a bury pear, and of a red or yellow colour; it abounds in a sweet juice, slightly acrid, but which is much esteemed by the Antiguans in punch or lemonade; from the apex of the fruit grows the seed, in shape like a hare's kidney, the upper part of the receptacle being the largest. The shell is thick and cellular, and abounds in a dark caustic oil, which blisters the parts it is applied to; it is said to be used by some West Indian ladies to improve their complexion—it must prove a very painful wash, I should think; far unlike Rowland's inimitable Kalydor. When roasted, the kernel is very sweet; they are often sent to England as presents. It is a common practice in Antigua, to place the young fruit, when growing, in a shallow-necked bottle, which is attached to the tree; when the fruit is full grown, it is severed from the tree, and the bottle filled with high wines, which keeps it in a state of preservation. Thus prepared, it is sent to England as a curiosity, where it raises surprise from the fact of so large a fruit having entered at so small an aperture as a bottle's mouth. The milk which oozes from the tree stains of a deep black, which no ablution will remove.

MANGO-TREE, *mangifera*, belongs to the polygamia class of plants. This tree sometimes rises to a great height, and is covered with a roughish bark. The leaves are often eight or nine inches long, and about an inch and a half in breadth, and the flowers start from loose umbels at the end of the branches. The germen afterwards becomes a large, oblong, fleshy fruit, of a fine yellow colour, and containing a flat seed covered with a woolly substance. When good, it has something of the flavour of a ripe apricot, but the generality of mangos are so strongly impregnated with turpentine, that it is almost uneatable. When fermented, an agreeable drink is said to be procured from the fruit. This tree was introduced into the West Indies from some part of Africa. In 1798, Admiral Lord Rodney planted it in Jamaica; he had taken the plants in a French prize from the Isle of Bourbon.

BANANA, *musa sapientum*, rises to the height of six or ten feet; the leaves are about eight inches broad, and three feet long, and of a bright green colour, deeply veined. The wind, as it blows them backwards and forwards, severs them at these several veins, so that in a few days, from unfolding, the banana branches hang in tattered shreds. The fruit is oblong, and about four inches in length; the outer covering is yellow, and the flavour something like that of an over-ripe apple. When cut longitudinally, a representation of the crucifixion of our Saviour is said to be perceived, but this, I think, is a vagary of the imagination—at least, I never could find anything of the sort, although I have cut many bananas.

The CUSTARD APPLE, *annona reticulata*, is a genus of the polygynia order, class polyandria. This tree rises to about the height of a common apple. The cup of the flower is three-leaved, from whence start six petals of the heart-shaped kind, and antheræ are numerous. The pointal becomes a large roundish fruit, of a pulpy consistence, and containing a great number of black seeds; it is not held in much repute, and is scarcely eaten except by the negroes, although Ligon speaks of it as being very delicious.

STAR-APPLE, *chrysophyllum cainito*, belongs to the monogynia order, and petandria class of plants. It rises to the height of thirty-five or forty feet, with a smooth straight trunk, from which shoot several branches at regular distances. The foliage is of a deep green on the upper side, with the underneath of a russet colour. The flower is campaniform, divided into ten segments, but of no great beauty; from the calyx rises the pointal, which afterwards becomes the fruit, of a globular shape, and divided into ten cells, in each of which is a flattish glossy seed. It derives its name from its internal arrangement, which, when cut transversely, presents the form of a star.

PAPAW, *carica papaya*, a genus of the decandria order, class diœcia. The trunk rises in a simple hollow stem, marked in lozenges, to the height of eighteen or twenty feet; the trees are male and female; the leaves are large, and divided into several lobes, and come out upon very long, hollow footstalks, from the acros or summit of the tree. The male flowers are tubelous, and divided into five segments; the calyx small, and the filaments short and long alternately. The colour is a bright primrose, and, seated as they are upon their pale green flower-stalk, they present a very beautiful appearance. The female flowers are also primrose colour, and expand in form of a star, so deeply cut into six segments, that they appear to consist of so many distinct leaves. The calyx is quinquedentated; and from the centre rises the pointal, surmounted by a crest of four leaves. This pointal afterwards becomes a fleshy fruit, of an oblong or globular form, covered with a thin rind, and containing, as in a melon, numerous small black seeds of the pungent flavour of pepper. The fruit, when good, has the colour, and something of the taste, of an apricot; when unripe, the internal part is quite white, and in such state is boiled and dished up in the manner of turnip. It is also cut into various forms, and, mixed with peppers, cucumbers, &c., forms the West Indian pickles. The milk which exudes from it is said to be efficient in making meats tender; and, accordingly, its good qualities are often put to the test by notable housewives, who wish to pass off their old fowls, of five or six generations, for young chickens. From all parts of the tree flows this acrid milky juice, or *albumen,* which may be used instead of egg in clarifying sugar or liquors. It is also said to be a specific for the toothache.

SOURSOP, *annona muricata,* of the polygynia order, polyandria class. It is a richly foliaged tree, rising to the height of about twenty feet. The flowers have a grateful but rather heavy odour. The calyx is three-leaved; the corolla is large, composed of six petals—the three outer ones concave and coriaceous, and of a yellow colour; the three inner ones somewhat smaller and spherical. The flowers are deciduous, and when they open they make so loud a report as to occasion a start from those who stand beneath the tree. The fruit is pulpy, and covered with a thick green rind, of the consistence of leather, studded over with green prickles, cone-shaped, and attains a great size; the interior is cellular, and furnished with oblong glossy seeds, which spring from the spear-shaped core. The juice makes an excellent transparent jelly; but in its crude form the fruit is never introduced at genteel tables, although of a very grateful flavour: all manner of stock are fond of it, and the little negroes luxuriate most freely upon it when in season.

MAMMA SAPOTA, *achras mammosa,* is a splendid lofty tree, belonging to the monogynia order, class pentandria. The pistil of the flower is rather long, and is surrounded by six stamens. The fruit is globular, and is covered with a thick brown rind; the eatable part lies between that and the large round seed, which is covered with a fine thin skin. It is very indigestible when eaten in its crude state, but makes a luscious sweetmeat, which is generally esteemed.

BREAD FRUIT, *artocarpus,* belongs to the order monandria, and the monœcia class of plants. It was brought from Otaheite to these islands by Captain Bligh, a gentleman well known for his trials in the "Mutiny of the Bounty." This tree rises to the height of about forty feet, and is covered with a thick foliage; the leaves are sometimes a foot and a half long, of an oblong shape, and when broken, exude a milky juice. The trunk is of a pale ash colour, with a smoothish bark; the catkins, or male flowers, have no calyx, but are formed of valves hanging down in the form of ropes; the corolla has two petals, and concave; the female flower has neither corolla nor calyx, but the germs are numerous, connected into a globe. The fruit is globular, and about the size of a melon; the rind is thick and green, and is divided hexagonally in the form of net-work; the internal part is covered with a substance like thick wool. The edible part of the fruit lies between the skin and the core; it is perfectly white, and something like new bread, but it must be roasted before eaten. The taste is insipid, but is said to afford great nourishment. The milk which oozes from the trunk, when boiled with cocoa-nut oil, makes an excellent bird-lime, and the wood is useful for building.

SAPPADILLA, *achras sapota,* of the monogynia order, class pentandria. The calyx is a perianthum, with six erect concave leaves; the corolla bears one petal, the full length of the cup; the germen is globular, and becomes a pulpy fruit of a similar form, having twelve cells, each containing a glossy oblong black seed. The fruit is very luscious to the taste, and ranks among one of the first at an Antiguan table. The tree is about the size of the oak, and continues to bud and blossom throughout the year: there are three species of this tree.

SUGAR APPLE, *annona squamosa,* another genus of the polygynia order, polyandria class. The flower is insignificant, and nearly scentless; the pointal changes to a cone-shaped fruit of a dead green colour, divided into oblong compartments, each one cellular, and furnished with a flat glossy seed. The fruit abounds in saccharine juice, from whence its name. It grows to the height of about fifteen feet, and is thickly covered with oblong leaves, the upper part of a dead green, the underneath approaching to white.

SEA-SIDE GRAPE, *coccoloba uvifera;* of the order trigynia, and octandria class of plants. The calyx is divided into five segments, of a velvety texture; there is no corolla, but the berry, containing one seed, is formed from the calyx. It luxuriates most freely in a sandy soil, where it sometimes attains the height of from eight to fifteen feet. The trunk, or rather trunks, for it sends up from the root several stems, is covered with a smooth brown bark. The leaves are orbicular, and are from five to six inches in circumference; they are of a bottle-green, and deeply veined, and stand upon short, thick foot-stalks. The fruit is of a red colour, but when quite ripe, approaches to black; it contains one seed, in form, like a cocoa-nut. There are fourteen species of this shrub, of which the chigery grape, *coccoloba nivea,* is another denizen of Antigua. It is not, however, much esteemed for the flavour. The flowers, which afterwards turn to the fruit, come out at the wing of the stalk, in racemi of about the length and appearance of white currants.

The SHADDOCK, *citrus decumana,* order polyandria, class polyadelphia, is a native of China; it was brought first to the West Indies by Captain Shaddock; hence its name. It is another species of the tribe *citrus,* belonging to the same class and order as its sister shrubs, the lime and orange. The fruit is of two kinds—the one with a white pulp, the other of a reddish colour; the latter is the most esteemed. The fruit is of much larger dimensions than the orange, with a thick rough rind, which is capable of being manufactured into a very superior kind of *bitters.* This tree grows to the height of from eight to twelve feet, with thick broad leaves, slightly serrated.

LIME-TREE, *citrus limonum,* of the polyadelphia order, class polyandria. The calyx is divided into five segments, the corolla is quinquefid, and of the most delicate white, and with numerous antheræ tipped with yellow farina. The scent of the flowers is most delicious; and their silvery whiteness, contrasted with the glossy green of the foliage, renders it one of the most beautiful of shrubs. The lime-tree is said to resemble the holly of England in appearance; it sometimes attains the height of fifteen feet. Oldmixon, speaking of this shrub, says—"Fifty years ago, the planters made hedges of them about their houses; their prickles served for a fortification against the naked negroes." The fruit is very fragrant, of the colour and shape of a lemon, and about the size of a hen's egg; the juice is a strong acid. Galisco mentions that it was the lime-tree and the box which Harpalus found so much difficulty in cultivating at Babylon.

The ORANGE, *citrus aurantium,* is of the same class and order as the foregoing. The trunk rises smooth and straight, from six to ten feet in height, when it divides into several branches, forming a green canopy. The leaves are oval-shaped, and of a glossy green; and its beautiful and fragrant flowers spring forth from numerous flower-stalks at the side of the branches. The fruit, when gathered, is in a green state, which afterwards attains a yellow colour. An orange-bough just severed from the tree, bending gracefully from the weight of its fruit, and shewing its clusters of pearly blossoms, is a very lovely picture.

AVOCADA PEAR, *persea gratissima,* order trigynia, class Enneandria, is a lofty tree, crowned with a dense foliage, and bearing one of the best fruits the island produces. The shape is that of a quince, covered with a tough, ligneous rind, and containing one large, compressed globular seed. In flavour, it somewhat resembles a broiled *vegetable marrow.* It is sometimes eaten with wine and sugar, but more generally with pepper and salt.

BLACK CHERRY, *cerasus occidentalis,* is a genus of the natural order rosaceæ. It rises to about the height of 20 or 30 feet. The wood is much used by the negroes in their wattled houses, as it is of a flexible nature. The leaves are obovated, and the delicate-looking flowers hang from every branch.

The ACACIA rises to about twenty feet in branching stems, armed with long and sharp thorns. The flowers are globular, and of a bright yellow; they hang from every spray, and load the air with their fragrant odours. The pointal afterwards becomes a legume, containing several flat brown seeds, like those of lupins; these seeds have been found useful in setting dyes, and the gum produced from the trees is the best that can be used in calico printing; formerly the flowers were made use of in the materia medica, but this age of wisdom has expelled those various conserves which once loaded the shelves of an apothecary's shop.

LIGNUM VITÆ, *guaiacum,* or pack wood, as it is sometimes called, is another beautiful forest tree of Antigua. It attains the size of a large oak; the trunk is covered with a hard, brown bark, although the branches are of a greyish-ash colour. The foliage is magnificent, and of the sweetest green, while the beauty of the tree is enhanced by the clusters of cerulean flowers, which hang in loose umbels from almost every spray.

Perhaps the most beautiful and fragrant flower which grows in Antigua is the *frangepanier,* or *plumeria.* It rises to the height of from ten to fifteen feet, with a rough, greyish trunk, from whence start numerous fantastic-shaped branches, convolving and wreathing their long, naked arms on all sides. From the end of these branches start large, oblong leaves, standing upon three-inch footstalks, and forming a beautiful cluster. These leaves are deciduous, and as they fall off, are succeeded by bunches of flowers, which grow in umbels, rising from one centre stem, of about three or four inches in length. These flowers are of the most delicate pink, shaded off to white, and of a velvety surface, the lower part of the petals being yellow. They are divided into five or six segments, and the scent of them is so delicious, that it ravishes the senses while inhaling its odour. All parts of this tree abounds in a milky, acrid juice, which drops freely upon breaking off the least part, or making the slightest incision.

GUAVA TREE, *psidium pomiferum*, order monogynia, class icosandria, rises in the manner of a shrub, to the height of from two to twelve feet. The leaves are ovate, and of a dusky green; the flowers consist of five segments, produced in a circular form, with numerous stamens surrounding an ovary of an oblong form. This becomes a fleshy fruit, of the shape and colour of a lemon, surmounted by a crest of small leaves. The interior of the fruit is of a rose-colour, or a pure white, containing numerous small, yellow seeds; the flavour is exquisite, and the jelly made from it surpasses the whole world of confectionary. The celebrated Sir Hans Sloane is said to have been particularly fond of it; indeed, it is a universal favourite, and cattle and birds greedily eat the fruit in its crude form.

BAMBOO, *bambusa arundinacea*, belongs to the order monogynia, class hexandria. It rises to a great height, sometimes fifty or sixty feet. The young stalks are almost solid, and are filled with a sweetish kind of liquid, which, as they progress in age and become hollow, falls to the bottom of the joint, where it is stopped by a woody membrane, and concretes into a kind of sugar, called *tabaxir*. This tabaxir is said to possess strong medicinal qualities, and was held in such esteem by the ancients, that it was often sold for its weight in silver. The bamboo is used in Antigua for spouts, fish-pots, or as posts for fences: it forms a pretty screen, and as the wind wantons through its lanceolated leaves, a pleasing melody ensues.

PHYSIC NUT, *jatropha curcas*, belongs to the same order and class as the cassada, &c. It grows to the height of ten or twelve feet, with a knotty stem, and the leaves (cordate and angular) starting from the ends of the branches. The flowers are green, and hang in umbels; they are succeeded by nuts, with the outward covering green, and containing an oblong kernel, separated by two milk-white leaves, of a perfect shape. This plant is often used for fences, and according to old Ligon, is "of so poisonous a nature that no animal will approach it." This is not correct in every point, for it produces no ill-consequences, unless taken to excess, when it acts as a violent cathartic.

The FRENCH PHYSIC NUT, *jatropha multifida*, is another species of this tribe. It rises in a shrubby manner, from eight to ten feet in height, the main stem being covered with a silver-grey bark, and dividing into several branches at the top. The leaves are large and lobed, and the flowers, of a purple colour, grow from the extremity of the branches, in groups. They are succeeded by nuts, of the same size and appearance as those of the *jatropha curcas*.

PEPPERS, *capsicums*, genus of the monogynia order, class pentandria. There are twenty species of this tribe, the principal of which known in Antigua is the bonnet or bonny pepper, *capsicum angulosum*, of a bright yellow; the goat-pepper, or *capsicum annuum*, of an oblong figure, and red colour, not much esteemed for flavour; the cherry-pepper, or *capsicum cerasiforme*, also red, in form like a large Kentish cherry—from whence its name; and the bird-pepper, the most esteemed of all capsicums. This last is a most beautiful shrub; the leaves are of the deepest green, and the fruit, with all the rich glow of the coral, bursting from their light green cups, cluster upon every bough. It is from the bird-pepper the best cayenne is produced; when mixed with the yellow bonny, the colour becomes paler, and is less esteemed. The London adulterators, in order to keep up that bright red tinge, are in the habit of colouring their cayenne with red lead.

The JASMINES are of great beauty and variety in Antigua. The principal among them are the Arabian jasmine, *jasminum sambac*, and the Cape jasmine, *jasminum fragrans*. The leaves are large, and of a beautiful green, while the silvery blossoms, of a rose-like form, fill the air with their delicious fragrance. This shrub is a genus of the monogynia order, belonging to the diandria class of plants.

KING OF FLOWERS, *lagerstrœmia indica*, is a genus of the monogynia order, belonging to the polyandria class of plants. It is one of the ornaments of the Antiguan flower-garden—its rosy corolla peeping from its bright green leaves; still it is not near so worthy of praise as its fair consort, the lovely

QUEEN OF FLOWERS, *lagerstrœmia regina*, which does not throw out her delicate pink petals until her slight limbs are bent down beneath her flowing burden.

"LADY OF THE NIGHT," *cestrum nocturnum*, of the monogynia order, and pentandria class of plants, one of the sweetest and most poetical of all the Antiguan flowering shrubs. The flowers are of a delicate white, and elegantly shaped. As the day draws to a close, they unfold their lovely petals, which emit the most delicious odour, and that so powerful, that a single flower will perfume an entire suite of apartments. It is not "*labour lost*" to sit up until midnight, to watch the unfolding of this darling child of Flora's in all her glory; for, in the words of the poet,

"Her beauty hangs upon the cheek of night,
Like a rich jewel in an Ethiop's ear."

The FLOWER FENCE, or Barbados pride, *poinciana pulcherrima*, is a very beautiful aculeated shrub, of the order monogynia; the flowers, of a bright red and yellow, are papilionaceous; the pistilum is long, and the stamens numerous; the seeds are oblong and glossy, and when beaten up with borax and water are said to form an excellent cement. There are two species, the red and the yellow, each equally admired, and which form a most beautiful garden fence, from whence the name. The leaves of the shrub are supposed to contain some medicinal qualities, and are consequently much esteemed by "old women."

TRUMPET FLOWER, *bignonia unguis,* is a genus of the angiospermia order, class didynamia; the calyx is quinquefid, the corolla of an elegant bell-shape, and is also quinquefoliated. It is one of the most glowing beauties of the West Indian florist's world. By some it is called the scarlet jessamin, from its colour.

The NOYEAU-VINE, *convolvulus dissectus,* belongs to the order monogynia, class pentandria; the flower is campiform, but expands beneath the influence of the light into the figure of a star. The petals are of a delicate pearly white, the lower parts of a deep purple, the leaves of a deep green; and the seeds, black and very hard, are contained in a three-celled capsule. Noyeau is said to be extracted from this plant, from whence its name; but setting aside this doubtful good quality, it is one of the most admired parasites Antigua produces, and forms a great ornament to a verandah or balcony.

Among the other beautiful vines to be met with, are the passiflora tribe; they are—

1st. The GRANADILLA, *passiflora quadrangularis.*

2nd. The WATER LEMON, *passiflora maliformis,* and

3rd. The CONCH NUT, *passiflora maliformis.*

The granadilla bears a large, oblong fruit, with a thick, fleshy covering, and containing a most delicious pulpy consistence, of a slightly-acid flavour, with numerous flat seeds.

The fruit of the water lemon is of a similar flavour, but of smaller growth, in size and shape more resembling a lemon—from whence its name—and with a covering more ligneous. The conch nut is the most acid, and of an inferior quality. It is of a globular form, with a smooth woody shell. All these varieties form an elegant arbour, with their glossy green leaves, and their lovely blossoms, of the same fair form and colour as the passion-flower—a genus of their own tribe.

ALOE, a genus of the order monogynia, class hexandria: there are thirteen species of aloes, the most common of which found in Antigua is the aloe plant, *aloe vulgaris.* The leaves are broad and thick, and about from two to three feet long; they are full of strong fibres, which can be manufactured into cordage, &c. The aloe plant is commonly used for fences, its long sharp-pointed leaves proving an excellent repellant to any intruder. From the centre of the plant rises a smooth green stem, or column, of about twenty or thirty feet high, broad at the base, and tapering to the top, where it branches out into numerous pedunculuses, or flower stalks. This plant has no calyx; the corolla is monopetalous, and of the colour of the brightest gold, which produces a splendid appearance when in bloom. They are very hardy plants, and can scarcely be destroyed even if wished.

SPANISH NEEDLE, *bindens leucantha;* of the natural order, compositiæ oppositifoliæ. The leaves are composed of strong fibres, which are capable of being manufactured into a ship's cable or a skein of lace thread, a sail for a man-of-war or the finest cambric handkerchiefs.

CACTUS, *cacteæ,* is an order of plants that abounds in all parts of the island. They consist of a calyx adhering to the ovary, the corolla divided into several segments, and the petals variously coloured. The fruit is a succulent seedy berry, in some species of a beautiful red colour. The stems are covered with small tubercles, containing tufts of sharp spines, varying in size. The "Turk's cap," *melocactus communis,* is one of the handsomest of its tribe. It rises in a globular-shaped stem, deeply channelled, of a green colour, and covered with long spines. The top is surmounted by a spherical spinal crest, of a beautiful rose colour, with fleshy seeds of the same glowing tinge. It grows wild in all the sun-dried plains of Antigua, and forms a singular contrast to the withered-looking herbage. The prickly pear is another member of this family; the leaves are thick and oblong, covered with long spines, and filled with a muculent substance. The fruit is in form like an English pear, and of a slightly acid flavour; the rind is thick, and of a red colour, marked near the base with streaks of yellow; the pulpy interior is of the finest crimson, and of the consistence of syrup, which is sometimes used to colour sweetmeats, and affords at times a rich treat to the little negroes. The fruit starts from the leaves without any footstalks, and leaf succeeds to leaf, until it attains the height of from five to six feet. It loves a sandy soil, but on every bank, or in every pasture, it may be met with; while from its formidable spines, and thick fleshy leaves, it forms an excellent fence. There is another species, called the French prickly pear, the succulent leaf of which is sometimes used as a vegetable.

The EGG-PLANT, *solanum melongena,* or *ovigerum,* is a curiosity in the vegetable kingdom. It attains the height of from two to three feet, and is covered with downy leaves of an ovate form. The fruit is of a globose fleshy berry, of the size, shape, and colour of a hen's egg, from whence its name.

There are three species of lilies indigenous to the country, the most common of which is the LILY-ASPHODEL, *amaryllis equestris,* a genus of the monogynia order, hexandria class of plants. The flower rises from an oblong emarginated spatha; the corolla consists of six lance-like petals, of a clear white, with long slender stamens. The seed-bag, or *capsule,* is composed of three valves, and contains numerous seeds.

COTTON SHRUB, or *gossypium,* rises to the height of six or seven feet. The flower is bell-shaped, and consists of one leaf deeply cut into several segments, enfolding one another, and of a pale primrose. From the centre of the flower rises a kind of hollow cylinder, adorned with chives or filaments. The pointal becomes a globular fruit, or pod, composed of five cells, containing small, hard, black seeds, closely enwrapped in the wool, (or cotton, as it is more generally termed,) which, when ripe, bursts open at the apex, and discloses the snowy interior.

CASTOR PLANT, or *palma Christi,* is a very pretty shrub, rising to the height of about fifteen feet. It expands into numerous branches, from which spring dark green leaves, deeply lobed, and standing upon long footstalks. The flowers are insignificant in appearance; the germen becomes a three-celled, globular pod, covered with slender spines, and contains three beautifully-polished, oblong seeds, of a black and silver-grey colour. The best castor oil is obtained from these seeds, by pressure; but the common practice in use among the negroes is to boil them in water, and skim off the unctuous matter as it rises to the top.

CASSADA, or cassava, is made from the roots *jatropha,* or *janipha manihot.* This plant belongs to the natural order *euphorbiaceæ,* and abounds in a juice, the smallest dose of which is highly dangerous from its poisonous qualities. It, however, forms a nutritious food after the juice is well expressed, when it is baked in the form of thin cakes, and supplies the want of bread. *Farina* and tapioca are other preparations from this root, half a pound of which, per diem, is said to be sufficient to support the strongest man.

ARROW-ROOT, and *tout-les-mois,* is the fecula obtained by a similar process from those several roots, the nutritious qualities of which are too well known in the sick chamber to call for further mention. The petals of the arrow-root are of a clear white, while those of the *tout-les-mois* are of a fine crimson, and start from long sheath-like leaves. The French gave the name to this latter plant, from the fact of its flowering every month.

There are a great variety of grasses to be met with in Antigua, the principal of which are—the Guinea-grass, cent. per cent. grass, (*panicum colonum,*) devil-grass, (*cynodon dactylon,*) and nut-grass, (*cyperus hydra.*) The Guinea-grass was introduced into the West Indies, from the coast of Guinea, as its name declares. Jamaica was the first island in which it was propagated, and that by mere accident. The seed of this species of herbage was brought from Africa, as food for some curious birds, natives of that clime, which the captain of a slaver intended to convey to Jamaica as a present. Soon after their arrival, the birds died, and the seed was thrown away as useless. It, however, took root, and flourished surprisingly. The cattle grazing in that part of the island found it out, and eagerly feasted upon it, which being perceived by the planters, the remaining roots were protected for seedlings, and thus the growth of this species was established, and finally distributed throughout the other islands, where it now ranks among the most esteemed of grasses.

The different species of grain propagated in Antigua are the INDIAN CORN, or MAIZE, and the GUINEA CORN—both of them included in the botanical name, *Zea*. The Indian corn rises to the height of about five or six feet; the leaves are eleven or twelve inches long, and two broad, with the edges deeply serrated. The corn, when ripe, is of a bright golden colour, and the ear is covered with a brown silken substance, and then enwrapped in a husk composed of many leaf-like envelopes, which are dried and used by the negroes for stuffing their beds.

The Guinea corn attains the height of about seven or eight feet; the stalk is about the thickness of a small rattan, and is, it is said, capable of being manufactured into sugar. The main stalk branches at the top into several pedicles, each of which bears an ear of corn; the grains are small and round, like shot; they are inclosed in a black shell, which, as the corn ripens, bursts, and forms two small leaves. This grain is used chiefly for feeding horses, &c., although the negroes sometimes manufacture it into meal, and boil it into a kind of pudding.

Of the esculent roots, the yam, *dioscorea sativa*, is the most valuable the island produces. There are several varieties of this plant, the roots of some of them weighing from 20 to 30lbs. The flowers are green, and consist of six segments, the male flowers having six stamens, and the female three styles. The leaves are broad, and strongly veined, and are seated upon long spreading vines. The internal colour of the root varies according to the species—some being quite white, others white and red blended together, which are called by the negroes *moonshine*, and some of a reddish purple.

The SWEET POTATOE, *convolvulus batatas*, is the most common in Antigua. It grows upon a twining vine, and vegetates best in a clayey land. The flower is campiform, and the leaves deeply lobated. There are several varieties of this root, some of which attain a great size; it abounds in a saccharine milky juice, which stains the flesh touched by it.

EDDOES, *arum maximum Ægyptianum*, are small edible roots, abounding, in their crude form, in a slimy juice, but when thoroughly ripe and boiled, attains a dry floury consistence. The natives consider it as one of their standing vegetables, using it in soups, &c.; but to an English palate it is generally distasteful at first trial.

SQUASHES, *cucurbita melopepo*, is a pomiferous herb much esteemed by the Antiguans. The yellow bell-flower is succeeded by a small, oblong fruit, which, when boiled, is very similar to the English vegetable marrow.

SOAP-BERRY TREE, or *saponaria*. The flowers are white and small, and are succeeded by acrid berries of the size and colour of small cherries. They were formerly imported to England, where they were used for waistcoat buttons. If pounded and thrown into water, it is said they cause the death of all the fish therein. These berries answer the purpose of soap in washing linen, (from whence they attain their name,) and are recommended as a specific for the disease of yaws in poultry.

There are a great variety of peas in Antigua, but none of them of the delicate flavour of those usually cultivated in England. The principal sorts are the pigeon pea, the black-eyed pea, and the white bean, or Barbados pea. The general use made of these vegetables is to boil them in soup, which forms a grand dish in negro cookery; they are used either in their dry or green state.

GINGER is a genus of the monogynia order, class monandria. There are ten species, each natives of tropical climates; the common ginger, or *amomum zingiber*, is the one most known in Antigua. The flower-stalks rise by the side of the leaves, (which are of a light green, and very narrow,) directly from the root; they are scaly, and from every joint issues a single blue flower, five-leaved, and shaped like the iris. The ovary afterwards becomes a triangular fruit, the seed being contained in three cells. The use of the dried root is too well known in England to descant upon the virtues of it; the green root is preserved in sugar, and forms a much admired sweetmeat.

PINE APPLE, *ananas*, is the queen of Antiguan fruits. There are two varieties, the "black pine," and the "white pine;" of these the first mentioned is the most esteemed. The flavour of the pine is exquisite, not to be *described*, but *eaten* to have its excellences fully appreciated; it forms, indeed, a perfect ambrosia not to be surpassed by that of *Mount Olympus*.

WATER MELON, or *anguria*, a genus of the diandria order, class monœcia. The calyx is quinquefid, and the flower quinquepetalous. The fruit belies not its name, abounding in a sweet water; it is three-celled, and contains numerous flat seeds; the scent is very fragrant. There are three kinds of melon in Antigua, all of which are esteemed for their cooling qualities.

Of the CAPREOLATED PLANTS, the gourd (*cucurbita*) is the most common in the island. The flower consists of one leaf, an expanded campiform, but so deeply divided that it appears upon first view to be five distinct segments. The germen becomes an oblong, bottle-shaped fruit, divided into six cells, containing flat, oblong seeds. The bitter flavour of the gourd is extreme; but both the fruit and leaves are said to be of great efficacy in some diseases of the viscera.

Among the acroydra tribe, the principal found in Antigua is the GROUND NUT, *arachis hypogæa*. It is a genus of the decandria order, class polyadelphia. The flowers are papilionaceous, and the leaves of a light green; the nut, which grows from the root, is not dug until the plant withers. It is roasted before eaten; the kernel, which is twofold; is very sweet, and forms an important article of traffic to the petty hucksters.

CHAPTER LIII

Government—Governor-in-Chief—Council—Assembly—
Government officers—Judicial officers—Ecclesiastical establishments—
Schools—Fortifications and military defences—Revenue—Exports and
imports—Population returns.

Antigua is the usual residence of the captain-general and governor-in-chief of the Leeward Islands; and in his absence, the oldest member of council, who is styled president, acts as his deputy. But in case of the death of the governor, or his removal from the office, according to a recent arrangement, the lieutenant-governor of St. Kitt's takes up his residence at Antigua, and officiates as governor until a fresh appointment is made.

The colonial government of Antigua is confided to the governor-in-chief of the Leeward Islands—a council, nominated by the governor, and confirmed by the crown—and a house of assembly, consisting of twenty-five members, representing the capital town of St. John's, and the twelve divisions, which the six parishes of the island compose, elected by the freeholders. The council act in two capacities—the one as the advisers of the governor in the administration of the executive branch of government; the other, as an upper house in the legislative assembly.

As the appointed advisers and assistants of the governor, his "privy council," as they are termed, when acting in that capacity, the members of the council enjoy the title of "honourable;" and their concurrence, or that of three of their body, is required to most of the acts of the governor in his executive capacity. Their appointment, sometimes, is immediate from the crown, though the governor may, in case of a vacancy, appoint *ad interim,* until a confirmation, which is seldom withheld, is obtained. Leave of absence from the colony may be granted to a member of the council, by the governor, or his *locum tenens,* for six months, which may be extended by the crown to two years; but by a longer absence, a member incurs the forfeiture of his office. The governor, moreover, has the power to suspend any member of the council from the exercise of his office, until such time as the pleasure of the sovereign may be made known.

In their legislative capacity, the council assume to themselves, with regard to the members of assembly, as nearly as may be, the relation of the House of Lords to that of the Commons in England. Their officers are, a clerk and marshal, the former being the first colonial secretary, and often assuming the functions of the usher of the black rod. The senior member presides, under the title of president. They deliberate in private, excluding strangers, and enjoy the same freedom of debate as do the house of assembly, as the English parliament.

The house of assembly, assimilating itself, as it does, as closely as possible, to the usages of the English House of Commons, needs no further particular notice.

The governor, however, discharges two important functions, which are usually exercised by separate individuals. He acts as chancellor, or rather, as commissioner of the great seal, and, as such, presides in the court of equity; and up to the present time, he has also exercised all the functions of an ordinary, though, we believe, in practice, seldom going beyond granting licences for marriages, and admitting the probate of wills—acts for which he is not allowed to grant deputations; but this interference in matters of ecclesiastical jurisdiction may probably soon be dispensed with.

The chief officers of the island are—

1. The *Governor*, who receives a salary of 3000*l.* sterling from the British government, besides certain fees of office—as, on administering oaths on admission to certain public offices; on granting letters of administration, probate of wills, marriage licences, signature and great seal to writs of execution, letters of guardianship; on every motion made in the Court of Chancery, and on various other occasions; but the fees on granting leave of absence to a member of the council, or commissions to public offices, are usually the exclusive perquisites of his excellency's private secretary.

2. *Public Secretary.*—His income, arising from fees, is said to equal, if not exceed, that of the governor.

3. *Treasurer.*—Receives from 800*l.* to 400*l.* per annum, and 2½ per cent. on all taxes and other moneys received; and also the same on all moneys paid away. He is required to give security on this appointment, from the governor, to the amount of 10,000*l.* currency.

4. *Master in Chancery.*—His income varies with the amount of business occurring. His fees are, 15*s.* 2*d.* for every hour, with other charges in proportion, when accounts are passing before him.

5. *The Registrar of Deeds* was formerly paid in sugar; but now, for every ninety-six words recorded in his office, he receives 2*s.*, and the same sum for every year in which a search is made for any particular deed in his records. The returns of this office, as of the two preceding, being wholly dependent on fees, it is not easy to estimate their average amount.

6. The *Provost Marshal* receives a fixed salary of 600*l.*, which is paid from fees, out of which the gaoler also receives a salary of 160*l.* All incidental expenses attendant on these two offices are also discharged from the same

fund; and there is always a surplus remaining, which is placed at the disposal of the governor.

7. The *Harbour Master* receives 50*l.* per annum currency for boat-hire, and a fee, varying from 4*s.* 6*d.* to 22*s.* 6*d.*, on certain vessels coming into the harbour, according to tonnage, from 30 tons to 300, and upwards. This officer seems less adequately provided for than any other, considering the attention required, and the responsibility attendant on his office.

8. The *Postmaster,* who is paid by the home government, receives 80*l.* sterling per annum.

The judicial officers connected with the colony are numerous, considered with respect to the population; but as none, with the exception of the chief judge, receive pecuniary remuneration, and he only 300*l.* sterling,[72] and from fees, the appointments, although high-sounding, are, with this exception, only honorary, and almost parallel with that of the unpaid, though not less useful, magistracy of England. The appointments are as follow:—A chief judge; four assistant justices; a chief baron of the exchequer; judge of the vice-admiralty court; registrar of the vice-admiralty court; two masters examiners of chancery; registrar in chancery; provost marshal, advocate, and attorney-general; procurator and solicitor-general; three king's counsel and a coroner, (the latter receiving 300*l.* per annum sterling from the colony.) The office of coroner is filled by Sir Robert Horsford, the attorney-general. To these must be added two stipendiary magistrates, appointed under the provisions of the act for the abolition of slavery, and paid by the home government.

The ecclesiastical establishment now comprises a bishop, receiving 2000*l.*; an archdeacon, receiving 500*l.* sterling from the British government; the rector of the parish of St. John, receiving, with a curate, 330*l.* from the colony; the rector of the parish of St. George, who receives a stipend of 230*l.* sterling; the rector of the parish of St. Paul's, who receives 250*l.* sterling; the rector of the parish of St. Peter's, who receives 300*l.* sterling; and the rector of the parish of St. Philip's, who receives a stipend of 275*l.* sterling.

The stipends are raised by rates on the several parishes; and in addition to these, the clergy receive the usual surplice fees.

There are several day and night schools belonging to the Established Church—viz.,

St John's—one boys' and one girls'; two infant-schools at the Rectory; on Manning's Estate, Cedar Valley, Marble Hill, St. James's, St. Luke's, African Hospital; three evening-schools in St. John's, and four Sunday-schools, besides at the various parishes in the island. The instruction which is generally given is reading and repeating the scriptures and church catechism, and also certain lessons and hymns. The number of children instructed by the clergy may be reckoned at about 2300.

There are twelve churches, including four chapels of ease. One of these chapels of ease is the private property of the Honourable and Reverend Nath. Gilbert, the descendant of the founder of Methodism in this country, which contains 400 sittings.

	Sittings.
St. John's church contains	1600
St. George's	600
St. Peter's, (town of Parham,) old church	300
St. Philip's, (near Willoughby Bay)	433
St. Paul's, (Falmouth)	400
St. Mary's, (Old Road)	250
St. John's parish has three chapels of ease—one at Popehead, called St. James's	420
Bendall's Bridge, St. Luke's	400
And one in town	150
St. Peter's, one chapel of ease, (private property of Nath. Gilbert)	400
St. Philip's	260
St. Paul's, (a temporary chapel at English Harbour)	350
St. Mary's, (in Ffryes Valley)	250

There is also a temporary chapel at the common gaol, which may be supposed to contain 150 sittings. The Rev. Robert Holberton volunteered, in the early part of 1829, to deliver a religious discourse every Sunday morning, between the hours of seven and eight o'clock, and has not grown weary in this laudable cause. He attends the prison at all times when serious consolations are required, and more particularly those who may have to suffer death by paying the penalty of the law.

ACCOUNT OF BAPTISMS, MARRIAGES, AND BURIALS.

		Baptisms.	Marriages.	Burials.
	Parish of St. John's	310	112	150
	St. George's	74	38	36
	St. Peter's	116	52	24
1836	St. Paul's	74	47	39
	St. Mary's	60	40	14
	St. Philip's	122	40	19
	Total	756	329	282
1837	Church	662	246	393
1838	"	528	316	313
1839	"	723	468	420
1837	Wesleyan Society	96	0	112
1838	"	108	0	114
1839	"	95	0	85
1837	Moravians	383	0	318
1838	"	249	0	256
1839	"	265	0	254

The Wesleyan society has several Sunday-schools, also day scholars, exclusive of night-schools, which may be reckoned as follows:—From the "Ladies' Society," and the "Wesleyan Missionary," conducted by voluntary contributions:—

	Scholars.	Teachers.
Sunday-school	1782	155
Day-school	962	19
The Moravian Mission has	1115	0
Besides infant children, whose number may be estimated at about	1800	0

Scholars. Teachers.

The members of their church may be estimated at about 9000.

FORTIFICATIONS.—There are seven forts—namely,

Sterling.

Fort James, which costs the country for captain's salary 150*l.* 0*s.*

Fort George   112*l.* 10*s.*

Fort Johnson's Point   60*l.* 0*s.*

Fort Byam   50*l.* 0*s.*

Old Road   59*l.* 12*s.*

Goat Hill Battery   60*l.* 0*s.*

Rat Island   60*l.* 0*s.*

The amount expended for the military defence of this country, sustained by the colony exclusively, not under the control of the ordnance department, amounts to near 2500*l.* sterling; and that incurred by Great Britain in this time of peace is sometimes over 24,000*l.* sterling. Some years it may be 1000*l.* or so under, and particularly now the island has no militia, as it ceased to exist in July, 1838, by order of her Majesty in council.

REVENUE.—The comparatively yearly revenue may be estimated at about 19,000*l.* sterling. The expenditure is generally more, which is raised by ¼*d.* assessed upon all lands; 1*d.* on every 100 lbs. of sugar; 3*d.* on every 100 gallons of rum and molasses; a street-tax, and a per centage upon all dwelling-houses or merchant-warehouses, according to the exigencies of the case; also a cistern-tax upon all dwelling-houses of the annual rent of 60*l.*, not having a cistern on or belonging thereto; (while this is a very necessary precaution in cases of fire, it brings in a very good revenue;) an import duty imposed by the British parliament on all American importations, (part of this only is paid into the island treasury, as a per centage is first detained by the collector of her Majesty's customs for defraying the expenses of officers' salaries; however, the surplus paid into the treasury may be computed at 9000*l.* currency annually, but has at times amounted to 16,000*l.*;) also another import duty, levied by our colonial legislature on all goods imported not coming under the act of the imperial parliament, but such as upon all British or other articles of foreign manufacture may not be considered dutyable, in that case, 2*l.* 10*s.* upon every 100*l.* is paid; also an annual sum is paid by every retailer of spirituous liquors, wines, and beer;

and a customs duty on wine imported, (except it be brought from Madeira and the Western Islands.

AMOUNT OF EXPORT IN THE YEAR 1770.

	£.	s.	d.
To Great Britain	430,210	0	0
To North America, United States, and the West India Islands	35,806	17	6
	£466,016	17	6

AMOUNT OF EXPORT, IN THE YEAR 1787.

To Great Britain, North America, the West India Islands, United States, and Foreign Ports, consisted of 284,526 casks of sugar, 716,545 gallons of rum, 5910 gallons of molasses, £59 160,510 pounds of cotton, 4*l.* sterling worth of dyeing woods, 2,596 and 48,000*l.* worth of other miscellaneous articles, which together amounted to

Shipping Inwards, 1831.

	No.of Vessels.	Tons.	No.of Men
From Great Britain.	55	11783	634
From North America.	50	4410	256
From West Indies.	142	6997	730
From United States.	58	6692	375
From Foreign Ports.	80	2608	336
Totals.	385	32,490	2331

Shipping Outwards, 1831.

	No.of Vessels.	Tons.	No.of Men
To Great Britain.	55	11498	628
To North America.	39	3334	197
To the West Indies.	191	10482	982

Shipping Outwards, 1831.

	No.of Vessels.	Tons.	No.of Men
To the United States.	31	3686	211
To Foreign Ports.	91	3522	399
Totals.	407	32,522	2417

AMOUNT OF EXPORTS FOR 1831.

	£.	s.	d.
To Great Britain	228,612	0	0
To North America	12,803	10	0
To West Indies	37,766	19	6
To United States	10,372	18	0
To Foreign Ports	7,090	15	0
	£296,646	2	6

SHIPPING INWARDS, 1840.

	Number of Vessels.	Tons.
From Great Britain	51	11,334
From North America and the West Indies	254	10,968
From the United States	79	11,657
From Foreign Ports	158	3,650
Total Number of Men		2,925
Total Number of Vessels		542
Total Number of Tons		37,609

SHIPPING OUTWARDS, 1840.

	Number of Vessels.	Tons.
To Great Britain	56	12,953

SHIPPING OUTWARDS, 1840.

	Number of Vessels.	Tons.
To North America and the West Indies	251	10,297
To the United States	26	3,844
To Foreign Ports	142	10,781

Total Number of Men   3,133

Total Number of Vessels 475

Total Number of Tons   37,375

AMOUNT OF EXPORTS, 1840.

	£.	s. d.
To Great Britain	401,624	4 6
To North America and the West Indies	328	0 0
	£401,952	4 6

Population.

Year	Number of Whites.	Number of Coloured.	Number of Negroes.
1673	no account taken.	no account taken.	500
1690	600		no account taken.
1707	2892	no account taken.	12,892
1720	3672		19,186
1724	5200		19,800
1729	4088		22,611
1734	3772		24,408
1756	3412		31,428
1774	2590		37,808
1787	2590	1230	37,808
1788	no account taken.	no account taken.	36,000

Population.

Number of Whites. Number of Coloured. Number of Negroes.

	Number of Whites.	Number of Coloured.	Number of Negroes.
1805	3000	1300	36,000
1810	3000		37,000
1817	no account taken.	no account taken.	32,249
1824			30,314
1827			29,839
1831			29,537

Census Taken in 1821.

Area in miles square.	Number of White Males.	Number of White Females.	Total number of Whites.	Number of Coloured Males.	Number of Coloured Females.	Total number of Coloured.
St. John's	17,955	644	563	1207	1210	1623	2833
St. Philip's	10,881	116	46	162	62	99	161
St. George's	6000	56	35	91	24	44	68
St. Mary's	14,190	81	43	124	65	94	159
St. Peter's	8310	100	37	137	53	65	118
St. Paul's	11,941	142	117	259	292	435	727
	69,277	1139	841	1980	1706	2360	4066

Number of negroes in six parishes, 30,985.

No census has been taken since 1821, but the population now may be estimated at about the same. The greatest bulk is employed in agriculture; the manufacture is sugar, rum, and molasses. The island is supposed to contain 69,299 miles, or 108 square miles, consequently the average population is estimated to the square mile in this island to be about 343.

---

[72] It most be remarked that this salary is not a determined one. The judge receives it as a boon from the existing legislature. His successor may, perhaps, only obtain the *honour* conferred by the appointment.

Supplemental Chapter

Since the foregoing pages have been written, many and great events have occurred in Antigua. St. John's, the capital of the island, has been raised to the dignity of a city, by the mandate of her most gracious Majesty Queen Victoria, (as announced by official letter of his excellency the governor-in-chief, Sir Charles Augustus Fitzroy, K.H., dated 10th November, 1842;) the church constituted a cathedral church and an episcopal see; and our former worthy archdeacon has become the Right Rev. the Lord Bishop of Antigua. The rector of St. John's, the Rev. R. Holberton, has most deservedly been appointed archdeacon, (as well as rector,) in the room of Dr. Davis, the present bishop. The first ordination held in the island took place on Tuesday, the 25th July, 1843. The governor-in-chief. Sir Charles Augustus Fitzroy, has ably conducted the government, and made himself universally and deservedly beloved and respected for his zeal and strenuous exertions for the common good. His excellency first met the council and assembly at the court house, on Thursday, the 21st of February, 1842, where he was received by a guard of honour, (of part of the 81st regiment, then stationed in Antigua.) After taking his seat in the council chamber, his excellency delivered in person a most flattering inaugural speech to the legislature; addresses were then returned by the council and assembly, to each of which his excellency made most gracious answers. Upon the breaking up of the meeting, his excellency returned to government house, where he held a levee, (which was numerously attended,) and received congratulatory addresses from the clergymen of the church of England, the Moravian ministers, the Wesleyan missionaries, and the members of the Presbyterian association.

The Scotch kirk has been nearly completed, and opened for divine service; an able preacher from Scotland, the Rev. A. Brown, is the officiating minister. Until the opening of the new church, the court house was kindly lent to the members of this persuasion to hold their Sunday service in; and where the Rev. Mr. Brown poured forth a strain of pure, unaffected devotion, and delivered a series of sermons, whose beauty lay not only in words, but in the grand religious truths they inculcated.

Agricultural societies have been formed, much to the interest of that useful class of men, the agriculturists. In these societies, prizes have been awarded to the following:—

To manager who makes the largest quantity of sugar per acre, on average crop—a silver tea-pot, value 8*l.*

To manager who makes best quality of sugar—a silver cup, value 7*l.*

To manager who makes the largest quantity of sugar per acre, from second ratoons, being not less than five acres—a silver ladle, value 4*l.*

To manager who has been most successful with his stock during the year—a silver knife, value 3*l.*

To the overseer who shall produce the best plan of a plantation, pay, boiling-house, and still-house books—a pair of silver spoons, value 2*l.*

To labourers who have worked the greatest number of days in the year on one property—five prizes, from 10*s.* to two dollars each, currency.

To those parents who have the largest number of children employed in agriculture—five prizes, from 10*s.* currency, to two dollars each.

To stock-keepers who have remained during the year, and have been most successful with the stock—five prizes, from 10*s.* to two dollars.

A popular institution for intellectual improvement has also been instituted at St. John's, in which several lectures have been given upon various interesting subjects.

On the 12th of June, 1842, a very bright and beautiful meteor passed over the town of St. John's, in a direction from east to west. Its form was globular; and as it passed rapidly along the heavens, it emitted bright spiral flashes of fire, which gilded the sky, and threw deep shadows upon the earth. During its progress, it was attended by a rushing noise, sufficient to call the attention of those who did not even notice its extreme brilliancy. Possibly this meteor might have belonged to the class termed *aerolites;* many of such phenomena have appeared, from time to time, in this quarter of the globe: one fell at Bahia, in Brazil, which weighed 14,000 pounds, and another, (still preserved in the British Museum,) which fell at Buenos Ayres, weighed 1400 pounds.

The next great event to be recorded, is the awful earthquake, with which Antigua and many of the other Leeward Islands was visited, on Wednesday, the 8th of February, 1843. About half-past ten o'clock A. M., a low, hollow, rumbling sound arrested the attention, and announced, in its own peculiar solemn tone, the coming of an earthquake. Immediately after this awful warning, a tremor of the earth was felt, which gradually increasing in violence, led the frightened inhabitants to rush from their houses, and seek safety in the open air. Heart-rending were the screams, fervent and numerous were the calls for mercy, from the assembled groups. The air was darkened with the dust from the falling buildings, as well as from the sulphureous exhalations which issued from the opening earth, and almost stopped respiration. In Antigua, the extent of damage was immense.

Out of fourteen parish churches, (including the chapels of ease,) only two remain uninjured. St. Paul's, situated at Falmouth, was entirely destroyed; as also St. Stephen's chapel of ease, the district church of All Saints, and the chapel schools of St. Bartholomew's and St. Mark's, not long ago erected. The new church of St. Peter's, which has been mentioned in these pages as being in a state of progress at Parham, and which was expected to be completed and opened for Divine service in 1843, was also much rent and injured. The pretty parish church of St. Philip's was cracked from top to bottom, and rendered unsafe, and the school-house was levelled with the ground. St. James's chapel of ease was severely injured, and the north and south wings fell. The school-room at St. Barnaby's was rent in several places; and at St. Stephen's a similar building was entirely levelled. The school-room at Brecknocks was also rendered unsafe. There were 172 sugar-mills upon the island, most of which upon that eventful morning had been "put in the wind," and were merrily going with the breeze, crushing between their powerful machinery the golden canes, and sending a rich stream of luscious juice through the several pipes into the boiling-houses; of these thirty-five were entirely levelled with the ground, eighty-two split from top to bottom, and the remaining fifty-five almost all of them injured, requiring numerous repairs. Among those most seriously injured may be mentioned—

"Bellevue, Messrs. Shand's—down.
Renfew's—down.
Belmont's—down.
Bath Lodge, property of Walters—down.
Green Castle's, Sir Henry Martin's works and mansion—down.
Lower Freeman's—down.
Sir Geo. Thomas's works, and part of the mansion—down; the manager was obliged to take up his quarters under a shed.
Little Duers—down.
Big Duers—down.
Ffrys—down.
Elliot's, part of sugar works—down.
Potter's—down.
La Roche's—down.
Baijer Otto Baijer's—down.
Mount Pleasant—down.
Rock Hill—down.
Delap's—down.
George Byam's—partly down.
Patterson's new steam-mill, and works—down.
Monterea's—down.
Paynter's—down.

Gunthorp's—down.

Claremont's, the seat of the Hon. W. E. Williams, untenantable, and works of two estates—down.

Gambles, Admiral Tollemache's—down.

The Wood—down.

Fryar's Hill—down.

McKinnon's—down.

The newly erected sugar-works of Wm. Williams, Esq.—down.

&c. &c. &c."

The city of St. John's suffered severely, and after the earthquake, presented a most dismal appearance. About one-third of the stores and dwellings were levelled with the ground; and the remainder (with the exception of those buildings erected of wood) so shattered and torn, that they were rendered untenantable. Some of the houses were completely twisted round, presenting an acute angle to the street, instead of their usual position. The cranes at the water's edge were many of them lifted out of the ground; and in several of the stores, streams of water bubbled up through the interstices of the pavement. The court-house, police-office, (formerly the old jail,) the arsenal, the new jail and barracks, the registrar's office, treasurer's office, governor's secretary's office, (recently erected,) colonial bank, Antigua library-rooms, &c., were all of them rent and torn, and several rendered unsafe. The cathedral of St. John's was damaged to a great extent, the tower being rent from top to bottom, the north dial of the clock precipitated to the ground, and part of the east wall of the tower thrown upon the roof of the church. The handsome altar-piece was entirely destroyed; and many of the monuments which graced the walls of the cathedral were hurled from their resting-places, and shivered into atoms. Of these were the tombs of Lord Lavington, Warner, Kelsick, Ottley, and Atkinson. The font was thrown off its pedestal, seven of the large pipes in the front of the organ knocked out, and much damage done to the interior of that instrument. The whole of the south-east walls of the cathedral were thrown into the churchyard, carrying with them some of the ornamental ground-glass windows. The north-west walls fell in one mass of ruins, while the north-east protruded beyond the perpendicular. The north and south vestibules were almost blocked up by the piles of massy stones and bricks. The churchyard also presented a melancholy appearance, many of the tombs being rent open, and split in various places.

Before this awful event, it had been the intention of the vestry to enter into a contract for raising the tower, and improving its architectural adornments, as also to make some alteration in the chancel.

The school-room erected near the rectory of St. John's was also very much dilapidated; and the national-school for girls was so much injured as to require being taken down.

The new Wesleyan Chapel was fearfully rent, and doubts were at first entertained for the safety of the building; but upon a mature deliberation, it was determined to repair it without pulling it down; which has since been done.

The nearly finished Scotch kirk met with a severe injury, its walls being cracked in several places.

The ministers of the established church in St. John's performed service under a large tent, erected to the east of the Daily Meal Society's buildings, and also in the Conversion Society's school-room, and the African hospital.

The Scotch and Wesleyan ministers were accommodated at the Mico and Moravian school-room, or beneath a grove of trees, near to the spot where Governor Parke met his fate; and for one day in the week, at the Moravian Chapel.

Almost every kitchen and oven in the island was destroyed; and many of the capacious cisterns ruined. In some of them, the water was so deeply impregnated with sulphur, or mixed with the fallen mortar, as to be perfectly unusable.

Oh! awful indeed was this fearful visitation of the Almighty! The loftiest looks of men were humbled, and the stoutest hearts were bowed down. Tremendous—terrible was the shock! The earth reeled as if about to be over-thrown; and scarce could the strongest man keep his footing. The island shook from its very centre; and in many parts the ground opened, and emitted columns of noxious sulphureous water. The sea felt the powerful hand of its Maker, and rose several feet above its highest mark; while in some parts it dashed up the streets to the distance of many yards.

The excess of terror occasioned by this awful throe of Nature was so great, that many individuals threw themselves over the wharfs, and sought refuge in the treacherous waves. Still their fears were not allayed; for the sea was so turbulent that they were under the necessity of again seeking dry land to save themselves from being engulfed in its yawning abyss. The legislature met at government-house on the 13th, (the court-house being in an unsafe condition,) by special command, to take into consideration the best way of averting, as far as human endeavours could, the direful results likely to accrue from the late calamity. A grant of 500*l.* currency was placed at the disposal of a committee, for the purpose of supporting the roof and plate of the cathedral, and rendering it in some measure safe for divine worship. The vestry met on the 24th March, under the tents, and among other resolutions agreed to make a record of the event in the church books. The dock-yard at English Harbour—the pride of the Caribbee Islands—has suffered greatly; the excellent wharfs racked and rent; in some places they sank down to the level of the sea, in others, they were heaved up and down, like the billows of the great deep; the massy stone and brick buildings erected within the yard were nearly all of them injured; the officers' quarters severely rent; the cordage stores, &c., cracked from top to bottom; the fine capacious cisterns ruined. The superintendent's office, &c., was also much impaired and rent; and the stone platform which ran along the commissioners' room moved out of its place, and the pavement beneath literally wrested up. The guard-house and midshipmen's quarters were greatly damaged, and the stone building near presented an awful appearance, one side of it having sunk some depth into the ground, while that part of the wharf contiguous to it was fearfully rent. In the boat-house, the massy stone circular pillars which supported the shed were very much cracked, and one of them was separated from its pedestal and hurled to the ground. The blacksmith's shop, paint stores, &c., were left but as "tottering walls," while the long line of cliffs and stone walls that topped the hill at the back of the yard were shivered in all directions. St. Helena was also much injured, and the embattled walls of Fort Berkley, at the mouth of the harbour, were overthrown. The superintendent of the yard, Jos. Hart, Esq., estimated the damage at about £20,000. In many parts of the yard the ground looked as if ploughed up, while in others, deep and broad fissures, strongly impregnated with sulphur, opened their yawning mouths. It was, at first, asserted that the mouth of the harbour had been obstructed by the fallen rocks; but upon a careful survey, the water was found to be deeper, if anything, than before the awful occurrence. At the Ridge, the terrible effects of the earthquake were also felt. The stone stores and barracks were either thrown down, or so severely rent that they were unsafe, and the privates were accommodated under tents for some time after. The small stone building, situated at the extreme point of Shirley Heights, (erected for the accommodation of the signal-man,) fell at the commencement of the shock, burying beneath its ruins a baby of four months old, but which was afterwards extricated and restored to its distressed parents unhurt, with the exception of a trifling scratch. The town of Falmouth presented but a mass of ruins—its church was levelled with the ground, and the tombs in the churchyard rent open, as if the last great day was come. The fortifications at Monk's-hill were cracked and rent in many places; and near to the spot, a huge rock was lifted up by the oscillations of the earth, from the place where it had reposed for centuries, and hurled to the opposite side of the road.

Dows Hill, the country residence of the governor, suffered great injury, and his excellency Sir C. A. Fitzroy lost furniture to the amount of 1000*l.*

sterling. De Witts, the seat of Sir Robert Horsford, Knt., solicitor-general of Antigua, was nearly levelled with the ground, and several other delightful country residences partly destroyed. The lately established villages were nearly all dismantled—their neat little stone cottages in ruins. Many of the Moravian and Wesleyan settlements throughout the island have suffered very much, as well as several of the forts. Rat Island battery is also much damaged, as well as the new lunatic asylum erected there. In many parts of the island, pools of water were formed, where hitherto no appearance of moisture was to be found; while in other places, established ponds were completely dried up.

The boats and ships in the harbour were fearfully affected. The island could not be seen for the space of ten minutes, from the dense cloud which arose from it. The hills which encircle the harbour were fearfully shaken; and at that part known as "Hatton's-hill" the effects were truly terrific. The whole of this eminence, which rises rather conically, is rent into yawning fissures to the extent of about eighteen or nineteen acres. This spot had been appropriated to the negroes' provision ground; and in one place, a portion of their well-cultivated gardens slipped from the brow of the hill, and, still clothed with its vegetable productions, half way filled up one of the chasms, (in breadth from three to four feet,) cleft in the solid ground. Upon the margin of the sea, another deep abyss presents itself. The solid rock is rent asunder, in extent to about forty feet long, thirty feet deep, and near seventy feet wide. That peculiarly shaped rock known to mariners as "Ship's Stern," and which has proved for so long a time a sure landmark to pilots, was shivered to pieces; and McNish's mountain (the highest in the island) very much rent and fissured. Several shocks were felt during the next forty-eight hours, and the ground appeared to have a tremulous motion for several weeks after. A proclamation was issued by his excellency Sir Charles Augustus Fitzroy, setting apart Friday, the 14th of February, a day of "public humiliation and thanksgiving before God, in acknowledgment of his Divine power, so fearfully and wonderfully displayed, as well as his mercy and forbearance in sparing the island from utter destruction," which was kept throughout Antigua. At Barbuda, the earthquake was also severely felt—all the stone buildings, with the exception of a small school-room, fell.

Barbados, St. Vincents, Martinique, Dominica, and St. Thomas, felt the shock but slightly. Guadaloupe was the greatest sufferer of the group. One whole town. Point à Pitre, was entirely destroyed, and upwards of 4000 souls perished, while about 600 were severely wounded. A few days after the earthquake. Admiral Gourbeyre, the governor of Guadaloupe, despatched the "Papillon" man-of-war to Antigua to inquire into its state, and render all the assistance possible. She brought the intelligence, that out of the inhabitants of one entire street, only one individual (a female) was saved alive. Soon after the earthquake, a fire broke out, and consumed what the earthquake had spared. An American master of a ship was taken into custody for secreting many articles of value, (the property of the sufferers,) on board his ship. His sentence would have been death; but on account of his having been seen to render assistance to some of the poor creatures who were partly buried beneath the fallen buildings, it was mitigated, and he was condemned to serve on board the galley for a certain term.

At Monserrat, the effects of the earthquake were severely experienced. Scarcely a house in the island that had the least particle of brick-work about it was uninjured; and some were so rent, that they were obliged to be pulled down. A great many of the buildings on the sugar estates were levelled with the ground, and otherwise severely injured. The fall of earth was so great from the mountain, and the dust so thick, that it was at first supposed to be a fresh eruption from the *Souffrière*, a volcanic mountain.

The following is an extract from a letter from a resident upon the island:—

"I was about five hundred yards from the sulphur pit, opening an old spring of fresh water; the earthquake commenced gradually—the oscillation slow. Though sensible it was an earthquake, I was under no apprehension, till of a sudden I heard a dreadful noise. On looking towards the mountain over the sulphur, it was enveloped in one mass of smoke as I thought. It was then time to move my quarters, but I was thrown upon my back by the violent motion. The path that I returned I observed cracking; I called to the man to be cautious—it was giving way—he came instantly forward, saying it was well we got over as we did, for the path was fallen in. The mountain, to the extent of a mile, is rent in various places. A man this moment has returned from the sulphur, stating that the crater is open, but does not perceive any greater appearance of smoke from it than usual."

We passed Monserrat three days after the earthquake. From the deck of the steamer we could perceive that large slips from the mountains were still falling; and every now and then a cloud of dust arose.

St. Christopher's also suffered very severely, the damage done being immense. The stone dwellings and stores in Basseterre, the capital of the island, fearfully shook and rent,—some of the finest, but a mass of ruins, and others rendered unsafe. The north and south vestibules of the parochial church of St. George were severely injured, as well as the walls of the main building, which in some places were rent from top to bottom. The clock stopped at half-past ten, the time the earthquake commenced; many of the mural monuments which adorned the interior of the church were also destroyed. The Female Benevolent Institution was much damaged, and the West Indian Bank rent and split. The reading-rooms also suffered, the south gable having fallen into the street beneath. One large dwelling, situated in the square, and known as "Wall House," fell a complete prey to the violence of the rockings. The entire side walls fell down, which striking upon a horse-stable beneath, buried the unfortunate animals in the ruins. Some of the private dwelling-houses were completely gutted, nothing remaining of them but the exterior walls. The gaol was so shattered, that the prisoners had to be removed, and accommodated for the night in the hospital adjoining. The square was crowded with a concourse of persons of every age, sex, and condition—pride, rank, power, were alike forgotten—as upon bended knees, or with clasped hands and pallid lips, they invoked the aid of that Great Being *"who rideth upon the wings of the wind,"* and at whose rebuke *"the earth shook and trembled, and the foundation also of the hills moved, and were shaken."*

The estates in the country suffered greatly; steam-engines, windmills, boiling-houses, proprietors' dwellings, &c., the labour of many years, were in one moment levelled with the ground. The works and dwelling-house at Bevan Island, (in the parish of St John's,) situated upon a cliff, were lifted from their foundations, and hurled into the ravine below. St. Peter's church was also greatly injured, as well as the Moravian church at Cayon. Upon one estate, report said, that three negro-houses sank into the earth; and in the vicinity, the ground opened, and a pool of water, of a particularly white and clear quality, was formed. In the neighbourhood of Sandy Point, at an estate belonging to the Payne family, the earth also opened, and vomited forth from its secret depths fumes of sulphureous vapour. Fort George, at Brimstone Hill, has felt the shock in a serious manner; while the mountain itself is, in many places, despoiled of its beauty, from the land-slips which have taken place. From Mount Misery, the highest point of the island, a long spiral cloud of white smoke was seen to ascend during the time of the earthquake; and the sulphureous spring situated in its centre is said to have overflowed its bounds.

At Johnstone's, or French River, a melancholy catastrophe occurred. It is a spot chosen by the washerwomen of Basseterre as the scene of their necessary avocations; and upon the eventful morning of the earthquake, about ten of these females were busily employed in washing, in a natural basin, (formed by huge rocks,) at the moment of the shock taking place. Seven of these women fortunately escaped by flight; but the three, who were exactly underneath the cliff, met a more melancholy fate. At the commencement of the awful commotion, an immense rock parted from this cliff, and fell into the stream below. The affrighted females fled from the scene of danger; but, alas! the increased oscillations of the earth caused it to rebound with fearful velocity, and striking against a larger rock, it split into three or four pieces, and thus dealt destruction to each of the poor panic-stricken women! From some parts of St. Christopher's, the Dutch island of St. Eustatia was seen to tremble like an aspen-leaf. Nevis also felt the dire commotion; the streets of the capital presented but one mass of ruins. The bath-house, an immense pile of the strongest masonry, was split and rent in every direction, and some of the massive stones riven in two. The court-house was greatly injured—many of the finest of the stores and dwelling-houses levelled, and the busy marts become mere heaps of rubbish. In many parts of the island, the earth was rent open to the extent of several inches—cliffs toppled down—columns of water were thrown up, and pools formed, where, prior to the awful visitation, nothing of the kind was to be perceived. Many of the estates also suffered great devastations; and some of the inhabitants left their tottering houses, and took shelter beneath sheds and outhouses.

It is impossible to describe the appearance presented in these different islands; indeed, it baffles all description. The scene cannot be painted, and language fails to impart the terror and alarm which prevailed. It was a beautiful day throughout the archipelago—the sun was abroad in all its glory, shedding a fervid ray over every object, and gilding the waters of the blue Caribbean, which lay quietly smiling beneath its influence. The breeze was as soft as an infant's sigh, and the wide canopy of heaven was spread aloft in all its beauty. Little then did

"Coming events cast their shadows before them."

A few minutes more, and darkness brooded over the land; and then, as it cleared away, the devastations presented themselves to the wondering gaze, and caused the strongest mind to quail! Yet, who could repine? for how signal was the mercy of God, who, amid all the dire convulsions, spared the lives of so many of his trembling creatures!

At the Savannah, besides many other places in the Union, the shock, which extended north as far as New York, was felt.

On the 8th February, the day of the great earthquake, the waters of the river Tiber, which washes the city of Rome, rose suddenly to such an immense height, as to inundate the houses to the first story. In Portugal, about the same time, loud subterranean thunder was heard; and soon after, the earth opened, and sent up large volumes of water, which overflowed the country for some miles. In the course of the following month, (March,) shocks of earthquake were felt in several places, from Liverpool and London north, as far as Van Dieman's Land south. In Jamaica, several smart shocks were experienced, which caused great excitement, and a day of public fast and humiliation was set apart by the government. The Grand Cayman (one of the three islands called Caymanas, lying between Jamaica and Cuba) has disappeared. This group of islands is inhabited principally by the descendants of the old buccaneers, who used to frequent these seas in former years, and negro turtle-fishers. They take their name from being a resort for the *cayman*, or alligator, who frequent these shores for the purpose of depositing their eggs in the sand. Trinidad has also been visited by several shocks of earthquake.

These several instances shew how very general these awful convulsions have been within the space of a few weeks; and prove to us (setting aside superstitious notions) that we ought seriously to consider "the signs of the times." Great fears were expressed by many of the credulous in America, upon feeling, or hearing of the earthquake; as on 1st January, the same year, a proclamation had been issued, by an American Millerite, in the following alarming words:—

"Great Earthquake!—To all the people far and near, to dreadful warning give ear. Jan. 11, 1183, there will be a great earthquake; three shocks in succession in all the whole world. Let all the people believe, and tremble before God; for the time will come when the saints will possess the kingdom. Jan. 31, 1843, the door of mercy will be shut against the whole world.—Now, my dear friends, I would advise you to flee for mercy, while the door of mercy is open. The Spirit of God testifies these things which are coming on the earth."

As soon as the events of this distressing earthquake became known in the sister colonies, meetings were held by the legislature, to take into consideration the best means of alleviating the wants and distresses of the Antiguan and other sufferers. Barbados was the first island which despatched a grant for the relief of the sufferers in the several islands. Trinidad granted 1000*l.* sterling; St. Vincent, St. Lucia, Jamaica, the Bahamas, &c., joined in their benevolence.

The subject of the great earthquake, and the loss met with by Antigua, was brought before the House of Commons on the 14th of March, 1843, by W. A. Mackinnon, Esq., M.P. for Lymington. A meeting was held in London on the 11th of March, for the purpose of taking measures for the relief of the sufferers in Antigua. The agent for the island, Dr. Nugent, presided at the meeting, at which also the bishop, Dr. Davis, was present, and was requested by the meeting to attend Dr. Nugent in his interview with the principal secretary of state for the colonies, for the purpose of soliciting aid from government.

Extensive subscriptions have been entered into at London and Liverpool,[23] &c. Her most gracious Majesty Queen Victoria, Prince Albert, the Duchess of Kent, and that exemplary and benevolent lady the Dowager Queen of England, with many of the nobility and commoners of England, have all most kindly and liberally bestowed that aid, so truly wanted by the distressed colonists.

It must be remarked, that the sufferers by this most awful and unprecedented occurrence are not to be found among the humbler grades of life, but in most instances are those who move in the higher and middle classes—individuals who are, generally speaking, endued with keener sensibilities, and who will thus feel more the change which, no doubt, will reduce many of them from comparative luxury to extreme want, unless most effectual aid be rendered to them.

Soon after the earthquake, the Royal Mail Steam-packet Company's ship Actæon was dispatched from St. Thomas's, to learn the fate of the colonies.

The "Thames," the Royal Mail Steam-packet Company's ship, Capt. Haste, was passing Antigua at the moment of the shock. Capt. Haste says, "The Thames was brought up as if on a reef of rocks, to his own dismay, and the dismay of all on board, and continued for a short period to jump and kick as if beating on rocks."

The shock was felt severely at sea. "The brig British Queen, Capt. Kennedy, from Whitehaven, lat. 17° 3' north, long. 58° 45', ship going six knots, felt a severe shock of earthquake, which stopped her way when 160 miles due east of the island, on the 8th, which lasted about four minutes." A French brig coming to St. Thomas's, "off Tortola, felt the shock so severely, he (the captain) thought that the vessel had struck on a rock."

Soon after the earthquake. Admiral Sir Charles Adams arrived at Antigua, in order to inspect the dock-yard. Before the earthquake, the barometer was noticed to vary from 30° to one-tenth higher; and on the 8th of February it stood at 30·2 in.

The next event of importance was the appearance in the heavens of a most beautiful comet. The first time this beauteous stranger was observed in Antigua, was on the 3rd of March, 1843. Its first appearance was like a scarf of clear white, shooting up from the horizon, and forming an arch of about 30°. The nucleus not being above the horizon, this phenomenon was supposed to be similar to the *aurora-borealis;* but as it gradually ascended the heavens, this idea was dissipated, and it was clearly seen to be a comet. Upon the evening it was first observed, a very splendid meteor passed over the town. Admiral Sir Charles Adams, on his way from Port Henderson to Spanish Town, Jamaica, observed this wondrous traveller, and made the following observations upon it, on board her Majesty's ship "Illustrious:"—

"March 4th, 1843. About fifty minutes after sunset, observed a strong ray of light in the west-by-south quarter, supposed to be a zodiacal light.

"March 5th. The same seen.

"March 6th. It proved to be a comet, the tail subtending an angle of 37° 14".

"March 7th. At forty minutes past seven, P. M., angular distance from Sirius 83° 50", length of tail 34° 28"

"March 8th, At forty-seven minutes past seven P. M., angular distance from Sirius 80° 19'; length of tail 29° 54"

"March 9th. Cloudy.

"March 10th. At fifty-four minutes past seven, P. M., angular distance from Sirius, 74° 48' 20"; length of tail, 24° 16'.

"March 11th. The same was seen,—much less brilliant."

The appearance of this eccentric body caused great excitement, occurring as it did so recently after the earthquake. When first perceived, it was supposed by many to be a lunar rainbow; but its steady movements and long continuance soon dispelled this idea. At times the stars could be distinguished through it, while at other periods they were hidden from observation. This comet, it appears, was discovered by Mr. Glaisher, of the Cambridge Observatory, as far back as the 28th of October, 1842. When discovered, "its north declination was nearly 69°, with right ascension of 16h. 40m. Now (Dec. 3) it has south declination of 34°, and right ascension of 19h. 16m. From the immense rapidity of its motion as it approaches its perihelion, it is probable that it is a comet of very long period. It seems this comet is not identical with the Chinese one of 1301, but coincides with the comet of Halley." This is Mr. Glaisher's own statement of the appearance of this wonderful heavenly body.

On Good Friday, being the 14th April, 1843, the cathedral of St. John's was re-opened for public worship, after being temporarily repaired for that purpose. An appropriate and impressive sermon was preached by the archdeacon, to a numerous congregation. All the other places of worship were crowded with attentive hearers. About eight o'clock in the evening, a sharp shock of earthquake was felt, which caused many of the inhabitants to rush from their houses, or from the respective chapels they had congregated in. Providentially, it did not continue long, and no accident happened; but from the recent awful convulsion of a similar nature, it was a moment of extreme terror to many.

During the month of April, 1843, another comet made its appearance. This coincides strangely with events of the year 1690, the period of the great earthquake in Antigua, which devastated great part of the town of St.

John's, and rent "Hatton's Hill," and which was followed by the appearance of two comets.

Up to the time of this work going to press, more than 35,000*l.* currency have been received from the British West Indian Colonies, and subscriptions raised in England, for the relief of the sufferers in the late awful earthquake. Since that dreadful occurrence, agricultural wages have risen from 4*s.* to 8*s.* currency per diem; and great complaints are made by the planters for not being able to obtain a sufficient number of labourers to carry on with expediency the culture of the sugar-cane.

---

[73] Francis Shand, Esq., gave 100*l.*

Printed in the USA
CPSIA information can be obtained
at www.ICGtesting.com
LVHW100237150823
755272LV00017B/143

9 789355 399625